The New History

*In memory of
Professor João Eduardo Rodrigues Villalobos,
a brilliant teacher, thinker and conversationalist*

The New History

Confessions and Conversations

Maria Lúcia Pallares-Burke

polity

Copyright © Polity Press 2002

First published in 2002 by Polity Press in association with Blackwell Publishing Ltd

Editorial office:
Polity Press
65 Bridge Street
Cambridge CB2 1UR, UK

Marketing and production:
Blackwell Publishing Ltd
108 Cowley Road
Oxford OX4 1JF, UK

Distributed in the USA by
Blackwell Publishing Inc.
350 Main Street
Malden, MA 02148, USA

A catalogue record for this book is available from the British Library.

Library of Congress Cataloging-in-Publication Data

Pallares-Burke, Maria Lúcia G.
  The new history: confessions and conversations / Maria Lúcia Pallares-Burke.
    p.cm.
Includes bibliographical references and index.
  ISBN 0-7456-3020-0—ISBN 0-7456-3021-9 (pbk.)
  1. Historians–Interviews. 2. Historians–Great Britain–Biography.
  3. Historians–Europe–Biography. 4. History–Philosophy.
  5. Historiography. I. Title.
  D14.P35 2003
907'.2022—c21

                                                                          2002006217

Typeset in 10 on 12 pt Times by Kolam Information Services Pvt. Ltd., Pondicherry, India
Printed in Great Britain by TJ International, Padstow, Cornwall
This book is printed on acid-free paper.

Contents

Acknowledgements   vi

Introduction   1

1   Jack Goody   7

2   Asa Briggs   31

3   Natalie Zemon Davis   50

4   Keith Thomas   80

5   Daniel Roche   106

6   Peter Burke   129

7   Robert Darnton   158

8   Carlo Ginzburg   184

9   Quentin Skinner   212

Index   241

Acknowledgements

I am deeply grateful to each and every historian I interviewed: Jack Goody, Asa Briggs, Natalie Zemon Davis, Keith Thomas, Daniel Roche, Peter Burke, Robert Darnton, Carlo Ginzburg and Quentin Skinner. Without the sympathy and generosity with which they received me, the writing of this book would not have been such an enriching and rewarding experience.

I am also very grateful to Christopher Tribe who did a wonderful job in translating from the Portuguese the original versions of the Introduction, the introductions to each interview and the interview with Daniel Roche.

Introduction

André Gide (1869–1951), a writer who liked to include an interlocutor in his works to help him put across his ideas in an informal, direct and personal manner, placed the following words in the mouth of his 'imaginary interviewer': 'The readers are not happy...It is my fault; I should have questioned you better. Your ideas, as you said, can be found in your books. The role of an interviewer is to invade privacy; it is to get you to talk about things that you would not mention by yourself.'[1]

My aim in conducting these interviews was partly just that: to get each of the historians gathered together in these pages to reveal things that a reading of their works does not reveal, or does not reveal so clearly; to encourage them to make explicit that which is so often implicit or assumed in their works and is therefore relatively inaccessible to the reader. As suggested by the word 'interview' itself – which derives from the Old French *entrevoir*, meaning to glimpse, see briefly or suddenly, or realize and understand vaguely – this is a fluid genre based on a convention of informality and yielding a relatively unstructured and unsystematic end-product. Thus in contrast with the finished, coherent academic paper, the interview can be seen as a genre somewhat intermediate between thinking and ordered writing, a genre that can catch an idea in movement, and as such it should be regarded not as a substitute but rather as a complement to more structured texts. What the interviews offer the reader is a series of snapshots, pictures of what individual historians thought on a particular occasion or even at a particular moment.

The idea of bringing internationally renowned historians together in one book to talk informally about themselves and their work arose quite

1   *Interviews imaginaires*, Yverdon and Lausanne, Editions du Haut-Pays, 1943, p. 31.

by chance. On the publication of the Portuguese translation of a work by the American historian Robert Darnton, who at the time was temporarily living in Oxford, the cultural supplement of a São Paulo newspaper commissioned me to interview him, not necessarily to focus on his translated book but rather to discuss more general issues. As soon as part of this material was published, a number of my colleagues, students and friends suggested to me that conversations of that kind with other historians might be useful not only to those who already knew their work and wished to gain a greater insight into it, but also to a broader, more diverse audience that had a vague interest in historical matters.

The scholars included in this book were selected because they are recognized by their peers to be authorities within their profession and also because of the prominent place they occupy in the so-called New History. They are all eminent, innovative and influential historians who stand out in the field of social and cultural history – the field in which the innovations of New History are most marked. They could be described as those who pronounce 'discourses of authority', in Bourdieu's words, and are considered to set the standard in their various specialist fields. Even Jack Goody, who is more famous as an anthropologist, is considered one of the group by major New History figures and admired for his talent and boldness. In other words, the nine historians interviewed are not simply original – all good historians are original by definition – but also particularly innovative in their styles and intellectual approaches. Having said that, it cannot be denied that many other historians could also have been chosen on the basis of the criteria adopted.

The questions put to them were not always the same, because the intention was to reveal something of the person behind the historian and to provide them with an opportunity to voice ideas and feelings that the rigour of more academic texts must generally suppress. The questions were individually tailored and in general were designed to make the respondents talk about the directions their lives had taken, their intellectual options, the implications of their work both within academia and outside, and their reactions to the intellectual trends and movements of today. As a rule the questions were not sent to the interviewees in advance unless they asked for them, which only happened in one case. Admittedly, had my strategy been to ask all of them the same questions, their points of agreement and disagreement on historical themes and approaches would have been more explicit; this approach would, however, have compromised the aims of spontaneity, flexibility and respect for their various individualities. In any case, it is interesting to note in connection with the interviewees' points of agreement and disagreement how certain great names were repeatedly cited as having been major influences either in their own professional development or in that of historians in general, while other names were absent. Whereas most of the interviewees spontaneously mentioned Marc Bloch and Jacob Burckhardt, Quentin Skinner was the only one to refer to Thomas Kuhn, only Carlo Ginzburg mentioned the linguists and literary critics Auerbach and Jakobson, and Skinner was the only one to describe Foucault as an important figure in the training of a historian.

Reflections on general issues of historiography often arose spontaneously when these historians were talking about their own work, and one could even imagine them discussing such matters with each other. But when this did not happen naturally I tried the next-best thing, so to speak, trying to push them towards the subject, and even attempting sometimes to introduce an element of dialogue not only between them and myself, but also among the interviewees themselves. In such cases I tried to steer our conversations not only onto 'tailor-made' questions but also onto more general subjects raised by one or other of their colleagues, depending on the time they had available and their willingness to reflect on topics like the history of mentalities, micro-history, history from below, comparative history, the history of women, the relevance of anthropology to history, etc.

I conducted all the interviews in person, and in two cases – Keith Thomas and Daniel Roche – I was joined by my husband, Peter Burke, who also figures as one of the historians interviewed. I must admit that my curiosity was not limited to the intellectual side of my interviewees: there was also a more mundane aspect. What would Daniel Roche, the historian of fashion and specialist in 'the culture of clothing', be wearing? Would Lord Briggs's and Sir Keith's titles lead them to behave differently from other mortals? How difficult would it be to play the journalist with Robert Darnton, himself an outstanding interviewer in his time as a journalist and reporter for the *New York Times*?

The separate answers given by the historians and the nine interviews themselves varied considerably in length. Such variation was basically due to the time they could spare to talk and their individual personalities, which of course also determined how personal and intimate the tone of the conversations was. Some of them, including Jack Goody, Quentin Skinner and (for obvious reasons) Peter Burke, met me on several occasions and for up to eight hours altogether; others, such as Asa Briggs, however, I met only twice and for no more than two hours in total. In Cambridge Jack Goody's expansive and easy-going nature contrasted strongly with Quentin Skinner's greater prudence and qualified enthusiasms. In Oxford Keith Thomas's caution and subtle irony counterbalanced the passionate and even audacious verve of Carlo Ginzburg in Bologna, almost as if their words had been commissioned specifically to display and contrast the Latin and British temperaments. With his relaxed yet vivacious conversation, characteristically punctuated with laughter, Robert Darnton stood out as one of those who were most willing to talk about their family lives, in which he was outdone only by his Princeton friend and colleague Natalie Zemon Davis. The only woman interviewed, Natalie Davis was memorable for the warmth with which she spoke about her work and her gift for expressing her emotions and feelings – perhaps a significantly feminine trait – even when talking about essentially academic matters. Asa Briggs, always in a hurry and the one whose answers tripped off his tongue most readily, also stood out as one of the most direct and impersonal of the interviewees. He was similar in this respect to Daniel Roche, who, with his calm, serene and unemphatic tone, revealed himself to be surprisingly and unjustifiably modest. Recently elected to the select group of professors at the prestigious Collège de France – an internationally famous institution founded in the sixteenth century, which in recent years has attracted eminent figures like Fernand Braudel, Michel Foucault, Claude Lévi-Strauss and Pierre Bourdieu – the modest Daniel Roche belies the image usually associated with French intellectuals.

The shift from an oral to a written medium raised some problems. To what extent does the transcription capture the expression of the original spoken word? To what extent does the absence of gestures, facial expressions, looks and tones of voice distort what is transcribed here and make it more liable to be misunderstood? There is no doubt that something has been lost when you cannot see Ginzburg's distinctively Italian gesticulations, hear Natalie Davis's quick, warm voice, watch the expressions on Skinner's face while listening to his amazingly fluent speech, and so forth. Yet when editing these interviews from the full, verbatim transcription of our face-to-face conversations, my concern has been not only to be faithful to the speakers' ideas but also to preserve, as much as possible, their characteristic modes and tones of expression. For this reason, when trying to convey the emphatic tones that I heard during these conversations and preserve a little of what was sometimes a highly expressive or passionate manner of speaking, I made use of exclamation marks. These exclamation marks are more frequent than my literary friends would think permissible, though less common than in my original version, since a few interviewees claimed that they did not 'use' exclamation marks – even when speaking! Similarly, every effort has been made to preserve as far as possible the original character of the interviews as informal, spoken conversations. Of course I have had to interfere by cutting out the most obvious repetitions, pauses and circumlocutions, condensing passages, reordering and recomposing sentences, etc.; that is, doing the kind of editing that as listeners (but not as readers) we do automatically in our heads. But I did my best to keep the oral features such as hesitations, imprecision, repetition, rapid changes of subject, or vague and incomplete answers without any major change, provided they did not affect the understanding of the ideas expressed.

The interview situation and the interviewer–interviewee relationship can have their problems. Ever since the publication of interviews became a relatively widespread cultural activity over a century ago, mistrust of interviews and interviewers has been a recurring theme, and history is full of examples of unwilling interviewees.[2] Uncomfortable with the role they have agreed to take on, many are suspicious – sometimes with good reason – of the ability of the interviewer, and even of the interview, to show them in their true light. Lewis Carroll, for instance, never agreed to be interviewed on account of his 'hatred of interviewers', while Conan Doyle once swore 'never to see an interviewer again'. Many others, however, such as H. G. Wells, who referred to interviews as an 'ordeal', and Rudyard Kipling, who thought it an 'immoral' activity, adopted the role they apparently detested when Wells interviewed Stalin and Kipling the American writer Mark Twain. More recently the introduction of the tape recorder seemed to offer a means of escaping from the interviewer's control and guaranteeing the accuracy of the interview. Thus the actor Warren Beatty, the film director Roman Polanski and the former British Prime Minister Margaret Thatcher, for instance, insisted on making their own recordings of the interviews they gave![3]

Some decades ago the writer and journalist Ved Mehta published a highly successful book based on interviews with several famous British historians who were at that time embroiled in a great debate about historical theories.[4] Well prepared intellectually and determined to get to know them better as thinkers and as individuals, he set about meeting them, often in their own homes. Their conversations, he recalls, were not always very friendly. Once, for example, he received what he interprets as 'a parting jab' from A. J. P. Taylor: as he was getting into his taxi on leaving the famous man's house, the latter pointedly remarked, 'After you have lived with books as long as I have, you start preferring them to people.'[5]

Nothing similar happened during the interviews gathered together here, all of which were marked by an extremely friendly, polite and good-humoured atmosphere. Certainly, some historians were much more

---

2   The title of an article in the *Idler* of December 1895 shows how controversial interviews had become: 'Are interviewers a Blessing or a Curse?' Significantly, a play by T. Thomas, *The Interview* (London, Samuel French, 1975), deals with the vicissitudes of an interviewer trying to interview a 'very famous man' who prevents him from using a tape recorder and spends the time contradicting himself.
3   C. Silvester, ed., *Interviews: An Anthology from 1859 to the Present Day*, London, Viking, 1993, 1–48.
4   Ved Parkash Mehta, *The Fly and the Fly-Bottle: Encounters with British Intellectuals*, London, Weidenfeld and Nicolson, 1961. Mehta (b. 1934), an Indian author who was naturalized an American, became well known for his contributions to the *New Yorker* magazine, where the material in *The Fly and the Fly-Bottle* was first published.
5   Ibid., p. 147.

tense than others, much more worried about the risk of making some careless remark, less willing to answer certain questions and more concerned to review the transcription in the original language or in the Portuguese and English versions.[6] None of them, however, showed a fear of having his or her words and ideas distorted, and hardly made any changes when checking the draft of the Portuguese version. Even the cautious Keith Thomas, who on several occasions had interrupted the recording by saying 'Off the record, please,' did not take the opportunity to alter what he had said. For the English version, however, some passages were reworked by a few of the interviewees so as to express various afterthoughts.

The interviews that follow are arranged in order of the seniority of the speakers, Jack Goody being the oldest and Quentin Skinner the youngest. For want of any other, this criterion seemed to be the most appropriate for presenting these practitioners of a craft which deals basically with the passing of time, and also for revealing the development of historical writing over the last few decades. The introduction to each interview is intended merely to provide the readers with some background information on the historian concerned which may be useful in understanding the discussion that follows. After each interview there is a select list of the interviewee's publications.

Ultimately I hope that my interference as editor – translating speech into written prose – will allow the reader to share with me the pleasures of these rich, stimulating conversations, which reveal that the serious and the profound can coexist without difficulty with lightness and humour.

---

6   These interviews (except for the one with Peter Burke) were first published in an abridged form in the Brazilian newspapers (*O Estado de S. Paulo, Folha de S. Paulo* and *Jornal da Tarde*), and then as a book under the title *As muitas faces da história: nove entrevistas*, São Paulo, Editora Unesp, 2000.

1

Jack Goody

The British anthropologist and historian Jack Goody (b. 1919) is acknowledged as one of the most versatile intellectuals of our times. His work, marked by great erudition, breadth of interest and a distinctly 'Goodyan' approach, has attracted the attention and admiration of not only anthropologists and historians but also philosophers, educationalists and economists. The great French historian Georges Duby, for instance, characterized Goody's work as a disconcerting but 'superb lesson in thoroughness' and acuteness that greatly broadens the horizons of historians. Amartya Sen, the philosopher and economist and 1998 winner of the Nobel Prize for economics, recommended it as an excellent remedy for the distorted view that the West has of East–West differences. The repercussions and impact of Goody's ideas have been so great that a few years ago his work was the subject of a conference in France, something which does not usually occur during an intellectual's lifetime.

The path that led Jack Goody to anthropology and history was not a straightforward one. He began his higher education in 1938 reading English literature at the University of Cambridge, at which time he associated with E. P. Thompson, Eric Hobsbawm and Raymond Williams, three other giants of English intellectual life. But the Second World War soon took him off to fight in the African desert, where he was captured by the Germans; he spent three years in prisoner-of-war camps in the Middle East, Italy and Germany, escaped from prison, and then spent six months living under cover in Italy. After a long time when he was deprived of books, ironically it was when he reached the German prison camp at Eichstätt (which surprisingly had its own library) that Goody came across two books that were to make a significant impression on his intellectual life: *The Golden Bough* by the anthropologist James

Frazer, and *What Happened in History* by the archaeologist Gordon Childe. On returning to university in 1946, he abandoned his literary studies and transferred to the faculty of archaeology and anthropology. After devoting himself to adult education (like his friend E. P. Thompson he wanted to 'help change the world'), he started his career as an anthropologist with fieldwork in an African village, where he became a 'friend of the ancestors'. Since then he has opened up several new fields of study: always rethinking his ideas and constantly moving from one subject to another, he has tackled themes as diverse as the impact of writing on societies, cooking, the culture of flowers, the family, feminism, the contrast between Eastern and Western cultures, etc.

His reputation as an anthropologist among his British colleagues was acquired primarily through the fieldwork that he carried out in Gonja in northern Ghana and the series of studies that resulted from it: studies on property, the ancestors, the relationship between forms of technology and the state, and so forth. He consolidated his reputation at an international level with broad comparative studies on the society and history of Africa, Europe and Asia. He was originally interested in the subject of literacy among Africans, ancient Greeks, Assyrians and traditional societies in general. His controversial 1963 article on the consequences of literacy, written in collaboration with the historian of English literature Ian Watt, was the first of a series of studies on this subject, the best known of which is his book *The Domestication of the Savage Mind* (1977). Another field in which Goody has used his talent for comparison is the history of inheritance and the family. His most famous contribution in this area is *The Development of the Family and Marriage in Europe* (1983), in which he explains the Church's ban on marriage between relatives as a reaction to practices that could deprive it of property. More recently Goody has broadened his comparisons to embrace food and flowers. *Cooking, Cuisine and Class* (1982), *Flowers* (1993) and *Love and Food* (1999) are studies in which he uses his knowledge of Africa to contrast the culture of that continent with that of Eurasia, an area which, as he explains, developed in a different direction after the rise of cities and writing caused by the Bronze Age 'revolution'. In short, anyone examining Jack Goody's work has to acknowledge that the all-embracing view of society and long-term history that lies behind it is so broad that it makes even the German sociologist Max Weber and the French historian Fernand Braudel appear limited and Eurocentric in comparison.

Jack Goody taught social anthropology at the University of Cambridge from 1954 to 1984, but throughout his life he has also been an itinerant researcher and lecturer in all four corners of the world. The dynamic, productive life that Jack Goody still leads at over eighty arouses admiration and astonishment in many of his colleagues. His academic production remains enviable both in its quality and in the number of his publications; his performance at seminars and conferences is always marked by a mixture of spontaneity and brilliance which captivates and inspires his audience. When at last a gap appeared in his tireless schedule of activities, Jack Goody gave me this interview in his room in St John's, the Cambridge college to which he has belonged since 1938, first as a student and subsequently as a fellow. In a conversation full of surprises and fertile digressions, during which he was extremely expansive, polite and good-humoured, Goody spoke at length about his interests, his experiences and his intellectual development.

MARIA LÚCIA PALLARES-BURKE   *You have written about an amazing number of issues, that range from the consequences of literacy and educational reforms to family and marriage patterns; from contemporary Africa and nineteenth-century Brazil to ancient Greece, China and Mesopotamia; from flowers and rituals of death to love, lust and food – just to mention some of your interests. How do you explain this breathtaking curiosity and encyclopaedic range?*

JACK GOODY   Well, maybe partly this is due to the peculiar situations I experienced in the war. At one time, for instance, I was in the desert fighting and coming up against Bedouins, and then, the next time, I was a prisoner of war living with Indians, South Africans, Russians, etc.; at another time I was escaping from prison and hiding in the houses of Italian peasants from the Abruzzi, and so on. I think that when I came back from the war, somehow or other I wanted to make some sense of all this diversity. But I think that it's only partly that, because reading Marx and Weber made me interested in broad sociological problems, such as why things happen in one place but not in others. That's something that has interested me for a long time. When I was doing fieldwork in a village in northern Ghana, I never wanted to stay locked into it, but rather to understand it in a wider framework: in its connection with the desert trade, the routes across the Sahara and its relation to the gold trade from the East and from South America, and so on. I've always been interested in that kind of connection. So, that's why I like to think that I am a specialist in the area that I've worked in Africa, but I don't like to see myself as an Africanist. Nor did my teacher Meyer Fortes. Like some other anthropologists, he didn't like to be seen simply as a specialist on one continent, but rather as someone able to discuss family systems in different parts of the world. This is why when the African Studies Association was founded in England, Fortes and most of the other senior anthropologists didn't join it. They wanted to be much more like the economists who had some kind of more general approach and were not seen as African economists or South American economists, or something like that. I don't think they were altogether right, because there is something much more concrete and specific in anthropology than there is in economics, but, nevertheless, the general principle was that you shouldn't be an Africanist or an Oceanist, in that kind of way.

What relationship do you see between your personal experiences and the anthropologist and historian you became?

I'm not sure that any early experiences led me to anthropology. I was much encouraged in school by my parents, who had left school early, especially by my Scottish mother. I grew up first of all in the new town of Welwyn Garden City in Hertfordshire, and then the family moved to St Albans, so that my brother (who taught astrophysics at Harvard) and I could attend the nearby St Albans [Grammar] School. There I got interested in archaeology, since Mortimer Wheeler was digging up the Roman town of Verulamium, which was next to the school.

But my main interest, apart from English literature, which was the sexiest subject at school and university, was current affairs and history. My schooldays were overshadowed by the expansion of Germany and Italy, and above all by the Spanish Civil War (more so than by the 'colonies', although the future of India was a concern). So my interest in literature had a more 'social' aspect to it than some of my teachers at Cambridge – above all Leavis – would allow.

During your fieldwork in Ghana, in which you became 'the friend of the ancestors', you defended their independence and even joined the Convention People's Party. How do you reconcile this with the anthropological ideal of impartial observation?

When I was in Ghana I was not only concerned with looking at some so-called primitive tribe, but also at what was going on politically. And you cannot do any observation unless you are, to some extent, a participant as well. I mean, unless people allow you to see what is going on. And if you want to see what is going on in politics you really have to belong to a political party. But since at the same time as I was a member of the party I also knew very well the local district commissioner working for the colonial government, I could more or less see both sides.

But my joining the Convention People's Party was not just a strategy. I was really interested in the process of independence and obviously was not a completely neutral observer. In fact, all of us who were working in Africa after the war were in one way or another committed to the idea of independence, to the idea of social change in these countries, and we were working towards those aims, perhaps overrating the role of education in society.

Your interest in educational issues – as part of your effort 'to change the world' – goes back to the time you worked with adult education after the war and was encouraged by your observation of the educational systems of many African and European countries. Almost two decades ago you proposed a radical reform of education that would involve the 'partial de-schooling' of the youngsters. How do you reconcile this proposal with your interest in literacy?

My interest in the social changes which followed the introduction of writing made me aware of two things. On one side, the means of oral communication do not disappear with the arrival of writing. On the other, the dominance of written culture (and of literate people), and the contempt for illiterates associated with it is deplorable. One of the reasons for my becoming interested in this issue was the experience of having a dyslexic daughter who at the age of ten or eleven developed an aversion to school when she realized that she had great difficulty in reading and writing. Well, people like her should be valued for something else they can do well. Some, for instance, go into gardening, and you can actually find excellent college gardeners who have reading and writing problems. And this is not an individual problem (it is known that 10 per cent of the population have this problem), but a general phenomenon associated with alphabetic literacy. So, when I made that proposal of de-schooling I was not thinking that it is possible to reverse the historical trend, even if that was desirable, but that one ought to evaluate non-written work and oral achievements in a more positive way. One of the disastrous things about education is that it takes people away from productive activities, the living activities in society, and locks them into a classroom. This is certainly not the way to learn respect for other types of labour besides the intellectual ones. When I worked in education in England after the war, in certain country districts children were allowed to spend some time in an ordinary productive system, learning, for instance, what a potato is and how it grows by observing the real thing and helping with the potato picking. The sad thing is that the experience didn't last very long because schoolteachers became very anxious to get rid of that living activity and bring back the students to their enclaves.

But I also had another thing in mind when I wrote that. I was thinking about the problems derived from the discrepancy between the educational system and the productive system, something that is particularly dramatic in the case of Africa, where there is not much functional reason for literacy. I must admit that at the time of the independence movement I went along with other intellectuals and politicians and also thought that with good schools and universities the economy would take off, the whole society would develop. But things didn't work out like that. While education – at an enormous cost – has been rather successful, even producing great novelists and playwrights (many now living in the USA or Europe), the productive system remains more or less the same. This means that a lot of money is spent in training people to be migrants and to have rather minor jobs abroad, because after having studied for seventeen or eighteen years, let's say, they don't want to go back to hoe agriculture, and yet there is no other job for them to do; they are taken away from traditional farming but they are not provided with any alternative. That's why you have now got an extraordinary number of Ghanaians in Chicago alone – about 10,000 of them, some with twenty years of schooling – working as taxi drivers and in other low-status jobs. The irony is that we, in the West, think that we are doing a great thing when we cancel debts or send them some help, while in fact we are probably taking more from them than we are giving to them, when we consider the jobs they are doing for us. I mean, the USA, for instance, gets very good taxi drivers in this way!

When I argue, then, that education has to be adjusted to the economy, I obviously don't mean this in any absolute sense, but in relation to certain particular situations. Alone, universal literacy cannot change the world, and certainly couldn't change Ghana! So, besides keeping education more in harmony with the economy, I'm defending the revaluation of oral achievements as well as of the literary ones, so that the great ballad makers and the great singers of tales can be praised alongside the great writers of books.

You have recently written an ethnographic and historical book about the culture of flowers, and from the outset you alert the reader that the topic was not as narrow as it might appear, but that, as in the case of cooking, it had a lot to do with 'the serious things of life'. Could you develop this idea?

It all started a long time ago when I was in Africa studying the funerary rituals and realized that you couldn't find the culture of flowers, which is so widespread in Asia and Europe. Not only is there very little use of flowers in Africa, but also very little symbolism attached to flowers, in either songs or stories. That's usually the way things start with me; the contrast arouses my interest. In this case, the contrast between the situation in Africa with, say, the situation in India, China or Europe. The question why people don't make use of flowers in Africa is posed against the background of the fact that in India, for instance, people are putting garlands around politicians all the time.

Assuming, then, that the use or non-use of flowers says a lot about society's attitudes and characteristics, I decided to write a historical and anthropological book on this theme. Wherever I went I started collecting tales of flowers, walked around cemeteries, talked with florists, visited

flower markets, and did some research in libraries. That is how I discovered the great symbolic meaning that flowers can have in certain
societies and the clashes that might exist between different cultures of
flowers. Once, when my assistant from Hong Kong retired, an Italian
friend tried to stop me giving her yellow chrysanthemums, because that is
a flower that you give to the dead in his part of the world. Little did he
know that in China the same flower carries a message of long life.

As to the reason why there is no culture of flowers in Africa, I would
say that this continent never adopted the changes of the Bronze Age, of
the Urban Revolution, which had such an enormous impact in Europe
and Asia, as the archaeologist Gordon Childe showed so well. With no
writing system, no plough, no intensive agriculture, not a large range of
crafts, no proto-industrialization, no accounting system, the African
societies did not have the large estates, the leisure class and the economy
of waste that allow for the development of the culture of flowers as well as
for a special cuisine. Yes, because a differentiated cuisine and the aesthetic
use of flowers require economic stratification. You can go to the house of
an African chief, who may be politically higher, but he will be eating the
same food as anyone else in the community. So, there is much less cultural
stratification in Africa than there is in the societies that have gone
through the Urban Revolution of the Bronze Age. By and large you
hear the same music, you eat the same food and you perform the same
rituals wherever you are in Africa. In this context, there is no room for the
use of domestic or even of wild flowers. They are regarded as a preliminary to the fruit or to the tree, and cutting them down is considered a
waste. That was in essence the same attitude that my mother would have
about cutting a branch from an apple tree: you would be spoiling the
fruit. And if the Africans never domesticated wild flowers, as happened in
China or India, where there was an enormous development of controlled
agriculture, it is partly because they were much more concerned with
domesticating the essentials of life, and saw the use of flowers as rather
frivolous.

*In your book on the culture of flowers you discuss the relative scarcity of
flowers in graveyards and at funerals in Protestant northern Europe and
contrast it with their abundance in the Catholic south, for instance in Italy,
where respect and love for the dead is shown in the language of flowers. How
would you then explain the tons of flowers (sent in a hurry from Israel,
Thailand, Holland and Kenya), which the Protestant British offered to
Princess Diana before, during and after her funeral?*

I think this is very intriguing, because it is true that the Protestant
Reformation with its condemnation of luxuries and elaborate rituals
drastically affected the culture of flowers. So flowers are used in the

Protestant countries in a much more limited way. My mother, as a Scottish Presbyterian, would have been horrified to see that waste. If someone offered her flowers, she would say quietly: 'I'd rather ha'e eggs.' Things have, nevertheless, changed since the seventeenth century and the historical compromise that produced the Church of England has allowed flowers to come into vogue. But even so, we never give anywhere near as many flowers as they do in France or Italy, and not only at funerals. In nineteenth-century France, for instance, there were very interesting publications about the language of flowers which every young lady should know. So I cannot make very much sense of the Diana event, which was certainly a unique demonstration. A little earlier something similar – on a much smaller scale – had happened in Brussels when people poured spontaneously into the street to protest against the government after the murder of a child by a paedophile. In the case of the Diana event, the demonstration also came from below. It was a great expression of sympathy, also with an element of anti-establishment involved – because the royal family had rejected her. I wouldn't say that it was a media event at all, although the media stimulated it, provoking a certain amount of contagion. Watching what was happening, more and more people were drawn to London to participate in the event. As in the case of Judaism, where people are not supposed to make an offering either to God or to the dead, but they go to the cemetery and leave a stone on top of the grave to show that they've been there, the British wanted to make their mark, to add their piece by throwing those flowers. And yet it is intriguing to see re-enacted a Catholic practice that, together with many of the saints, had been abolished in England so long ago.

As a result of your comparative study of Asia and Europe, you have argued that, contrary to what sociologists, anthropologists and historians have assumed, the West did not have a special predisposition towards the development of capitalism or modernization. In fact, you even suggested that, instead of talking about the 'uniqueness of the West', we should rather talk about the uniqueness of Eurasia, and especially about Asia's considerable contribution. Do you mean to say that the idea of stagnant oriental societies, put forward by Marx and so many others, is really a myth of the West?

Yes, I think it is very much a myth of the West, since all societies have been stagnant at certain periods, and the East has certainly had very dynamic periods. The deep-rooted cultural difference that, according to Marx and to some extent Weber, divided the East from the West, one being stagnant while the other was dynamic, is simply not true. The view of the Western sequence that dates the advance of the West from the ancient Greeks in a direct line, with no interruption, is just part of the folk wisdom of Western Europe. Contrary to what Marx thought, you could find in the East institutions of civil society and systems of commercial law which allowed for the development of mercantile capitalism.

There is a more or less common view that thinks of the enormous population of India and China as being somehow an index of failure. That is absolute nonsense! An enormous population like that is, on the contrary, an indicator that the economy has been very successful; otherwise they'd not have survived! The great work of Joseph Needham has shown so well that until the fifteenth century China was in many aspects in advance of Europe.[1] In the Middle Ages European societies, in any comparative sense, were pretty stagnant types of society, whereas Asia was more dynamic in terms of the accumulation of knowledge, the agricultural economy, and also in the manufacturing economy, with the sophisticated production of silk and porcelain in China, for instance, and the production of cotton cloth in India, products which were exported in vast quantities to Indonesia, to Africa and even a little bit to Europe well before the Portuguese took over the trade.

It is true that we have to explain the fact that in the sixteenth century the balance started to change and Europe began to be in advance in certain ways. But the explanation cannot, in my view, be in terms of claiming that one society was stagnant and the other was dynamic. We should remember that, in a sense, the Industrial Revolution was partly concerned with copying Asian manufactured products and producing them on a mass scale. Cotton cloth in Manchester was an import substitute for textiles from India and silks from China, while the Wedgwood and Delft industries were copying Chinese porcelain.

Is it fair to say that the main motive behind your extremely wide-ranging work is the will to undermine the notion of the 'uniqueness of the West'?

Well, that is one important element. While studying inheritance practices in Africa I became interested not only in their specific features, but also in the similarities and dissimilarities to those in the West. If in every society people have to pass on their goods and values to the next generation, there will be different ways of doing it, but also certain problems in common. When I started my work on flowers I travelled in Indonesia, Bali and India. On seeing the intense use the people make of flowers – wearing garlands around the neck and so forth – I started to wonder why in Africa they were almost completely absent. That was when I was rather surprised to find that Keith Thomas seemed to think that the concern with nature had been a uniquely European, and more specifically an English process, part of the sensibilities and the mentalities of Western

---

1   Joseph Needham (1900–95), historian of science, author of *Science and Civilization in China* (7 vols), Cambridge, Cambridge University Press, 1954–.

modernity. But that was contrary to all the evidence that showed that there was a much more intensive garden culture in China than there ever was in England, that the symbolism of flowers was so much more important there. Thus, the idea of England as the home of the intensive cultivation of flowers and of college gardens, an idea held by so many people, could not be sustained by a comparative approach. So I thought it important to show not only that Asia had had a sophisticated culture of flowers (more sophisticated than that in Europe), but also that Europe had to go to Asia for flowers as well as for flower patterns. If this was true about flowers, the same point could be made about attitudes to the rest of nature. The earlier existence of the so-called animist religions, which can be seen as part of a dialogue between man and nature about the world, is another example showing that we did not invent ecological concerns. In short, on the basis of a broad comparison between attitudes and ambivalences towards the control and exploitation of nature, the claims to the priority and the uniqueness of the West cannot be sustained.

You have undermined the claim to the uniqueness of the West and argued that it distorts our understanding of the past and present not only of the 'others' but also of ourselves. Do you mean to say that there is nothing unique about 'us' or 'them', and that, therefore, this category is misleading in itself?

Not altogether, because there is nothing wrong with the idea that every country and every person is unique. But in what ways are we unique? I tend to think that I am unique because I consider myself a very generous person, or have some similar quality, but that may not be at all true if someone else comes and compares me with others. The idea of explaining modernity as the result of so-called Western singularities, like individualism, rationalism and family patterns, has prevented us from having a deep understanding of the East as well as of the West. What I'm trying to say is that the idea of the uniqueness of the West has got, in a sense, out of hand. Of course England is unique in some ways, Europe is unique in others, China in yet other ways, and so on. But the idea got out of hand because it became a common assumption to think that it is because we are unique that we could invent things like capitalism, modernization, etc. Well, this is possibly true if we're thinking of industrial capitalism. But if one is thinking of mercantile capitalism it is certainly not true, since mercantile capitalism was just as vigorous as or more vigorous in the East in the fourteenth, fifteenth and sixteenth centuries than it was in the West. As to modernization, who is to say that Hong Kong or Japan is not more modern than we are? So, things are always changing, and somebody is more modern at one time and somebody else is more modern at another. It is not a unique feature of my constitution as an Englishman or European that has allowed me to 'modernize'. And yet, that is the way historians like Lawrence Stone and others are thinking. Just look at the history of the family, for instance, and how this notion of the singularity of the West was overemphasized and then used in a theoretical way that is very misleading. You can only tell if the English family is unique by looking at other families, like the Chinese. You can't just claim that uniqueness on the basis of data on eighteenth- and nineteenth-century English families. That does not make any sort of sound theoretical sense at all. Was it unique in relation to modernization, to industrialism, to capitalism? Nevertheless, that is what's been happening.

And this is the reason why you strongly argue for the importance of the comparative studies as a way to avoid ethnocentrism and misleading notions. But could you say something about the dangers of making comparisons and contrasts?

Yes, there are lots of difficulties, an immense number of difficulties, starting from the fact that one never knows enough about even one society, let alone about several. So we are forced to rely upon the work of other people. But, in fact, in whatever field we work we are always doing that, quoting this and that without being able fully to verify the quality of the data and not having any recipe for perfection. This is particularly true in anthropology because there may be just one person who worked amongst a particular people, which makes it much more difficult to assess the quality of the work than in the case of European societies, say, which have been looked at from a variety of perspectives. Nevertheless, it seems absolutely essential that we should find out something about different societies before we make any sort of generalization. A good number of historical studies, especially on early modern Europe, tend to declare that something is happening for the first time in history (like the notion of childhood), without looking around to see whether what is being claimed might be quite untrue. English historians, particularly, tend to be rather island-centred and to overemphasize the uniqueness of England. The problem is that at the end of the eighteenth century England undoubtedly made some particular advances in the organization of production and the control of energy that were later taken up in the rest of the world. From this, then, English historians extrapolate and make assumptions about the uniqueness of English society without looking around to see whether this was truly so. This is particularly serious in family studies that assume, following Malthus, that the Asian patterns were very different and claim that it was the uniqueness of Western European patterns that promoted modernization, capitalism and so forth. The problem is that we are always having to adjust those ideas to allow for similar developments in other regions. At one time, people were saying that Japan was advancing because, like England, it was also a small island, or that Japanese feudalism (supposedly the only other system in the world like Western European feudalism), was instrumental in helping them to advance to capitalism. You can see that very clearly in Perry Anderson's *Lineages of the Absolutist State* (1974). But then, no sooner you've said that than you discover that China and Taiwan are developing in the same way and you have to make a series of further adjustments to the argument. So, yes, there are a lot of difficulties and this is why many people, postmodernists and others, have rejected comparison altogether.

But, however difficult it is, we have to engage in the kind of comparisons Weber, for example, was making about world religions. Even though we may get it wrong, it is better than simply saying that Christianity is unique without looking around to find out what is really unique about it. Although there is no recipe for perfection and we may not be able to do it terribly efficiently, comparison is one of the few things we can do in historical and social sciences to parallel the kind of experiments the scientists do.

One of the problems of the comparative approach is that of comparing and contrasting ideas, objects and practices in different cultures while ignoring the context that gives them their meanings, a criticism often made of the work of Frazer. Is it possible to solve this problem?

My predecessors, who couldn't imagine how studies on African societies could illuminate anything in the lives of European peasants, criticized Frazer heavily. On the other hand, I was fascinated by his work ever since I found the two abridged volumes of *The Golden Bough* in the library of the prisoner-of-war camp at Eichstatt in Germany. This is the book which made me interested in anthropology and I don't think I would have come into this field had it not been for Frazer. I agree that he treated some ideas very atomistically, like the ideas of the soul from all over the world that he discussed and compared. He had no experience in fieldwork, something we all have now. Whether we are historians or anthropologists, we all have done intensive work in a field, so we have some kind of touchstone, something to go back to in order to test our judgement and see how certain ideas fit together in a particular society.

But I think that the reaction against Frazer went much too far, because he helped to make it possible to understand the relationship of advanced societies with other cultures, in a way that no other anthropologist, except possibly Lévi-Strauss, has done! His influence was enormous not only on social and historical sciences, but also on literature. If you look at the notes to T. S. Eliot's *The Waste Land* (which was my favourite reading at university), they are full of references to Frazer.

So, with the better data we have now collected about particular societies, we should continue to look into the important questions that Frazer raised. Because the questions he put are the ones that human beings ask about society. To ask, for instance, if the beliefs we have are universal or local is a perfectly valid question.

You describe yourself as a Marxist, but you have also shown how Marx's views about the so-called 'stagnant oriental form of society' and the specific 'Asiatic mode of production' fed the ideological bias of the West. In spite of this, do you still think that Marxism has any contribution to make to comparative studies?

I'm certainly not a non-Marxist, because I think that Marx has a lot of good starting points for a number of questions. I've just today been writing a sort of critique of some of Marx's ideas, only because I think they are still worth taking seriously. He has certainly added a long-term historical dimension to the social sciences, which many social scientists don't have. He has a theory about the development from one type of social formation to another which has some value as a kind of general theory, although it may be, in many ways, crude and inadequate. So he might be wrong about Asian societies and also about special features of the European ones, but he certainly raises exciting problems and treats them in interesting ways. Archaeology is one field in which Marx's influence has been very positive, forcing it to attempt to see the flow of history in general terms. I'm thinking particularly about another fascinating book I read in the prison camp, *What Happened in History,* by Gordon Childe. This Australian Marxist historian transformed the study of prehistory in this country and made it much more socially oriented. He was especially important to me in giving a social dimension to major changes in history and prehistory. And his ideas about the great advances of the Bronze Age which took place first in Mesopotamia and then in northern India and China showed, contrary to what Marx and Weber had said, that you couldn't really differentiate Europe and Asia at this time. If anything, Asia was more advanced than Europe; therefore, its societies were not as stagnant and despotic as these authors thought them to be.

Of course, given their lack of knowledge of oriental languages, it was almost impossible for Marx and Weber to know about the commercial and manufacturing development of these societies. Now that the data available in Western languages, not only on the East but on Africa as well, have improved out of all recognition, the faults that were understandable in the past are much less forgivable. On the other hand, this increase in the amount of data that we now have has also increased the problem of controlling the data.

One of the consequences of the relatively recent convergence of history and anthropology has been the wider appeal and diffusion of micro-history. Following anthropologists, historians have acquired a taste for the study of small communities and obscure individuals. As you know, respectable historians have criticized this new trend. They express the fear that micro-history may tackle only micro-problems and trifling issues, and that those who write it become mini-historians. In a dramatic way, John Elliott, for instance, says that something is very wrong when 'the name of Martin Guerre becomes as well or better known than that of Martin Luther'. What are your thoughts about this?

I have a certain amount of sympathy for Elliott on that, but fortunately micro-history is not the only convergence between history and anthropology. On the other hand, there have been some interesting points coming out of these micro-studies, which shows that it is an exciting field. And the same is true of the study of particular individuals in particular places and times, points which might be relevant on a wider front. So I personally don't mind about Martin Guerre, provided that people don't look upon this as the only method of enquiry and dismiss wider comparative studies. That is, in fact, what sometimes happens in anthropology, when people become attached to fieldwork, to particular studies, thinking that general studies are of no value. And the further danger in anthropology is one of being caught not simply in a micro-study of a particular people, but in a micro-study of the observer's reaction to that people. In that case, you are not primarily concerned to learn anything about the people, let alone about the wider frame of reference.

What are then the advantages of the convergence between history and anthropology?

If you go into a culture that has no historical records, there is the terrible danger of thinking that it has been like that forever; that there is something natural in the way the Jivaros or the Zuñis, for instance, are behaving. Well, one thing that we can be pretty certain of is that this is never the case. On the contrary, cultures are always changing. I've recently become interested in the changes in people's attitudes to images, realizing that cultures are not always iconophiles or iconodules [image worshippers], but that they change over time. So a society that has been Catholic like medieval England, and has made much use of flowers, changes and pushes that aside when it becomes Protestant; and then, it changes again in the nineteenth century; and so on. Neither individuals nor societies are locked into particular attitudes over the longer terms. Now, if you are taking a snapshot view, a synchronic view of a society (as we used to say in anthropology), which is basically what you get when you do fieldwork in a society, you get the idea that culture is something which goes back in an almost material form to the beginning of time. That is the assumption that allows you to talk about the Ashanti culture, for instance. History, in a sense, is what saves us by giving us the time dimension and depth that is lacking in anthropology. It is true that it is not always possible to get time depth in anthropology, given the lack of early material on the cultures we study; nevertheless anthropologists can at least bear in mind the possibility that these world views, the attitudes they observe, are not necessarily permanent features; as in all society, such attitudes may contain contradictions which can potentially lead to changes over time. Certain recent studies of African peoples offer the evidence for this, since we can observe the changes in their attitude to images, which turn from figurative art into abstract forms.

Thinking about the problem the other way around, anthropology can be beneficial for history, influencing it by the theoretical and generalized way it looks at certain issues, like kingship. Anthropology can help historians to look at certain problems, like marriage rules and inheritance systems, with a wider range of data that has been analysed in a different frame of reference. I've myself found it very exciting to work with E. P. Thompson and Joan Thirsk on a volume for Past & Present Publications on different inheritance systems, in which the European systems when viewed in a wider framework raised interesting problems, especially as regards women.[2]

As someone who began by working on Africa and who now writes a lot about Europe, you have become a more or less unique intellectual in the world of the social sciences. How important do you consider your mediation between these two worlds?

Well, I consider my African experience very important, because whatever problem I'm considering, whether in Europe or elsewhere, I ask myself, how would this look in an African context? So it's been very important to me to look at some aspects of European experience against an African background. Observing the similarities and differences between certain aspects of African societies and Western societies – like the inheritance systems, for instance – I've also been trying to arrive at some kind of explanation for those differences and not simply point them out as being the result of savage mentalities. That was partly why I became interested in the role of literacy and writing in societies. What I was trying to say then was that some of the differences between Europe and Africa, which exist, are related to the fact that the Africans did not have a writing

2 *Family and Inheritance: Rural Society in Western Europe, 1200–1800*, Cambridge, Cambridge University Press, 1976.

system. In other words, instead of explaining African societies by talking about savage mentalities in contrast to advanced mentalities, if we look at them in a concrete and contextual way we can see things actually happening as a result of the introduction of writing and schools. In Ghana I could see a great deal of change taking place within a very short space of time; people's horizons being opened up, people performing different kinds of operation, writing books, etc. I've known people who came from simple villages in Africa where writing does not exist and who have become university lecturers, novelists, businessmen in the world at large and even the secretary general of the United Nations!

Having studied some African cultures which are marked by a relative isolation, what do you think about Edward Said's sweeping statement, 'the history of all cultures is the history of cultural borrowing'?

The idea that these oral cultures in Africa were stagnant just waiting for ideas to come in from abroad is definitely wrong. I think we should not play down the amount of invention that is going on in different cultures. You can only account for the great diversity that exists in human society by thinking not only of borrowing but of the element of invention which exists among human agents. These two processes go together in most cultures and I don't think one can put everything down to internal invention or everything down to external borrowing. We have to study the matter sector by sector, and in the case of Africa, for instance, there is a great deal of invention in the religious and artistic sphere, with new cults and new ideas emerging all the time, sometimes with a few borrowings of thematic elements involved. In other spheres, like the agricultural, technological and the writing system, the fact of cultural borrowing is important.

Brazil is not missing from your wide-ranging works. What made you interested in the 1835 slave revolt in Salvador, Bahia?

Partly because I am interested in revolts in general, but actually, in this particular case, because I was very fascinated by the local police chief's understanding of the event. He attributed the relative success of the revolt to the important role that writing played in its organization. It's known that the slaves and free men who participated in the revolt in Salvador – the majority being Muslims of Yoruba origin – were learning to read and write in Arabic characters in informal Islamic schools, and that many of the leaders were educated Africans who had travelled considerably and had excellent knowledge of Arabic. With these abilities, the rebels had been able to send notes to one another giving instructions, and it is these sources, which were confiscated and collected by the police, that were studied by Nina Rodrigues in 1900.[3]

In the aftermath of this failed revolt, a draconian measure was taken in order to expel dangerous elements from the black community: 400 literate blacks were sent back to West Africa, and this exodus removed them as a factor in future rebellions. So, as you can see, my earlier interest in the consequences of literacy was stimulated by this dramatic event, which showed that once these people had acquired the Arabic script they could operate in a much wider sphere of activity. This event, therefore, brings to light, in a dramatic way, the potential that reading and writing have for cultural transformation. As a result of this work I became interested in the role of literacy in other slave revolts in the Americas, but didn't do much more about it.

One of your main aims has been to refute the ethnocentric distinctions between 'we' (the civilized, advanced, logical-empirical people) and 'they' (the primitive, mythic people). At the same time, you refuse to accept cultural relativism, which you refer to as 'sentimental egalitarianism'. What is wrong with cultural relativism?

This is very much a postmodernist fashion, although there has long been this element in anthropology itself, since to some extent its practitioners have always wanted to point out, quite rightly I think, that some societies are not as different from ours as many people have thought. But it's also very important to recognize the differences alongside the similarities. Relativism, in its extreme form, is saying that the people in Africa are the same as the Chinese, the Japanese, and so on. Well, if they are the same, why are their achievements not the same? So the notion that arose in recent years that all human societies are the same goes against cultural history, I think, because it's not possible to equate the achievements of people without writing to those of peoples with writing. We have to take into account the fact that societies that do not have what I call the technology of the intellect are not able to build up knowledge in the same way as the ones that have. Of course, they have knowledge systems about nature but they cannot achieve the same as the societies that have books, encyclopaedias, dictionaries and all that sort of thing. Simply saying, as a philosopher like Derrida does, that reading nature is the same as reading a book is quite wrong. Reading the stars does not give the same kind of knowledge about Brazil, for instance, as the knowledge one can get by reading books. That's what I think is wrong with cultural relativism.

3   R. Nina Rodrigues (1862–1906), Brazilian anthropologist, author of *As raças humanas e a responsabilidade penal no Brasil* (1894), *Os africanos no Brasil* (1933), *O animismo fetichista dos negros baianos* (1935).

It is not that I am better or cleverer than they are, but I have the ability to use pen and pencil, to read and work with books, and this enables me to do things that people from another type of culture, however clever and gifted they are, cannot do. The same applies to the plough and tractor. With the plough, animal traction or the energy from a tractor I can produce a great deal more than I can if I'm a farmer who works with the hoe, as in Africa. It's only because systems of production have become so elaborate that they produce a surplus, that we can be sitting here like this for all these hours just talking. In a simple oral culture we would have to be out there farming to get our food most of the time. It seems obvious therefore that it is a mistake not to realize the existence of these differences. They are not moral differences.

You have strongly rejected the notion of mentality as an appropriate histor-ical explanation. The histories of mentalities, you argue, betray a certain intellectual laziness. Could you expand your reservations about this approach?

I think that it is too easy and even simplistic to discover changes in mentalities in history as Philippe Ariès, Lawrence Stone and so many others have done. The 'invention of childhood', for example, is unconvin-cing because a comparative perspective is lacking. In order to affirm that this invention took place in Europe at a given historical moment, it would be necessary to know, in the first place, what childhood was like in the previous period, and in the second place, how other societies, past and present, have regarded it. The same point could be made about the idea that conjugal love arose in Europe in the eighteenth century. All we have to do to see that this idea does not work is to turn back to the Middle Ages and to ancient Rome. It was along those lines that Ian Watt (my former Cambridge colleague and the author of a fascinating book on the rise of the novel) and I criticized the explanation of the great Greek achievements as the fruit of the 'Greek genius'. There is a kind of intel-lectual laziness in invoking the 'genius' or 'mentality' of the Greeks to explain their success. In this respect I share the criticisms made by Geoffrey Lloyd in his book *Demystifying Mentalities*. In order to escape this circular argument, which explains nothing, we have to try to discover the factors that contributed to the so-called 'Greek miracle'. This is what we tried to do in a rather polemical article of 1963, 'The Consequences of Literacy', in which we approached human development via the categories of literate and illiterate.

But in what way does your dichotomy literate–non-literate (which you contrast to the binary oppositions savage–civilized and logical–pre-logical

*used by Lévi-Strauss and Lévy-Bruhl), differ from the other oppositions,
which you claim to be ethnocentric and simplistic?*

The other dichotomies seem to treat human societies as fixed, since they
do not explain their differences and do not have any inbuilt notion of
change. Simply saying that societies are logical or pre-logical, or hot or
cold does not tell you anything about these differences and how you get
from one to the other. Whereas what I try to do with literacy is to show
what writing actually does in a human society that makes it different from
a society that does not have it; and introducing a dynamic element, I also
try to show how you get from one type of society to the other. So,
contrary to the other oppositions, I don't see them as being fixed for all
time because I point to the mechanisms of change, the coming of writing
being one important cause for the changing of the system. But in any case
my opposition is not binary, like the others, because I see all sorts of
changes in the mode of communication as being relevant. It is true that
the shift from non-writing to writing was of enormous importance; but
I also suggest that the changes which writing provoked differed
depending on what system was adopted, whether it was a logographic
system as in China, or an alphabetic system as in the later Near East. And
again, subsequent changes, like the invention of printing and the mech-
anization of book production, had an immense impact on the modern
world. Before these, the whole human experience went through a major
change with the development of a system of speech. So, I see a whole
series of divisions that make a difference to human society, and not, like
some of my colleagues, a single great divide.

Historians, for example, often talk about the difference between history
and prehistory, one with documents and the other without them, and, like
Lévi-Strauss's hot and cold societies, I don't think these divisions are very
meaningful if they don't try to show, through a particular mechanism of
change, what happens when, for instance, people start to write things
down. In fact, the idea of oral societies as being very fixed, rigid, is to my
mind quite mistaken because they have no fixed system of storage as we
have with paper and pencil; therefore, with no book to go to, they have to
be continuously creating something new. So far as religion is concerned, for
instance, I've always argued that writing makes things rather conservative,
whereas in oral cultures religion is usually very fluid, with a multiplicity of
cults coming into existence. When you have a written religion, you are
always going back to the book in some way or other, the sacred text
becoming a fixed text. So my aim has been to show what the differences
between writing and non-writing are and how these differences affect the
various spheres of human activity like the economy, religion, and so on.

When I wrote about 'the domestication of the savage mind', I chose the
title deliberately to stress the fact that I wanted to deal with a process and

not simply a dichotomy. I wanted to show the process of domestication, what was involved in that shift, because I thought that some of the things – not all – which Lévi-Strauss attributed to cold and hot societies could be better explained in terms of differences in the modes of communication.

Two experiences were crucial for the development of this special concern of mine. The first was that of having suddenly found myself without any book when I was a prisoner of war in the Middle East and Italy (as I said earlier, the German camp surprised me with its excellent library). After the war, when I met Ian Watt again, who had had the same experience (but without the library of Eichstatt), we decided to work together on the influence that modes of communication have on human society; and, above all, on the role of memory and on the consequences of the introduction of literacy in societies without writing. The second experience was my being able to observe the process of 'domestication of the savage mind' in action in Africa. Lévi-Strauss's discussion of the two opposite types of society seemed to imply that people were locked into that division, whereas my experience in Africa had suggested exactly the opposite, that is, that people were changing constantly, particularly with the establishment of schools that concentrated on the teaching of writing. The notion of property, for instance, was dramatically affected when people were asked to register the land that they had farmed for hundreds or even thousands of years. Until that happened, they owned a piece of land along with a lot of other people, in the sense that many people had rights over it. But when they were called to write down – 'I Jack Goody own this patch of land' – this act excluded everybody else. So introducing written transactions in that way changed the whole nature of ownership.

In your book on representation and ambivalence you introduced a notion of culture which includes an important and complex element that you call 'cognitive contradiction'. What is its role?

I'm sorry if all this is somewhat obscure, but it's a little obscure to me too! The notion of 'cognitive contradiction' arose from my conviction that societies are not locked into a fixed state, that a culture is not something which goes back in solid form to the beginning of things. With this notion I was trying to explain some aspects of cultural change by showing that there is an element of contradiction in each and every culture, however simple. It is in fact part of the human situation, something that is shared by everybody. Representation is essential to human life, and yet there is ambivalence about the whole process of representing things. And it is because a contradiction is implicit in each culture that there exists a potentiality for change.

The question which I initially faced, as I briefly mentioned before, was the shift from figurative to abstract forms of art that can be observed among peoples in Africa. Why, for example, do certain African cultures have figurative images, while neighbouring peoples have abstract representation? And why does this situation change over time? This distribution did not seem to be completely random, accidental, but, on the contrary, it appeared that there were some general doubts as to the form of the images. While certain groups saw no problem in making figurative images, others regarded them as inappropriate. The same phenomenon can be found in early Christianity, and later on with the Protestants who pulled down the statues from the front of Ely Cathedral, showing that there is a kind of movement back and forth within a culture over time. Similar movements or shifts from figurative to abstract and back again you can find, for example, in the history of Judaism and Buddhism. We think today of Buddhist temples as full of images of the Buddha, but in the first five centuries of Buddhism there were no such figurative images. They apparently began to be made by monks in order to spread the religion among the populace. Even now Zen Buddhism does not pay too much attention to images; the followers of Zen see themselves as practising a more refined form of religion that pays attention to the word rather than to images.

So the evidence that in many cultures you find great changes in the use of images over time suggested to me that there is a sort of ambivalence about the idea of representation, on the same lines of the old Platonic objections to representations as never being the thing itself. In Plato's words, they are a lie. This means that people who were using images would tend to ask the question 'what is the difference between the presentation and the representation?'; and from that they might, in the end, reject representations, as abstract artists did in Russia and France at the beginning of the twentieth century. The host, for example, regarded at one time as sacred, came to be viewed as a simple piece of bread.

So, with the element of 'cognitive contradiction' that I introduced into the concept of culture, I was trying to understand certain aspects of cultural change, some of them very sudden, like the people chopping off the hands of angels in Ely Cathedral, and then putting them back again ten years later. Or the complete disappearance of the theatre in London in 1648, followed by the great burst of theatrical activity with Restoration drama in the 1660s. What is intriguing is that these were the same people, the same Londoners, rejecting at one moment and accepting at another. So I'm arguing that these shifts are not simply effects of an imposition from outside. On the contrary, they show both the culture and the people being ambivalent about what they were doing; because people were also having doubts whether the theatre was a proper activity, whether the figurative images were appropriate, and so on. One dramatic case of this kind of shift you can find in Judaism. At first, the Jews took very seriously the Old Testament injunction that they should not make images of anything on earth, and definitely had no images. But then all that changed very suddenly. In the nineteenth century the Jews were not painting, were not active in the theatre, and yet they founded Hollywood and became extremely important in the world of films, painting, sculpture, theatre and arts in general. It's said that Marc Chagall at the beginning of the twentieth century was the first Jewish painter in history!

Of all the books in your area of interest which ones would you like to have written?

Well, there are a lot of novels that I'd like to have written. But in the area of non-fiction, and the nearest to my own field, it would've been a great achievement to write the two books that I discovered during the war at the prison camp of Eichstatt, before I took up anthropology: Gordon Childe's *What Happened in History?*, a magnificent synthesis of the early period of human history, and James Frazer's *Golden Bough*, a very inspiring book, which was greatly disapproved of by my predecessors. These books, which have influenced me a great deal, would certainly have fulfilled my greatest ambitions. But if I may refer to my own books, I think probably the one I'm particularly proud of is one that has not got any word of mine in it. It might sound odd, but it was the recording and translation of the myth of the Bagre that I regard as being my most permanent achievement. It's not that I created a work of literature, but by registering and translating this African myth I in a sense recreated a work of literature that discusses fundamental theological issues and reveals the philosophical element in an oral culture. What might appear to be theological questions that relate specifically to Christianity or Islam I showed to be widespread problems, which come up in many religions. Yes, because they are all there in this myth: the problem about the material and the immaterial nature of God, the problem of a creator God, the problem of evil – why did God create evil as well as good, and why does he not come down and change all that, etc.

So one of the things that I most enjoyed about doing that book is that, although this entire philosophical element was there, if I had not written down that particular version of the myth at that particular time, it would have vanished. And the extraordinary thing about this is that nowadays the people themselves look upon my translation as some sort of sacred text, a Bible; and I'm very much part of their history now. My version is interesting to them not because I wrote it, but because I took it down from old men fifty years ago. If someone decided to write it down nowadays, the version would be rather different because it would have been recorded fifty years later. So it is as if I've recorded the living memory of wise men. If I can think of an analogy, it is as if I had sat down with Homer and written down his recitation, while other people only had the poems of Homer in a version fifty years later, which was very different from my version. Unlike our own societies, which store culture in writing, in all oral societies cultures are stored in the memory. It is, therefore, an obvious remark that old people have a special place in oral societies, as a source of power and knowledge. They are the wise people because, by having longer memories, they are a store of information. If you then believe, as they do, that knowledge has come down from a long way back, then the people who are nearest to that period are the ones who know it best, who've got the truth.

I must explain, though, that I didn't take down the myth in the actual context of recitation. To enter into the room where things were happening I would have had to join a secret society, much like joining the Masons. Only this would have allowed me to participate in the initiation ritual of the society where the myth was recited. I had, then, to find someone who had participated in the ceremony, willing to recite it for me outside. And the reason why I never joined this secret society is partly because the initiation procedure meant that you had to sit silent under a tree for some six weeks, and that didn't seem the best way of passing my time out there!

Cambridge, October and November 1997

SELECT BIBLIOGRAPHY

Death, Property and the Ancestors: A Study of the Mortuary Customs of the LoDagaa of West Africa (Stanford, Stanford University Press, 1962).

ed., *Literacy in Traditional Societies* (Cambridge, Cambridge University Press, 1968); translated into German and Spanish.

The Myth of the Bagre (Oxford, Oxford University Press, 1972).

The Domestication of the Savage Mind (Cambridge, Cambridge University Press, 1977); translated into Spanish, French, Italian, Japanese, Portuguese, Turkish.

Cooking, Cuisine and Class: A Study in Comparative Sociology (Cambridge, Cambridge University Press, 1982); translated into Spanish and French.

The Development of the Family and Marriage in Europe (Cambridge, Cambridge University Press, 1983); translated into Spanish, French, Italian, Portuguese.

The Logic of Writing and the Organisation of Society (Cambridge, Cambridge University Press, 1986); translated into German, French, Italian, Portuguese.

The Culture of Flowers (Cambridge, 1993); translated into French and Italian.

The Expansive Moment: Anthropology in Britain and Africa, 1918–1970 (Cambridge, Cambridge University Press, 1995).

The East in the West (Cambridge, Cambridge University Press, 1996); translated into French and Italian.

Representations and Contradictions: Ambivalence towards Images, Theatre, Fictions, Relics and Sexuality (Oxford, Blackwell Publishers, 1997); translated into Spanish.

Love and Food (London, Verso, 1998).

The European Family (Oxford, Blackwell Publishers, 2000).

2

Asa Briggs

Asa Briggs (b. 1921) is one of the most eminent social historians in Britain today. Although he is the greatest living specialist on Victorian England, Briggs has never allowed himself to be confined to a single period, region or even subject. The breadth of his interests and his enormous capacity for work were displayed early on: while he was still reading history at the University of Cambridge he was also secretly studying economics at the University of London. For most people either one of the courses would have required absolute dedication and very hard work. It is said that Briggs sleeps only four hours a night, and the speed with which he writes letters, book reviews and even books has always made his colleagues envious.

A Yorkshireman born and bred, Asa Briggs was profoundly influenced by his region of origin. The whole of Briggs's vast contribution to the history of England is illustrative of his fascination with the conquests of the Industrial Revolution, the 'long revolution' which began in the North and in his view transformed the whole fabric of society without any barricades or coups d'état.

Like others of his generation Briggs found economic history fascinating, but unlike most of his contemporaries he broadened his interests and became one of the pioneers of social history in England. He published his study *Victorian Cities* in 1963, before urban history had become a subdiscipline in its own right. In that book he also developed a comparative approach unusual for those times. His discussion of Victorian Melbourne, Australia, contrasted with Birmingham with its small workshops and modern Manchester, a typical city of the Industrial Revolution, has yet to be surpassed, and *Victorian Cities* is still compulsory reading for anyone interested in the Victorian era or in urban and comparative studies.

Back in the 1960s Briggs announced he was preparing a book on 'Victorian things' at a time when the history of material culture was virtually unheard of, but the endless administrative duties that he took on meant that he finished *Victorian Things* only in 1988. Contrary to what one might imagine, this is not a study of antiques but a social history based on the study of objects as well as texts. When he announced this project in a lecture delivered in 1963, Briggs vividly illustrated his approach by suggesting that someone should write the social history of the lawnmower, relating this object to the rise of the middle-class suburbs with their spacious gardens, to the decline of domestic servants, and so on.

Asa Briggs was also the first British historian to show an interest in the history of modern communications and the development of the leisure industry, the subject of a lecture published in 1960, again at a time when such topics had not yet been discovered. It is therefore hardly surprising that he was invited to write the history of the BBC, a subject on which he has published several volumes over the years.

With such a background, it was only to be expected that Briggs would eventually write a social history of England, the first attempt to replace the famous *English Social History* (1942) by George Macaulay Trevelyan, a major historian in a more traditional mould. Given his long-standing interest in the Victorians and pre-Victorians, it was assumed that Briggs would begin his history in the eighteenth century or at the very earliest at the end of the Middle Ages. But with his customary boldness he exceeded everyone's wildest expectations and decided to go back to the very beginning, starting his *Social History of England* (1983) in prehistory! It is worth noting that Briggs found much of the inspiration for this book in the works of the Brazilian sociologist-historian Gilberto Freyre, the first intellectual, as Briggs himself admits, to make him aware of the relationship between the visual and the social and the importance of objects as historical evidence.[1]

In his early eighties, Briggs still displays the enviable qualities of energy and daring that have marked his whole intellectual career: he has recently written (in collaboration with Peter Burke) a general history of the media, from Gutenberg right up to the Internet, for which he made a trip to California, in order to understand the Silicon Valley phenomenon.

No general description of Asa Briggs should fail to mention his interests in education and politics, subjects on which he holds strong convictions. In the 1960s he helped devise the Open University and the

---

1   Gilberto Freyre (1900–1987), Brazilian sociologist and historian, most famous for his studies of racial and cultural mixture and the patriarchal family, including *The Masters and the Slaves* (1933) and *The Mansions and the Shanties* (1936), both of which are available in English.

University of Sussex, institutions that brought great innovations to the field of education. Briggs hired so many young Oxford academics for Sussex that the new university, established near Brighton on the south coast, was dubbed 'Balliol-by-the-Sea'. Yet Briggs had no intention of reproducing the Oxbridge system there: he wanted to create a centre of excellence in a different mould. He dreamt of a university without departments and strove, in his words, to 'redraw the map of learning' by introducing an interdisciplinary approach to Arts studies – something quite revolutionary for the times. At Sussex history could be studied in the School of Social Studies, combining courses in history with sociology and philosophy of the social sciences; or in the School of European Studies, combining history with philosophy and literature; or even in the School of African and Asian Studies, combining history with economics and anthropology. In the field of politics Briggs's support for workers' causes and the Labour Party received a boost in 1975 when he was made a life peer by the Labour government under Jim Callaghan.

Although he retired in 1991, Lord Briggs remains fully active as the president of several bodies, such as the British Social History Society and the Victorian Society, and as a guest lecturer in the United States, Japan, China, India and various countries in Europe. His multiple occupations keep him constantly on the move between Sussex, where he lives, and the House of Lords and the various London institutions to which he belongs, and it was not easy to find a slot in his diary for our interview. Eventually Briggs gave me a warm, jovial welcome at his London office, appropriately located in the attractive house in which the great Victorian writer Thackeray once lived. And as expected, it was with incredible fluency, speed and concision that he talked about his work, his interest in Gilberto Freyre, his intellectual trajectory, Victorian times, the future of the British monarchy, and so on.

MARIA LÚCIA PALLARES-BURKE *How did you decide to become a historian? Would you say that your family background and education influenced your future career? Did the Briggs family play a decisive role?*

ASA BRIGGS I never had the slightest intention of following this career when I was a child or even as an adolescent. I think that it was only when I went to Sidney Sussex College, Cambridge, that I began to think of becoming a historian. Indirectly, however, the Briggs family did play a role. My grandfather, born in industrial Leeds, might be described as a character out of a book by Samuel Smiles, and he actually went to some of Smiles's lectures. My grandmother, who came from a family somewhat higher in the social scale, had a strange experience which certainly helped to make me interested in history – she never knew her parents! Her mother died in childbirth and her father also died before she was born. Both my father and my grandfather were foreman engineers, both of them extremely skilled with their hands, and I think that my increasing interest in the history of technology has grown in part out of those family roots. My grandfather in particular was extremely interested in history and it was with him, when I was very small, that I visited every abbey, every castle and every old town in the neighbourhood of Keighley in Yorkshire. We talked a good deal and happily he lived long enough to see me go to Cambridge, which was a great thing for him.

On my mother's side, my ancestors were all farmers who became extremely successful as greengrocers, but my grandfather's enormous medical bills during his last illness, followed by the Depression of the 1930s, left the family business in a poor state. I grew up extremely conscious of the fact that I was living in a period of economic depression. When I was ten, I won a scholarship and went to an old grammar school where I had an extremely interesting education. When I reached the sixth form, the headmaster, who was a historian, played a great part in my future. It was entirely due to him – a persuasive man with an air of authority – that I went to Sidney Sussex, which was his old college. He insisted that I should read history, although it had not been my best subject. Up to that time I had been evenly divided between arts and science, and English had been my favourite subject. In any case, I am very pleased to have followed my headmaster's advice. I never had the slightest doubt about this.

What made you choose Victorian England as your main field of study?

I'm fascinated by the relationship between continuity and change in history, and there was an enormous amount of both change and continuity in Victorian England, as there was in the Yorkshire of my childhood. I'm less concerned with the queen, although I find her interesting too, than with the whole period. At the same time as changes of an unprecedented kind were going on, Queen Victoria was there on the throne providing an element of continuity. Throughout the whole period from 1837 to 1901 you see the queen's head on the coins. This in itself fascinated the great French historian of nineteenth-century England, Elie Halévy.

How important was it for you to challenge stereotyped views of Victorianism?

I challenged everything because, in fact, when I started writing there wasn't really very much interest in Victorian England. English historians were more interested in the seventeenth century, in particular, than they were in the nineteenth. And so I think I'm really partly responsible myself for a greater interest in Victorian England having developed, trying to take the Victorians more seriously and to look at them in perspective. I wasn't so much challenging recent views; I was challenging old-fashioned views of Victorian England, which were extremely stereotyped although quite brilliantly expressed at times, in Lytton Strachey's *Eminent Victorians*, for example. So, by challenging the version of the Victorians as limited, hypocritical, rigid and better at producing material things than culture, I was doing something that I think was essentially new. I was seizing on their diversity.

The period that you call 'the age of improvement', Hobsbawm named 'the age of revolution'. How would you compare your views on Victorian England with those of Eric Hobsbawm and also E. P. Thompson?

I think that both terms are appropriate for their respective users. My term 'the age of improvement' is better than 'the age of revolution' in relation to England. But Eric Hobsbawm, whom I know very well and who is a friend of mine, was talking about Europe, and 'the age of revolution' was more appropriate for Europe than it was for England. So, whereas I've concentrated on England in detail, he has looked more generally and kaleidoscopically at Europe and indeed the world. He wrote a very good review of *The Age of Improvement*, so he accepted my phrase, which was based on the way that contemporaries looked at it. Where we disagree is on a different matter, that is, my views are different from his in so far as I don't start from Marxism. Hobsbawm places more emphasis on historical phases than I do, moving from revolution to capitalism, from capitalism to imperialism, and so on. Well, this is really a Marxist phasing; and I think that history is more complex than that with pendulum swings and ambiguities as well as contradictions. Hobsbawm himself realizes that and shows himself to be more aware of the contradictions of his own time when he writes his volume on the twentieth century, which he calls *The Age of Extremes*, a curious title to my mind. As for Edward Thompson, whom I knew very well indeed when I was a young professor in Leeds, he limited himself to the eighteenth and early nineteenth centuries, and as far as his ideas about the working class are concerned, I agree with Hobsbawm rather than with Thompson and date the making of the English working class to the late nineteenth century rather than the early nineteenth century. Nevertheless, Thompson was important in three ways. First of all, he looked at the whole conception of class in England in some depth. Second, he was a historian who was more interested in experiences including the experiences of people left out of history, than in ideas; and that is a contrast between his Marxism and Hobsbawm's Marxism. Third, he inspired a generation to turn to historical research on themes that interested me as well as him.

Was there any special encounter which you see as decisive for the development of your style of history? Who are the people you consider your mentors?

The most brilliant lectures I attended were those by Eileen Power, when I was studying economics at the LSE. I came to know her quite well and thought her superb, absolutely marvellous. Her interest in broadcasting inspired me in my later work on the history of the BBC. I was also lucky enough to have Harold Laski as a teacher. His lectures were an incredible *tour de force*, dramatic and impressive. As for Hayek, his lectures were not very good but as a person he was fascinating, dignified, a true European with wide interests. In Cambridge I took a course in history in the traditional style of that university, spending more time on medieval than on modern history, with a good deal of constitutional (and economic) history and less political history. Michael Oakeshott was the best teacher, he really fascinated me. His lectures, whatever the topic, were quite unforgettable. My personal tutor Ernest Barker, then an old man, had considerable influence on me. My interest in political history and political thought I owe in large measure to these two teachers. It was Barker who made me read German writers. In the middle of the war crisis of 1940, he sent me a postcard in German with a long quotation from Gierke.[2] I remember being surprised when I received it that it had not been confiscated by the censors! I was also very much influenced by the people who were reacting against the liberalism of the years between the wars, by E. H. Carr, for example. As for Trevelyan, whom I had read when I was still at school, he had absolutely no influence on me at all. He was a poor lecturer, he had no style. I came to appreciate him more a long time afterwards.

You started your Social History of England *by suggesting that this country has a deep love for tradition, for maintaining things as they are. Unlike other peoples, as you say, for the English 'age is an asset, not a liability'. How would you then explain the paradox that the world owes to a country like this so many innovations that revolutionized people's lives in the nineteenth century, from electricity and the railways to fountain pens, matches and 'water closets', as you so well showed in Victorian Things?*

Because I think there is an element of enterprise in English society that goes back to the Middle Ages. It is very difficult, for example, to talk about peasants in England in the Middle Ages in the same way as we talk about them in Europe, where they would be wearing traditional costumes

---

2   Otto von Gierke (1841–1921), German historian of law, most famous for his studies of medieval corporations.

and be treated as one group. When you look in detail at village structures in England you find that there's a great variety of incomes and a certain amount of social mobility. So I think that enterprise is part, if you like, of my sense of continuity. When I talked about the English veneration of age, I did not mean to say that this was somehow incompatible with being interested in making new things, and the concept of invention itself, already there in 1700, was pushed very far in eighteenth-century England. So the paradox of the combination of innovation and tradition is, in fact, more apparent than real. In the interweaving of a historical tapestry, the two elements are always present.

I also think that this sense of veneration for the past which I wrote about in 1983, in the first edition of the *Social History*, has changed considerably during the course of the last fifteen or twenty years. The tourist industry still capitalizes on 'heritage', but we have destroyed some old institutions very effectively. We now often leave out history when we consider our future. The position at present is more complicated, therefore, and as we move into a new millennium, we try to leave more and more of the past behind. A fourth edition of my *Social History* would be different not only from the first but from the second and third.

Isn't the 'Victorian morality' which we hear so much about a misnomer for a European or even a Western phenomenon?

We hear less about it than we did. Yet I think that the conception of Victorian morality is worthwhile holding on to, so long as we recognize the diversity in the attitudes of the Victorians themselves. There are too many stereotypes still current. I think theirs was a period when new people were coming into authority and power, and when religion was being challenged by science and eroded by indifference. But many Victorians in England wanted somehow or other to hold on to the concept of there being an *ought* in life as well as an *is*. Now, that is not just English. You can find it in continental Europe and even perhaps in Brazil. I think that Victorian values moved from one society to another. They were very frequently misinterpreted in the twentieth century or handled superficially, but they were certainly there. It remains important to consider them not only in an economic or religious context but in cultural terms, taking into account industrialization and before that the Enlightenment.

It is a more or less common view that it was during the Victorian period that there was a widespread struggle for a higher institutional morality, for the development of a public spirit, which was more or less successful in overcoming a corrupt political system. Do you believe that this really happened? If so, to which agencies do you attribute the power to change a mentality?

Yes, there's a lot of truth in saying that around the 1860s things started to change for the better in England, and that this was related to the end of patronage and to the opening up of careers to talent. There has never been any really good English history of corruption and I believe that it would be most interesting to have a detailed cross-cultural study of corruption everywhere and indeed of the development of institutional as well as individual morality. I wrote an article years ago on the origins of institutional morality which I would like to have followed through. Gladstone was a very important figure in the story because he insisted on the importance of accountability in public finance. I'm not saying that this meant the end of corruption, because there was still a lot of corruption in elections and in local government, although on a far smaller scale than in most countries. What happened in the 1850s and 1860s was the result of the combined pressure of three different forces. First, there were ministers who genuinely believed that the most important thing to do was to account for money that was spent; rather than decide how to spend money. Second, a wide range of voluntary organizations, strong in Victorian England, were pressing for improved institutions. Third, there was a willingness to investigate 'scandals', and public opinion was aroused.

If the pressure of public opinion was so important, what was responsible for its formation and for making it consider institutional morality as a central issue?

Not just the press. Industrialists, in particular, men who did not rely on patronage but on the market, compared their own drive with what they thought was the laxity, the lethargy and the inefficiency of traditional public institutions, seeking to create new institutions which they thought were free from these features. Some of them were religious dissenters, treating the Church of England as one such institution. Meanwhile, there were novelists who made a great deal of play with the importance of institutional morality and had great influence on public opinion in general. One of the most important novels in English literature, George Eliot's *Middlemarch*, is very much about institutional morality. Trollope's novels frequently deal with institutional morality; Dickens often deals with a combination of confusion and folly in high places and the immorality of some of the things that went on there. There were some poets who did this too. Arthur Hugh Clough, for example, in his famous poem *The Modern Decalogue*, talked critically about all the sins of the time, including the adulteration of food.

Literary references like the ones you've just mentioned appear frequently in your work. Could you give us your view about the relation between history and literature?

I never believed that history was simply a social science, because I think that the historian should turn to literary sources as well as to facts and figures. I must add that it was long ago that I reached certain conclusions about the evidence of literature. In the first place, literature should never be used simply to illustrate a ready-made argument. The historian ought to try to enter into a particular work, as I did, for example, in the cases of George Eliot and Trollope. In my view, literature can do three things. It can give us access to common experiences which would otherwise have been lost. It can express individual experiences and link them to the common ones. Finally, it can transcend these experiences up to a point and deal with universal human problems. In this respect literature is obviously linked to philosophy, but it can stimulate the historian's imagination as well as enliven his analysis. I am deeply interested in knowing how human beings are viewed in relation to the whole kingdom of Nature, a key Victorian term, and even, perhaps, to the kingdom of God. I know that this is an ambitious task which I am normally unable to carry out. But I am sure that there is much more in literature than an apt quotation.

Is there any special field in historical studies that deserves more attention from scholars?

I am sure that some fields have not received as much attention from historians as they deserve. In my view, we need better political history, and we need diplomatic history more than ever. The crises of Bosnia and Kosovo showed quite dramatically that diplomacy cannot be replaced by modern weapons and computers and that the changing ways in which international relations were conducted over the long-term ought to be one of the central themes in new historical studies.

Margaret Thatcher used to speak about the need to revive Victorian values, and more recently, under John Major, Parliament talked a lot about what was called the need for a 'back to basics campaign'. Do you think that such a revival is possible? And were those Victorian values what Thatcher and the others thought they were?

No, at least not in the way some people think. Mrs Thatcher's phrase was a political phrase, and it was associated with one aspect of Victorian England which was the sense of the importance of the gospel of work and the feeling that drive, character and duty (which she had been taught about in the Methodist chapel where her father used to be a lay preacher), were the things that really matter. She had no understanding, however, of the fact that Victorian England was itself a place which was undergoing significant change, and that many of the values that she talked about were not equally important at all points in the reign. Indeed, there were critics of those values. If she had talked about the importance of society having certain values in order to cohere in an age of individualism, it would have been different; but that was not the way she thought. There is clearly a need in any society to have forces which bind people together, as well as separate them, and the more you become market-oriented and the more individualism is stressed, then the more you get involved in value questions. Blair seems to appreciate this, but does not know quite what to do about it. Citizenship classes in schools will have only limited value, and the new stress on discipline in schools may not work. Nor commitment to more and more grading by examination. There is another danger. Once you start talking about important issues, like what makes a society cohere, you are always in danger of trivializing them; and with a very powerful press, the scandals and the lapses from the values get more attention than the values themselves. John Major learned that.

Edward Said has been devoting a lot of effort to showing that imperialism, although officially over, is still very much alive in the Western world in the form of orientalism, that is, a cluster of Western ideas about the East, especially important in the nineteenth century. Considering that Victorian England was the greatest imperial power of modern times, could you comment on his views?

I think his views should be taken very seriously because there is covert imperialism as well as open imperialism, a cultural imperialism as well as an economic imperialism. But I think that in relation to the Victorian empire it is important to bear in mind that there were always articulate critics of empire, far more than there were in other countries where imperialism developed in various forms. There was what I and other historians have called 'the argument of empire'. No one, for example, would ever dream of calling Gladstone, who was one of the two great political figures of the period, an imperialist. Quite the reverse. The word 'imperialism' was not, in fact, used very much in England until the very end of the century. It was applied in the middle years of the century to the empire of Napoleon III more than it was to empires overseas. And when by the end of the century Britain had added an enormous amount of extra territory to the empire, alongside the pride taken in it, and expressed lavishly in 1897 at Queen Victoria's Diamond Jubilee, there also developed a sense of its impermanence. The war in South Africa (1899–1902), not over when Queen Victoria died, divided politicians and brought to the surface national feelings.

Going back to Said, I agree that many ideas which were developed in the nineteenth century concerning Britain's relation to other peoples are still strong and have survived the collapse of empires. Nevertheless, I would have liked him to have devoted more time to comparing the process of imperial expansion with the process of imperial contraction.

How far did the public schools have a role in making Victorian Britain what it was?

I think they had quite an important role, especially in forming the civil servants of the British Empire. Their main role was to provide education for the middle classes, quite a few sons of the gentry and also for some aristocratic children. Before the beginning of the nineteenth century they had taken in boys from a broader social range. When they were reformed in the nineteenth century, they virtually excluded the children of the lower class; they occupied new buildings, tried to inculcate their own conceptions of morality and became much more efficient institutions. When the civil service was opened to competitive examination, it was certainly the people who had been to public schools who won many of the places.

There is, nevertheless, a somewhat ambivalent element in their impact because for every Tom Brown that they produced, a man who believed in the virtues and values that he'd been taught at school, there was somebody who represented the opposite and who was a cad at school – that was the word that was used – and the opposite of a hero on the frontiers of empire. There were also rebels. Concentrating on the role of the public schools, male preserves, is something of a male preoccupation. That is one reason why women's studies are important. There are, of course, many other reasons too.

You are one of the few people in England to know the important work of the Brazilian Gilberto Freyre. How did you discover his work and what importance did it have in your intellectual development?

I discovered his work around the time I went to the University of Sussex. I had heard of him before and I had read some of his work in translation. But I can't say that I really realized how interesting he was until I started thinking about the relationship between visual history and social history. Freyre was very interested in houses and artefacts and made an immediate appeal to me as a historian. He was much in my mind when I was writing *Victorian Things*. There is also some evidence of his mark on me in my *Social History of England*. I was strongly interested in his ideas both on time (in the essay I wrote about him I talk about his Proustian attitude towards time), and place, especially his poetical approach to place. His acute sensibility to smells, colours and even noises also impressed me very much. Those were some of the things that appealed to me, and I wished my Portuguese were better to really read some of the many things that have not been translated.

My contacts with the Jamaican sociologist Fernando Henriques were also very important to my discovering Freyre. He was then running a University of Sussex centre in Barbados (which, alas, does not survive), the Centre for Multi-Racial Studies, and was extremely interested in Freyre's attitudes towards colour. Fernando had an aesthetic rather than a social sense of colour, and so did Freyre, who illuminated the significance of the mixing of colours in relation to Brazilian identity.

What do you think is Freyre's intellectual importance?

I don't think he has been taken as seriously as he ought to have been. One of the outstanding historians of the twentieth century, he has not been put on the historiographical map as he deserved. He had something very distinctive to say, but he is not easily related to a school, or indeed to a tradition of historiography. He should never be treated negatively in terms of what he did not say. He calls out for appreciation. I don't know anybody else besides Freyre who writes in detail and with so much originality about domestic arrangements or about plantation life.

I have not been able to find any person in Britain who has genuinely read very much Freyre. There are of course some people in the United States who do know about him, but it's true that Americans are generally more interested in Brazilian history than the English. In Britain, nobody ever asked me any question about Freyre until you did. And moreover, in the reviews of my volume of essays I cannot remember anybody picking out the one that I wrote about Freyre or remarking on the fact that I had chosen Freyre as one of the historians who has most interested me.

When I wrote my essay on Freyre, I thought it was useful to compare him with Trevelyan because both historians share a few important things: they are equally interested in places, in buildings, in the long-term continuities of the history of their own countries; and they were also, by temperament, rather hostile to certain manifestations of 'modern progress'. I was somewhat dissatisfied with David Cannadine's *Trevelyan*, for it seems to me that he left out precisely the kind of points we're talking about now. Comparisons matter, particularly when social history becomes cultural history.

Like Freyre, you make a lot of use of newspapers as a historical source. Were you inspired by Freyre's wide and early use?

I agree that his use of newspapers as a source was a remarkable achievement for his time, like his use of other little-tapped sources such as etiquette books, photographs and even recipes. But I've not been inspired by him so far as using newspapers is concerned. I used them an enormous amount, before I read or met Freyre. What I have subsequently done is to look at them very critically and in perspective to write about them in terms of the evolution of a media complex. I hadn't really developed my interest quite as fully in that direction when I got to know Freyre but, like him, I had always used newspapers to an enormous extent without thinking too much about what I was doing.

What do you consider to be the dangers involved in the use of this historical source?

It is terribly dangerous to rely too much on newspapers as a historical source, but the benefits of using them are as great as the dangers. If any student wants to work with me on a research thesis, I do not accept any outline of what he proposes to do until he has immersed himself in a considerable amount of the material of the time; and I think that reading newspapers for their topicality and their immediacy is a valuable exercise in total immersion. One thing that it does is to establish a notion of the working language of the time. It allows you to pick up recurrent words and key concepts, and to build up a lexicon out of the newspapers. But I wouldn't regard doing this as getting at what are the really significant elements of history. Newspapers should never be an exclusive source, and the nearer they are to becoming one, the more they should be treated with suspicion. They can be very biased, they are often extremely uninformed, and they cut up history into short segments. Having said that, they can be as interesting for the advertisements they contain and for their illustrations as for their 'news'.

Freyre has, as you know, been criticized by Brazilian intellectuals for his conceptual fluidity and for his role in producing and diffusing a powerful ideology which hides the contradictions of Brazilian social processes in the name of social harmony. To him, according to this view, we owe the myth of a Brazil which is distinctive for its cultural miscegenation and social democracy. Do you share these criticisms?

I'm fully aware of these criticisms, but I've never been too much bothered about conceptual fluidity. One of the alternatives to it is conceptual rigidity; and many of the people who criticize him on this account are working within Marxist frameworks of various kinds which can restrain the historical imagination. As for social harmony, only Brazilians can say much that is useful, but I think in any case he's predisposed through his own experience towards a notion of historical harmony being the key to the unity of a period. I know little about Freyre's views on the Brazilian political situation, but I suspect that he might have been insensitive to the dangers of military authority, and probably overestimated the natural harmonies of Brazilian society and underestimated the forces leading to conflict. But I do not see any inconsistency in his writings. I think that they are remarkably of one piece. I've not read two works by Freyre that take up a different methodology or reach different conclusions about Brazil. I think he was also anxious to show that there was a time dimension to Brazilian history and that it was different from the time dimension in North American history.

Freyre's greatest importance for me is as a cultural historian, a term that had only a limited use in his lifetime but has now become very common. I do not wish to make too great claims for Freyre either as a sociologist or as a social psychologist, but he saw the importance of taking the two together. He was sociologically aware even when he was not sociologically sophisticated, and he was psychologically aware when he made an effort to get inside people as well as to observe them. I feel, therefore, that I ought to compare him not only with British social historians but also with French historians of 'mentalities'. Therefore, if he were going to be fitted into a general historiographical frame, one would have to bring in French history as well as English history.

Did you find this mixture of 'physical and mystic love' he felt towards England, in other words, his Anglophilia, noticeable in Freyre's attitudes and work?

Yes, his Anglophilia was obvious to me, but at the same time it was a more agreeable Anglophilia than some which I've met in the United States. I'd rather meet people who are really critical of their own societies and critical of us. So I don't feel very happy in the company of Anglophiles. But it didn't really make me feel particularly overwhelmed in the case of Freyre because I could talk to him about history, about newspapers as historical sources, and many of the other topics that we've covered. His knowledge of English literature was deep and wide-ranging, including so-called minor writers and essayists. Yet there was no English writer he would mention where there wasn't a reason for doing so. He didn't put them in for the sake of effect. He genuinely knew them, he read them and he knew what he meant when he talked about writers like Gissing, Pater, Dickens and so on. He liked the English language and prose style, and preferred its conversational tone to the quite complex style of the French. It was also very important to him for a historian to write well and memorably.

Since I knew that he liked England, I felt that it was very important that an English university should give him an honorary degree, and it was on my initiative, which was backed very strongly by Fernando Henriques, that Sussex offered him the title of doctor *honoris causa* in 1966, when I was its Vice-Chancellor.

Freyre used to say that he saw Portugal through 'English eyes', 'impreg-
nated with English literature'. Would you say that you saw Brazil through
Freyre's eyes when you visited the country?

I really saw Brazil through my own eyes! I had been to Venezuela, to
Mexico and quite a lot to the Caribbean and I was interested myself in
questions of colour and culture. When I looked at Rio, for example, I was
comparing Rio with other cities, in a way that perhaps Freyre wouldn't
have done. I had already written about cities and was aware that in São
Paulo a completely different group of historians were working on the
growth of that city, some of them taking my idea of 'shock city', Manchester and Los Angeles being two examples, and applying it to São Paulo.
There was actually a conference in California once on Manchester, Los
Angeles and São Paulo as shock cities. Some of the things that I have
learned about Brazil after Freyre's death have come to me through different channels. Nevertheless, bearing in mind that Brazil has changed dramatically since then, and that there are forces in contemporary Brazil
demanding changes which Freyre did not contemplate, I would still tell
anybody going to Brazil to read him. Without any doubt.

Contrary to the French historian Jacques Le Goff, who felt completely out
of place at the University of Oxford, Freyre confessed that he felt amazingly
well there, as if he belonged there. Having met Freyre and knowing his work,
how would you interpret the attachment of this young Brazilian to an insti-
tution in which so many English people do not feel at home?

Because Oxford is a place in which the old coexists with the new, where the
new functions and flows within an old framework. There is a certain sensibility, of a quasi-romantic kind in Freyre, which makes him appreciate the
idea of ruins, Chinese clocks, the view of the swans on Worcester College
lake, and so on. I think one cannot understand Freyre without realizing the
importance of his attitude towards beauty. He's aware of the element of
decay in beauty, but he's also very much drawn to beautiful things, and
Oxford just seems to be beautiful, very different from the smoky industrial
cities he disliked.

Well, why does an Englishman not respond to that? Because we'd
approach Oxford through our experience of other parts of England,
which Freyre didn't have. And we also carry to Oxford our feeling of the
inadequacies of what has been studied and taught there. I could not share
Freyre's attitude to Oxford, which has far more contrasts inside it than he
ever knew about.

One of the British policies which most affected nineteenth-century Brazil
was the anti-slavery campaign. What do you think about the idea defended

by some historians that, instead of a demonstration of public spirit and moral idealism, this campaign was, on the contrary, aimed at undermining the economic power of other countries, and, furthermore, a strategy of distracting British public opinion from domestic demands for a broader franchise and extensive social reform?

I don't agree with either of those two points. Anti-slavery campaigns have been mixed-motivation campaigns. British people could be very hypocritical at times and there was an element of truth in the argument that some early nineteenth-century English industrial workers were being treated worse than plantation slaves. It has fascinated me that in Yorkshire, the part of England where I was born and brought up, the condition of people working in the mills was compared by factory reformers to that of the slaves. Never at any time, to my mind, was the anti-slavery campaign used as a decoy to distract people's attention from their own problems. Never. As to the wish to destroy other people's economies, the one old economy that was, I think, effectively destroyed in the nineteenth century was that of India, where there was no slavery. As far as Africa was concerned, I used to enjoy talking in Trinidad to Eric Williams, who raised quite different questions about the relationship between colonial slavery and British capitalism. These are still worth discussing.

For Brazilians, and perhaps for all societies with a republican background, it seems a bit odd to see a person with affinities with the labour movement and the Labour Party accept a noble title and enjoy the privileges that go with it. Could you comment on this?

This question is of much more interest to people outside England than it is to people here. When I was in China years ago and was going around with a very good young interpreter, he never asked me any question about England at all. We were talking about China all the time until, on the very last morning before I left him, he said to me: 'Could I ask you a very personal question? What does it feel like to be a lord?' And I said: 'It makes me feel no different than if I were not a lord.' The reason why I was offered a peerage by James Callaghan, a Labour prime minister, in 1975 was because I had been involved very deeply in university policy-making in Britain at the start of the new universities, and it was felt that that prominence in educational life in Britain should somehow or other be represented in Parliament. And the other reason was that I had been the chairman of a committee on the conditions of work of nurses and their education and training. It was, again, considered very important that while a Nursing Bill was going through Parliament, there was somebody present who really knew what it stood for, and would help to get it through.

Having made those two points, I should emphasize that I did not go into the House as a politician. If I had wished to be a politician, I would have gone to the House of Commons much earlier. The House of Lords, now different in composition from when I went in, plays a very minor part in my life. I use my peerage mainly as a means for gathering information. The title has not changed my attitudes in any kind of way, nor my behaviour. Nor does it confer any special privileges. I always write under my own name, Asa Briggs, and never refer to myself as 'Lord Briggs'. I never call myself Lord Briggs abroad either, but curiously it is abroad, as I have said, that this subject interests people most. I do not think that this is because they are more interested in continuity than in change, but because they are fascinated by status.

Turning now to the future, there has been in recent times a marked rise of controversy about the value of the Royal Family and one frequently hears references to the loss of prestige of the British monarchy and even to the lack of reason for it to continue to exist. Do you believe that there is a real trend in favour of abolishing the monarchy, or do you still think that there is something or a lot to be said in its favour?

I don't think there's a very powerful movement to abolish it. There might be pressure to change its role or to change the line of descent, but not to abolish the institution. It went through a very bad patch before Queen Victoria, and if you look at it in perspective it was Queen Victoria who developed the conception of a Royal Family. Her uncles were not looked upon with a great deal of pleasure by her or by other people who were her subjects. When Queen Victoria's husband died and she went into a kind of retirement, there was a certain amount of criticism and even republicanism, because it was felt she was not doing her job; but even then she received more sympathy than criticism.

I wouldn't say that any institution lasts forever, but unless something very foolish were done, I'd be surprised if there was any very great pressure to abolish the monarchy during the early twenty-first century. I should add that one reason why the last edition of my *Social History* was different from earlier accounts was that I had to introduce Princess Diana as well as Blair and 'New Labour'. There is still no great enthusiasm in England for the idea of a republic or a president. The British monarchy has very little real political power, but it still carries with it a lot of symbolic force.

Robert Darnton has been arguing that the French press had a crucial role in the fall of the Ancien Régime. *By publishing scandalous and defamatory stories about the sex life of Louis XVI, Marie Antoinette and other members of the royal family, the libels stimulated irreverence, desacralized the institution of monarchy, and in the end undermined its authority. Would you say that, as in the case of old regime France, the modern British media have a lot of responsibility for the present crisis of the monarchy?*

I think that while Bob Darnton was right to draw attention to this literature, it in no sense, in my view, caused the French Revolution. I think that the financial crisis and the inability of the French monarchy to solve it, plus the spread of Enlightenment ideas, were more relevant to its fall than was the spread of scurrilous scandalous literature. What this literature did, however, was to make people behave somewhat differently after the monarchy had fallen. In other words, it became important after the fall of the Bastille and the execution of the king.

In England this scurrilous scandalous literature is associated with a media system which is far more powerful than Darnton's largely underground literature. And certainly the media, which have an obsessive interest in scandal, not only royal scandal, make it difficult to ensure the cohesion of elements in society which hold it together; and very frequently a large sector of the British media, not just the tabloid press, plays on popular prejudices rather than on the desire to give information or to stimulate discussion. I think that it is odd that the same person who owns *The Times* owns the most popular newspaper, the *Sun*, which uses a high level of journalistic ability to produce a very low level of journalism!

The publication of the sex scandals of the Royal Family may have undermined its position, but I don't think one should take this too seriously. There is an element of soap opera in the sequence, which appeals to many people, English and foreigners alike, perhaps again foreigners more than the English themselves. Apart from the peerage, the subject I'm asked about when I go abroad is, what is the Royal Family up to?

London, July and October 1996
(Interview updated and enlarged, July 1999)

SELECT BIBLIOGRAPHY

Victorian People (London, Odham, 1954).

The Age of Improvement, 1783–1867 (London, Longman, 1959).

Mass Entertainment: The Origins of a Modern Industry (lecture, Adelaide, 1960).

The History of Broadcasting in the United Kingdom (5 vols, Oxford, Oxford University Press, 1961–; new edn, 1995).

Victorian Cities (London, Odham, 1963).

A Social History of England (London, Weidenfeld and Nicolson, 1983).

Collected Essays (3 vols, Brighton, Harvester, 1985).

Victorian Things (London, Batsford, 1988).

The Story of the Leverhulme Trust (London, Leverhulme, 1991).

(with Peter Burke) *A Social History of the Media: From Gutenberg to the Internet* (Cambridge, Polity, 2001).

3

Natalie Zemon Davis

Looking back in 1998 on her intellectual life, Natalie Zemon Davis described her efforts to insert a series of groups into history – workers, women, Jews, Native Americans and Africans – as though she were 'engaged in some rescue mission over and over again'. Some years earlier she had referred to her relationship with the past as being 'partly maternal', as if by writing history she wished 'to bring people to life again as a mother would want to bear children'. The tone of these statements reveals Natalie Davis's gift for expressing her feelings and emotions without ever allowing this to compromise the highest academic standards of her important work, in which she has been engaged for over forty years.

Natalie Davis is an undisputed authority on sixteenth-century French history and also one of today's best-known and most respected historians, not just in the field of the social and cultural history of the early modern period but also in that of women's history. The first course devoted to the history of women in Canada – which was to become the model for one of the most popular courses in Western universities in the 1970s and 1980s – was organized by Natalie Davis and her colleague Jill Ker Conway in 1971.[1]

1 Jill Ker Conway (b. 1934), an Australian specialist in nineteenth- and twentieth-century women's history. A former professor and vice-president of the University of Toronto, she currently teaches at MIT (Massachusetts Institute of Technology). She is the author of *The Female Experience in Eighteenth and Nineteenth Century America* (New York, Garland, 1982), but her more recent books have been autobiographical: *The Road from Coorain* (London, Heinemann, 1989: a best-seller in the United States for a year) and *True North: A Memoir* (London, Hutchinson, 1994).

The cover photograph of Natalie Zemon Davis reproduced by kind permission of Erwin Schenkelbach.

It was, however, as a specialist in the history of Lyons in the sixteenth century that Natalie Davis made her reputation in the 1960s, when she wrote a series of ground-breaking papers examining that city from various standpoints: urban spaces, trade, immigration, Catholic–Protestant relations, gender relations, etc. At that time she admits she was basically interested in the working classes, and the workers' revolts in Lyons seemed to be ideal material through which she could address the major questions that then fascinated her: class, class conflict, religious changes and the relationship between the social and the intellectual world. Although at the beginning of her career as a historian she had been guided to a great extent by Marxism, her study of anthropology broadened her frame of reference and added to her work a concern for the symbolic dimension of reality and the multiplicity of relationships involved in it. And so in the 1970s Natalie Davis's reputation grew along with her new historical-anthropological explorations. Her pioneering study of the rites of violence, for example, although focusing on sixteenth-century France, raised much broader questions on the uses of ritual to legitimize urban violence against outsiders. Anthropology can thus be said to have enhanced Natalie Davis's main characteristic, that of using local history as an opportunity to broach more general issues.

In the early 1980s Natalie Davis became even better known internationally as the author of an academic best-seller, *The Return of Martin Guerre*, and consultant to the 1982 film of the same name directed by Daniel Vigne. As she remembers, ever since she read the book by Jean de Coras, the Toulouse judge, relating the story of a famous case he had judged in 1560, she said to herself, 'This has got to be a film!' The case that went to court concerned the dramatic events involving a peasant family in Languedoc, when a man who had been missing for twelve years reappeared and was accepted as the real Martin Guerre by his family and community for three or four years, until he was finally denounced as an impostor by Bertrande, his wife. The story, which reached its climax with the arrival of the real Martin Guerre just as the impostor was about to convince the court that he really was the missing villager, had all the ingredients of a box-office success. Through his performance as both the real and the false Martin Guerre, the well-known French actor Gérard Dépardieu further helped to publicize the story and gain recognition for Natalie Davis as a historian able to reach both an academic and a lay audience at the same time. Again, she had showed her expertise in the art of using local history in order to raise general questions: on this occasion a micro-history – a case of false identity in a French village – was used to discuss questions of identity formation and class relations.

At about the same time Natalie Davis struck out in a new direction, showing her ability as a historian of Jewish culture and women's culture in the early modern period. These are the interests that have led to her most ambitious work so far, *Women on the Margins* (1995), in which she compares and contrasts the careers of three seventeenth-century women – one Jewish, one Catholic and one Protestant – and their adventures not only in France or even Europe but also on other continents. This was a project, she explains, 'that wove together all the strands of my past interests – social, anthropological, ethnographic and literary – and yet also cast me out on new seas and territories'. She is now writing another book along the same lines on cultural mixing, in which she even explores the caravan routes of North Africa.

The same daring that marks this work, which Natalie Davis published in 1995 at the age of sixty-six, reflecting her untiring determination to try out new paths, can also be seen in her personal life. She is unusually open and frank about this. Born in Detroit in 1929 into a wealthy Jewish family that remained untouched by the Depression of the thirties, she lived a quiet life until the start of the Cold War and her meeting with Chandler Davis, a young Harvard mathematician to whom she has been married for over fifty years. She had had an ideal education, first at a select private school in suburban Detroit, and then at Smith College, one of the so-called 'Seven Sisters', the most prestigious women's liberal arts colleges in the United States. During this period, however, as her social and political conscience grew keener she began to take an active part in political debates and action against racism and for freedom of expression, trade unions, etc. In privileged households such as hers, Natalie Davis recalls, 'people of colour entered only to clean, iron or serve at the table'; yet that did not prevent her very early on from demonstrating against racism and going against convention by deliberately sitting next to a black person whenever she got on a bus.

Her meeting with Chandler in 1948, however, turned her life upside down. First, because her decision to marry a 'goy' (and after only a few weeks of courting) was totally unacceptable for a young Jewish woman like her. Chandler, as she herself says, was neither Jewish nor rich. She was well aware that the fact that he was 'handsome, smart, on the left, and liked intelligent women' would make no difference to her family's opposition. So at the age of just nineteen she eloped and married without telling her parents or even Smith College (which exceptionally did not expel her). The second reason was that it marked the beginning of the family saga of dealings with the FBI and McCarthyism – during which their passports were seized and Chandler was imprisoned for a few months. These problems came to an end only in 1962 when they moved to Canada, where they both found positions in the University of Toronto. It was during this difficult period in the 1950s that Natalie Davis had her three children and did her doctorate for the University of Michigan. 'The joys of childbirth and childrearing far outweighed the political travail we were going through,' she says. And without any embarrassment she adds, 'Having children helped me as a historian. It humanized me; it taught me about psychology and personal relations and gave flesh to abstract words like "material needs" and "the body"; it revealed the power of the family, rarely treated by historians in those days.'

Natalie Davis has recently retired from Princeton, where she had taught since 1978 (after spending six years at Berkeley, California), but is still extremely active as a researcher and itinerant lecturer in many parts of the world. She remains unassailable as a role model, not just for the new generations of women academics but for historians in general. Her message to historians and the general public is that the study of the past can be seen as a lesson in hope, because it shows that, however domineering society may be, there are always alternatives open for people to make their own history. 'No matter how static and despairing the present looks, the past reminds us that change can occur.'

Extremely elegant and attractive in her petite way and looking younger than she is, Natalie Davis received me in London, in the flat of her friend Lisa Jardine, for a long, friendly and enthusiastic conversation on modern historiographical trends and the most varied aspects of her career and interests.

MARIA LÚCIA PALLARES-BURKE   *You were brought up in a Jewish family for whom, as you said, 'the past was too unpleasant for children to know'. What made you want to spend your life in the study of the past?*

NATALIE ZEMON DAVIS   To start with, I think it was a sense of dislocation from the past, of being, so to speak, rootless. On one side, my family was made up of Jewish immigrants from Europe, both my grandparents and great-grandparents considering that it was not worth talking about their Russian or Polish past, which was, in many ways, so grim. On the other side, there was no American past either, since their commitment, as for many other Jewish people in America, was to the future. The first impact of the past I felt when I was already in the high school and started to become familiar with students who came from old American families and were deeply rooted in the country's past. At that time I had a wonderful history teacher who initiated me into Greek and European history, the Enlightenment, the French and American revolutions, etc. That's when I suddenly felt a sense of belonging to these distant events and located myself in those extreme European pasts. At the same time, I became deeply fascinated by the idea of knowing the aspirations that people had had in the past. When I went to college that interest continued, at the same time as I also became extremely involved with literature and writing, an interest which has family roots, since my father had been a popular playwright. A few weeks ago, when my daughter made a speech of reminiscence, 'My Parent's Daughter', for my seventieth birthday celebration, she referred to her childhood memory of hearing the typewriter clack, followed by a pause while I was thinking. That reminded me exactly of what happened when I was a little girl, and my father was clacking away and stopping as he wrote his plays. So an interest in writing and imaginative creation became part of me very early. As for history, it was not only important because it gave me a sense of the past which I lacked; it also responded to my deep interest in politics. Since college, it has seemed necessary to me to know about history for political reasons. Marx had said that history was the only science that was going to give people guidance for the future, and I was fascinated by the thought that I – not as a woman or as a Jew, which identities didn't seem to be particularly interesting questions at that time, but as an individual person – belonged to the great wave of humanity.

As for my lifelong interest in history, what has always driven me is not the wish to find any easy answers to our present questions in the past, to obtain prescriptions or to learn any clear lessons from it. These lessons, if they exist, are extremely unclear. The opinion I have just expressed might be wrongly taken as a cynical view of history, but I am not a cynic. I often think of what the Renaissance humanist Pico della Mirandola said about human beings: they could reach up to the achievements of the angels, but they could also fall into doing terrible things, demonic acts.[2] Pico's saying gives us a feeling of hope as well as of the threat of the absolutely terrible. When I was younger I tended to be looking for the more upbeat features of human experience, even seeking where they could emerge out of the experience of oppression and domination. Today I can still write about this, with more soberness and sorrow, but I'm also prepared to talk about a humanity which I see as much more complex and with a wider range of experiences. So I'd say that my sense of the importance of the past has increased and expanded to include a variety of subjects. Twenty-five years ago, for example, I began to include women in my studies, and more recently Jewish history and non-European themes. And this expansion of my interests has given me more vantage points from which to study the past.

Since your schooldays you've been an active participant in the debates and events of the time. You've protested against the Marshall Plan, McCarthyism, and in the bus you always sat next to a black person to protest against race discrimination. Would you then describe yourself as an intellectual who is committed or engagée? And do you put the history you write at the service of this commitment?

I certainly want to be an intellectual who is *engagée*, but the way that I've been engaged has changed over time. When I was a student I was active in

2   Giovanni Pico della Mirandola (1463–1494), Italian humanist, author of the *Oration on the Dignity of Man*.

politics, until I began to have babies. Subsequently I've still been very attentive to what is happening, but my activity has become limited to signing petitions and letters and sending money, and more rarely to sustained organized campaigns. Of course, I marched up and down during the civil rights movement and during the Vietnam War. In recent years I was involved in a protest against the Gulf War (a terrible, terrible mistake on the part of the US government) and against the award of an honorary doctorate at the University of Toronto to ex-president George Bush. And I've been giving support to Israeli friends who are helping Palestinians rebuild their demolished houses and protect their lands against the encroachment of settlers. But besides my involvement in cases like this, my commitment has been in connection with my work, defending a more participatory form of university life, for instance, and an anti-hierarchical structure in the department. But I must add that if my work in the department is inspired by my political values, my work as a historian is not in the service of politics. In so far as my work has a critical edge – which I hope it always does – that seems to me to be a commitment. Because my first task as a historian is to understand the past, to do research about it in order to get as much evidence as I can, to check my evidence and do my best to interpret it in ways that do justice to the set of questions asked and to what the material shows. Even in my most activist days as a Marxist undergraduate I was never a doctrinaire. I found Marxism a helpful insight but I've always had pretty much respect for what my research found. History serves through the perspective it gives you, through the vantage points from which you can begin to look at and understand the present, through the wisdom or the patience that it gives you and through a comforting hope in the possibility of change.

Would you agree then with the common view that the historian should be neutral and impartial and never take a stand?

In the past ten years or so my study of scholarship in France during the German occupation has dealt directly with this question. I had already started thinking about it back in the early seventies, when I was working on religious violence during the sixteenth century. But now I've been trying to understand even the historians who collaborated with the Nazis, and so the importance of figuring out where the people we are writing about are coming from becomes even more evident. I keep asking what formed those historians and their morality. This is not to say that they are right in my eyes, but to make them intelligible in terms of their life trajectories and of certain values of their time. In other words, instead of explaining them by some kind of schizophrenia or mental illness or mere envy, which would imply a certain degree of reductionism, it seems to me a critically important task to understand them through their own voices, not my voice.

On the other hand, the historian might want – and this is a matter of style – to insert his or her own voice somehow within the body of the work. I tried to do this when I was writing about the sixteenth-century rites of violence. I was trying to make sense of those gratuitous and cruel acts of violence in a way that was not reductionist. At the same time I did not want to leave the topic without making any kind of judgement, without inserting myself at a certain point. So at the very end of the essay I said that the rites of violence are not the rights of violence, and made a comment for the present and with some kind of contemporary reference. Now, if we intervene in this way, it should be very clear to our readers what we are doing, where we're coming from and where we stand. In other words, we should show, by some expository or literary device, that the narrative voice is changing, and that it's our personal voice that they are hearing now. I'm fully aware of the fact that one's values influence what one is writing about at all times, but I don't think that the historian should be self-conscious and intervene at every moment, as some contemporary writings suggest. In fact, that can become very boring.

The 1950s, the period in which you had your three children and wrote your Ph.D. thesis, was also the time when you went through various dramatic experiences: you and your husband were persecuted for refusing to take the oath of anti-communism, your husband was put on a blacklist and could not find a permanent position in an American university, and was eventually put in prison for contempt of Congress. For your scholarly life 'the worst part of this period', as you put it, was your intellectual isolation. Wouldn't you say, though, that there were also great advantages in not being attached to any group and that much of the innovation you brought to historical studies is due to this involuntary isolation?

I think that is a very good point and the situation definitely did have this positive side. I did not have to be an assistant to anyone and didn't have to worry about pleasing people because I was not in a situation in which I needed to please them. I was not even doing the research in the city where I was going to present my thesis, and was not part of any student group after the first year of my graduate study at the University of Michigan. We were then living mostly in New York and I just went off on my own, subscribing to different journals, reading at the New York Public Library and going to academic meetings which, although interesting, were a little bit lonesome because I didn't know anybody there at the time. Actually, it would have been nice to have had one or two friends who were trying, like me, to raise children, yet were also very strongly interested in history. It was at this time in New York that I met Rosalie Colie from Columbia University, where I was teaching at night for one term.[3] I dedicated one of my books to her memory because the talks we had were intellectually very important to me. She wasn't in the position of my teacher, but rather of an older friend, and this allowed for an independent discussion, between two women, on more or less equal terms. Five or six years ago when I wrote about the painter and naturalist Maria Sibylla Merian in *Women on the Margins*, I think I was drawing upon some experience of my own when I was talking about her lack of patrons. I hope that my familiarity with such a situation gave me some insight and that I wasn't just projecting myself onto her when I referred to the advantages she had of being able to do things her own way. Like her, I had also done things my way, and certainly didn't worry about who would examine my doctoral dissertation. The only people I was thinking about when I wrote were intellectuals who were already dead, like Max Weber, and a few other people who were starting to write on the Weber thesis about Protestantism, but whom I didn't know personally. I wasn't thinking about what X or Y were going to say, and the main person I talked to was my husband, who isn't even a historian.

When you started working for your Ph.D. in the early 1950s you wrote a paper on Christine de Pisan, but decided, nevertheless, not to choose women's history for your dissertation, which would've been a real breakthrough. Keith Thomas, for example, said that what prevented him from continuing in this field in the late fifties was the lack of a general interest in the subject. What do you think prevented you from exploring this new territory at that time?

It didn't seem to me the right track to take then either intellectually or professionally, although I was fascinated and cheered by Christine's *City of Ladies* and enjoyed my work on her. So I'm glad I learned about Christine de Pisan but I don't regret it at all not to have pursued women's history at that point. First of all, I felt that it was more important to continue working on artisans, class and social change in the Protestant Reformation, a field in which nobody at the time seemed to be interested in doing the kind of archival work I was doing. Secondly, at that time I didn't see women's history as adding a new dimension to historical studies. When I did look at this first professional literary woman I tried to locate her socially, but from my Marxist point of view I didn't see much novelty in studying a highly placed woman. I preferred to turn to

3   Rosalie Colie (1924–1972), North American literary critic, author of *Paradoxica Epidemica: The Renaissance Tradition of Paradox* (Princeton, Princeton University Press, 1966) and *Shakespeare's Living Art* (Princeton, Princeton University Press, 1974).

something that was still uncharted, being much more taken by the intellectual issues involved in what I was discovering about the early trade unions, for instance. That was one of the reasons why I never revised or published my paper on Christine de Pisan, although the *Journal of the History of Ideas* had expressed interest in it. At the time I just put it aside and went back to my artisans! And thirdly, I think I didn't want to do a woman's thing just because I was a woman. There were also political reasons behind my choice. In the early fifties, when I wrote that paper, we were in the middle of the Cold War, the Korean War, and the real issue then was the problem of peace, rather than women.

In your youth Marxism and socialism seduced you because, as you stated, they 'offered some big ways to organize the past'. And now, do you still see some value in the work of Marx and certain of his followers?

I never really had an experience of conversion to Marxism. Although I always thought that some Marxist writing was interesting and valuable, I was actually rather eclectic. Marx himself is a fascinating man historically, really one of the great figures of the nineteenth century, and in some ways we're in a better position now to appreciate both his limitations and his greatnesses because the Cold War is over and we're not evaluating him polemically in terms of true or false. I would say, then, that I continue to find Marx and some other people inspired by post-Marxian questions extremely interesting and stimulating. They prevent us from thinking the world is only a text and also remind us of the importance of conflict in the understanding of a culture. Indeed, one thing that I feel quite strongly about (and used a lot in my teaching) is the notion that it's better to identify a period not so much in terms of the things that people deeply believe as in terms of the deep conflicts that divide people. That is, periods and cultures are held together by a deeply shared common argument or uncertainty. I think that is actually a much more helpful way of conceptualizing things than saying that a given period is held together because everybody believes in *x*. So that's my approach and maybe it's congenial to certain Marxist ways of thinking.

Do you have any philosophy of history yourself?

Yes, to a certain degree, but not one that involves a belief in stages of evolution. In 1998 I published a paper called 'Beyond Evolution', in a volume in honour of the Polish historian Jerzy Topolski, in which I deal with views – Marxist and non-Marxist – of modernization theory, theories which share the belief in evolutionary stages.[4] I don't agree at all with

4   'Beyond Evolution: Comparative History and its Goals', in *Swiat Historii*, Posnań, Instytut Historii UAM, 1998, pp. 149–57; repr. in *Society and Culture*.

this view, for I believe that there is no single trajectory. I might have to change my mind again as I get older, but today I reject the evolutionary scheme in which I believed when I was a graduate student. Now I like to insist on the notion that there are multiple trajectories, multiple paths. If there is a philosophy in this, it is one that looks for debates rather than consensus or coherence. It's not so much a philosophy as a vision of the past which is interested in the multiple ways of doing things within a common frame, and which looks for quarrels and cracks rather than agreements in historical movements.

For many years your work was concentrated on Lyons. What attracted you to that city? It also seems that you've chosen to write many essays on it instead of a book. Was this a conscious preference for the essay form, or was it accidental?

To start with, I wanted to test an argument about religion and capitalism, and I had learned from the works of Henri Hauser that Lyons had had all that I needed:[5] it had extraordinary artisan movements, publishing, bankers, merchants, industries, like silk, and even Rabelais, who had lived there for many years. It just had everything that one might possibly want for a test case. I was also attracted to the idea of working not in Paris, but in a marginal place, so to speak, outside the centre. The archives there were also extremely rich, so much so that the studies I made in the following years have been sustained by that material. I have, for instance, all the dossiers of all the wills and testaments of many notaries, a complete set for a whole neighbourhood. Even now, my book on gifts [published in 2000] makes a lot of use of the Lyons material.

But why didn't I publish a whole book on Lyons instead of essays? I could have published my doctoral dissertation for that matter. I think that this was the product of my isolation. I made the mistake I try to tell my students not to make. I became so interested in other things, like anthropology, for instance, that my intellectual ambitions made me want to redo the thesis on the basis of new material. At that time I needed some mentor to say that I should publish it as it was. A second reason was having had children in that decade, which meant that I was busy trying to manage the children, at the same time as I was starting to teach, and giving a paper here and there as well. Still a third reason is that I had so many interests and didn't just write on Lyons at that time, but also on very different subjects, like the two or three articles I wrote on commercial arithmetic. So it was a sort of combination of life history, stage of life and multiple interests that made me write mainly essays, instead of a book. There wasn't a philosophy of the essay behind it. But, if I look back at

5 Henri Hauser (1866–1948), French social historian, author of *Travailleurs et marchands dans l'ancienne France* (1920) and *La modernité du 16e siècle* (1930).

Society and Culture, I feel that each of its chapters grew out of the others, so that even though they were written separately over a period of fourteen years, there was a single intellectual issue behind them.

You've worked a lot on the sixteenth century and especially on Protestant-ism. Do you think it an advantage or disadvantage that you're not a Christian? Would you say that this position has allowed you to have insights which are denied to the insiders?

To me it was an advantage. But I wouldn't say that it is a necessary condition, because Jean Delumeau is a great example showing that it's possible to achieve a kind of detachment and a multiple perspective even when working within a Catholic frame. But I feel that for me there was a distinct advantage in not having confessional stakes at a time, the 1950s, when there was still a great deal of confessional writing, even if it was good history. The Protestants would publish in the Protestant journals, the Catholics in the Catholic journals and so on. And since I was not writing about the Jews and didn't have any stakes one way or another, I just stepped back. I would say that for me the biggest shift was moving away from the evolutionary position, or, to use the old term, the 'pro-gressive' position. When I began to be interested in anthropology and in women's history, I also began to look at Catholicism in a new light. It was the anthropological approach to religion and the study of many more forms of religion that opened up my horizons. It made me interested in Catholicism not so much as a system which was going to be left behind, but as an equal actor with Protestantism. And I believe that this shift was much easier for me to make by the fact of being an outsider.

And inverting the situation, when you write about Jewish questions, would you say that by being emotionally involved, an insider, you may lose a sense of perspective?

Yes, I believe that there is this danger. For me it was a better path to have come to the study of Jewish things as somebody who could bring to this research topic the experience of working as an outsider on the Protestant and Catholic questions. I would say that I try to work with the technique of empathy, seeing things from within, as well as looking at them from without. In regard to the Jewish case, I really try to do that, making a particular effort to see it as an outsider, especially when what is at stake are things at which I'm shocked, even though I'm completely familiar with them. In those cases, a sense of humour and the ability to laugh at one's culture and to be delighted by certain features of Jewish self-parody may be helpful. When I wrote the prologue of my *Women on the Margins,* for example, I raised a question to Glikl, the Jewish woman merchant I studied, asking her why she always called her sons Rabbi (a kind of honorific title), while never giving her daughters any special name. That was my way of referring to a sexist practice in the Jewish past, a feature of Jewish culture which is very irritating. So I was sort of exposing something of Judaism from outside. And Glikl, in her answer, accuses me of doing just that. By making fun of yourself you might, in a way, be able to distance yourself from what you're so familiar with. In short, I like very much the notion of trying to be an insider-outsider.

One of your most path-breaking articles is on the rites of violence in the sixteenth century. Was this interest mainly the result of what you found in your research, or was it a reaction to urban violence in your own time in the USA or elsewhere?

It was both things plus the Holocaust. First, I've had a long-standing interest in violence and uprisings in Lyons, and among them one that attracted me especially was the '*rebeine*' of 1529, that extraordinary grain riot already studied by Hauser. I wanted to examine my Lyons sources and find out whether he was right in pointing out that the motivation of the '*rebeine*' was both religious – that is, Protestant – and economic. And the evidence I found proved that he wasn't. The main riots I came across in my Lyons work were religious ones, while the grain ones had a specific focus and traditional legitimation. Secondly, that period, the early seventies, was a challenging time, with a great deal of violent action taking place in the USA in connection with the end of the Vietnam War, the Civil Rights movement, and also in regard to university administration, sometimes even leading to student takeovers. I was personally involved in a lot of anti-war demonstrations in Berkeley and elsewhere, which sometimes turned violent, not necessarily on our side, but on the side of the police. So I had seen quite a lot of this and was deeply interested in crowd behaviour. And thirdly, there was subconsciously the stimulus represented by the Holocaust, the terrible violence against the Jews during the Second World War. The examples in the United States weren't so extreme, because though there were martyrs in the Civil Rights movement and in the anti-Vietnam War movement, you didn't have that mass cruelty, which in many ways was similar to the sixteenth-century kind of massacres. Even the small-scale ones were reminiscent of what went on in twentieth-century Germany, including the ritual aspect. So when I was writing about the rites of violence of the sixteenth century, I think I was also trying to make sense of the Holocaust.

How relevant were Freud and other psychologists for your study of the rites of violence and of the human impulse to kill people?

Some of the insights of Freud have become part of our cultural way of looking at the world, like his views on the tensions in parent–child relationships, and I accept them and use them. Like Marx, Freud is also very interesting as a human figure, and he was one of the commentators who gave me helpful ideas when I was working on the carnivalesque. But I've never been interested in adopting Freudianism because to me doing historical work does not mean confirming a psychological or psychoanalytical theory, which is what so much psychohistory seems to be doing. That seems to me to be reductionist. An example of my use of a Freudian perspective is an essay I wrote years ago on the Calvinist leader Théodore de Bèze. I interpreted his breaking with his humanist friends in France, his conversion to Calvinism and his involvement with and marriage to a chambermaid as in part acts of rebellion against his father. I became very interested in Bèze's rebellion, and I made the point that the first book he wrote after he got to Switzerland was the tragedy of Abraham sacrificing Isaac, a play about a father and a son. So, as you can see, my Freudianism goes as far as using a Freudian insight which has become part of our general culture. I wouldn't want to go any further than that. That is not my aim as a historian.

You often cite scholars from other disciplines. In your article on the rites of violence you cited, for instance, Elias Canetti, Mary Douglas and Neil Smelser. What could they offer that the historians didn't?

I should mention that a number of the people I cited in 'The Rites of Violence' [reprinted in *Society and Culture*] were at Berkeley, so they were part of my local network. I think it's very important in scholarly work to look at the precise community the person is in, whom he or she is talking to, because we all have a general outlook but we also have a local one. But if many of the authors I used to cite were part of my local scholarly community, Mary Douglas wasn't. She was part of my interest in anthropology at the time, and her theorizing on the question of pollution (a theme the historians were not studying at that time) was extremely valuable. I was just beginning to work on women's things, and found her notion of menstrual pollution particularly useful and insightful. I guess I could say that my choices of intellectuals to be cited were determined by the role of eye-opener that they played for me, as a historian. On the one side, they were working in a wider frame, covering sources and periods that I might not have come across in historical work; on the other side, they were looking for certain kinds of theory, for general statements which historians sometimes make, but not necessarily in the field of violence.

Are there any specific theoreticians whom you find particularly important for your work, or do you simply choose them for instrumental reasons?

Mainly instrumental reasons, which doesn't mean I don't respect them. What I mean is that the people I have most responsibility for are not the theoreticians – whom I respect; I even have affection for some of them, whom I know personally – but the people about whom I am writing. My final responsibility would be to my sixteenth-century subjects and also to Rabelais and Montaigne, who were great observers of the sixteenth century. These are the two thinkers to whom I would always want to go back in order to check my ideas. They were not theoreticians, but sharp observers who knew their century very well, with the exception of women. That is why I feel that if I am on the right track there should be some echo of this in Rabelais and Montaigne. As for women, I would go back to Marguerite de Navarre. For my book on the gift, for instance, I felt I had to reread Durkheim and Mauss, who were important because they really spent a lot of time thinking about theories of exchange. But this doesn't mean that I feel that I have to salute them and revere whatever they said on the theme. The same applies to my work on cultural mixture, in which I try to see things from other viewpoints besides the European. I have used a very rich source material. I have my own ideas, but I also want to know what the post-colonialist writers and scholars are saying on this theme. I'm occasionally inspired by what some of them say, as in the case of a great literary critic from Morocco, Abdelfattah Kilito, whom I met recently, but even so I wouldn't consider them to be my absolute guides.

Your first book, Society and Culture in Early Modern France, *published in the early stages of the women's movement, helped to make you a model for women's history. Is there any development in women's history with which you would not like to be associated?*

I would like to start by saying that if I make criticisms of things that emerge from the women's movement I don't do it as an enemy. There is a great deal of fighting in the movement right now, but if I do have reservations, my criticisms are not expressed with the desire to expel people, or with the sense that I am the one who knows all about it. I don't subscribe to that at all. I don't like women's history that is written with the suggestion that it has the absolute key and that all the other things are a sell-out or just wrong. I prefer a women's history that doesn't look at women as victims (and I don't have a specific book in mind when I say this), and that doesn't fail to see the many situations in which women are in collaboration or even in complicity with men. In the seventies, when I wrote a kind of overview of the state of the field, I urged historians to move away from women's worthies, as they were called in catalogues of the seventeenth and eighteenth centuries. It seemed to me that we should not just produce a modern version of that genre, though it had had the merit of highlighting the exceptional women of those times. However, this doesn't mean that there can't be certain studies that happen to have women as their main characters. That is, in fact, the case in my *Women on the Margins*, in which, although there are men in it, I decided to focus on three women. But one should always remember the range of relationships and connections that women are in; otherwise one runs the risk of not seeing how they were placed. Lives have several systems going through them, and we must bear their existence in mind in order to see the whole. Just the other day I was in a Berlin workshop and my friend Barbara Hahn (who works on late eighteenth- and early nineteenth-century literary women Berliners, mainly Jewish), gave an extremely interesting paper about these German Christian men who had relations with Jewish women. Well, she had seen the sarcastic letters the men wrote to each other about their women, and which other scholars had already noticed. But she had also seen the affectionate and pleading letters these men wrote to their Jewish women. All of these letters have to be seen together if you want to have a better understanding of their relationship. You can't just take the ones in which they gossip with one another about their women, but you also have to see what they wrote to the women with whom they were sleeping. In other words, it's important that we should look at women in a wider perspective.

As a leading participant in and observer of the rise of women's studies, do you see it as an advantage or a disadvantage that this field has been associated with the militant movement?

I think the advantage was the enthusiasm that was shared by a whole generation and which was visible both in political action and in the wonderful and exciting teaching courses in this period. The disadvantage was the belief that militancy is the key to everything, which it isn't. In my case, as in others of my generation, the great difference is that I did not practise women's history at the start of my career. I was a historian of other kinds of things before I started doing women's history, and although I was encouraged to go into it by the women's movement, I was also fuelled by the previous interests I mentioned earlier. For me, this period represented a great challenge because I wanted to work on this new theme but didn't want to be restricted to it. In fact this was, I believe, the challenge, as I prefer to call it, rather than the disadvantage, of most women's historians of the first generation: not to narrow their scope, and to write about women without necessarily making them the exclusive topic of their research.

Years ago E. P. Thompson was considered a sinful anti-feminist historian for arguing that 'wife sales' were not only an expression of male oppression of women but also gave room for women to show their independence and sexual vitality. Do you think that such a reaction would not be possible today, or would you say that, up to a point, the history of women is still dominated by the idea of victimhood?

Not everybody reacted like that at the time. I certainly didn't, because it was clear to me that these rituals were sometimes engineered by both sides in order to have a divorce that would be face-saving for the husband and allow the wife to marry her lover, albeit in a humiliating way. But anyway, I think it would be less likely to happen today because the idea of the victimization of women which lay behind those reactions is much diminished now. I think the more serious people would just say that Thompson's work – with the exception of this fascinating article on 'wife sales' – was not particularly attentive to women at all, which is true, since his main interest was in the male English working class and in socialist and pre-socialist thought. So he would be questioned, I'd say, for this silence, this omission, since this is what's become more or less unacceptable. If I can think of another topic which might provoke today the kind of reaction that Thompson experienced, I'd say it is the issue of the Holocaust or racism, since there are scholars who interpret everything in terms of persecution and victimization.

It seems to me that women's history still finds it difficult to acknowledge the role of men in feminist thinking (Benito Feyjóo[6] and Poullain de la Barre,[7] for instance, who created the epistemological conditions for thinking about the equality between the sexes), the importance of some 'male' texts which tackled the problem of women's oppression by men, and the possibility of there existing a fruitful interweaving of texts by male writers with those of women. What would you say to those who believe that women own the history of women?

I don't think that this difficulty is inevitable, considering the way women's history is practised today. What I do think, though, is that we

6 Benito Jerónimo Feyjóo (1676–1764), Spanish Benedictine monk and a leading figure in the Spanish Enlightenment, author of the polemical treatise 'The Defence of Women', one of the discourses in his *Theatro crítico universal* (1726–39).

7 François Poullain de la Barre (1647–1723), author of the feminist-Cartesian treatise *De l'égalité des deux sexes* (1673). This text was partly plagiarized by the anonymous author of the British treatise *Woman not Inferior to Man* (1739), which was in turn translated complete into Portuguese in 1832 by the Brazilian feminist Nísia Floresta, who presented it as if it were a translation of the *Vindication of the Rights of Woman* by Mary Wollstonecraft. (see Maria Lúcia G. Pallares-Burke, *Nísia Floresta, o Carapuceiro e outros ensaios de tradução cultural*, São Paulo, Hucitec, 1996.)

have done a much less good job in studying social complicity and collaboration between men and women, not paying enough attention to the situations in which women are working with men. Because if a man like those you mentioned writes a text, there is probably a woman he is collaborating with; that is, he is not all by himself, just sitting in his Benedictine abbey, say, never meeting women. He has taken the initiative to write a book, but there is very likely some collaborative work going on here. And I think that we, women historians, have done rather little thinking about situations of collaboration across the lines, involving sides that were very unequal in power.

This is one of the reasons why I'm engaged in this cultural mixture project, and have been thinking about the difficult question, say, of close relations across the boundary between slave and free. These are all relations that involve questions of power and intimacy. The problem is that we don't have a very good language for talking about this, and there is a great need for one in order to describe co-operation across these lines. A lot has been written about love for years, but when you want to talk about love and power disparities, then you need a special language.

As for intellectual collaboration, we are familiar with it in academic settings but we haven't looked hard enough at informal collaboration. We haven't focused enough on the cross-fertilization of ideas coming from people of different ages and genders. And there are thousands of cases of this kind, in which ideas get interlaced in the history of science, in the history of learning of all types, and also in the history of women. Thinking about Poullain de la Barre, for instance, we know the texts he wrote but not the women that he knew, other than a little about his wife, and it would be very interesting to try to see him in interaction with them, exchanging ideas with them.

In one of your earliest essays, 'City Women and Religious Change' [reprinted in Society *and* Culture*], you've shown that the rise of Protestantism, by rejecting the female saints and by eliminating separate religious organizations for women, contributed to making women more vulnerable to subjection in all spheres. Were you consciously reacting against the common view that Protestantism opened the road for women's emancipation?*

I do think that the Protestants contributed to it, and I don't want to deny their long-term contribution to women's emancipation, especially sects like the Quakers. They did open up a common world of literacy and a common world of liturgy which were beneficial to women. The positive things they said about women's literacy and what I called in that article the 'assimilation of style' undoubtedly had positive effects. In other words, even though the men were on top, women were together singing psalms, reading the Bible, and so on.

But having made that clear, I was reacting in that article against the notion that Protestantism was the sole solution as a universalizing religion. I wanted to suggest the contribution of other factors, since there is a very important version of early feminism that arose in female communities such as convents where women were on their own, in a kind of separate space, not in the subject status entailed in law by marriage.

Your book The Return of Martin Guerre *has generated lively debates, and together with Le Roy Ladurie's* Montaillou *and Carlo Ginzburg's* The Cheese and the Worms *has been praised for belonging to the postmodernist tradition in historiography. Do you agree with this view?*

I don't think that postmodern is the most useful category to use for these three books which have, in fact, different goals, Ginzburg's being less ethnographical than the other two, which are more concerned with a total study of a community. When I think of the postmodern, I think of the focus on the importance of culture and language as conditioning everything, from the way we speak to the way we think; and also of the postmodern approach's undermining of generalizations and preference for speaking about fragments, rather than about coherent wholes. All three books take local culture very seriously but they are also concerned with experience and with long-term traditions and structures of thought. I don't think that the postmodern label adds very much here. And as to the claim that these books are postmodern because they refuse to generalize, I would reply that, although different, all these three works were hoping to generate insights into processes that went beyond the individual case they were studying. All were generating suggestions about other cases, not only through the possibility of analogy, but also through communication networks and systems of power. What I mean is that news travelled and judges and inquisitors came in from outside. News travelled about the Martin Guerre case, and news travelled about heresies and wild ideas in remote villages and mountain towns.

In which way do you distinguish your book on Martin Guerre from the other important micro-histories written by Ginzburg and Le Roy Ladurie?

I should perhaps start by saying that I don't mind being categorized as a micro-historian, although when I came to the project I was thinking of myself as an anthropologist who goes to a village and is interested not only in ethnography but also in performance. Because one of the advantages of being an anthropologist is that you are able not only to observe people and talk to them directly, but also to observe performances which can reveal how things are actually experienced and acted out throughout a life; things that often do not show up in a diary or in a document.

There is a very perceptive passage in the film *Elizabeth* by Shekhar Kapur which illustrates what I want to say very vividly. It's an insightful moment, even if it may not be historically accurate or verifiable. You see the future queen rehearsing an important speech before she gives it to Parliament. I loved that moment because although literally her voice might have been different, and she might have had a tutor present, still to see something acted out which would be concealed from us and not recorded in such a way in the documents is extremely interesting. The idea of imagining that kind of rehearsing attracted me a lot.

If I compare my book with Ginzburg's and Le Roy Ladurie's, one thing that stands out is that in addition to the ethnographic and anthropological interest which we all share, I had a special concern with a storyline. Carlo Ginzburg and Le Roy Ladurie were both telling a story, the story of trials, but they were less interested in the multiple versions. So, by 'storyline' I mean that there was the story of Martin Guerre (the man who leaves and the man who comes back), the story of his wife, the story of a whole village, and the story told by the judge. I became very conscious of these different versions, and this made me think about how a story is told and how people put different accounts together; that's why my project led me in a literary direction.

Your international reputation seems to have increased a good deal after you published this micro-history, and by restoring to history phenomena which were considered negligible and peripheral you led the way for an ever-growing number of works in this direction. Are you happy with these followers or do you share, in some degree, the criticism made by John Elliott, for instance, when he said that something is terribly wrong when 'the name of Martin Guerre becomes as well or better known than that of Martin Luther'?

Well, I hadn't heard about this criticism of John Elliott's, and it's certainly a very witty saying of his! He is, in fact, a dear friend of mine and I know he enjoyed my book very much. I think I know what he means, and I agree with him in the sense that I too would think that there was something wrong if that was the case. But I don't think it is. Many people seem not to know what a good micro-history should be. I would say that Carlo Ginzburg and Giovanni Levi and others who write micro-history would agree that, if it's done well, such a history should be an in-depth study that is rich in itself, but also reveals connections with other processes and events outside itself.

It might seem easy to write micro-history, but this is definitely not the case. Many people think it's just a question of finding an interesting story and telling this story. They believe it is easier than to write, for instance, a textbook where you have to cover so much ground. But the truth is that because a textbook is so general you may not have to do research on every little thing, whereas a good micro-history requires, at the same time, details, evidence and the ambition of *histoire totale*.

I would not recommend a historian to do nothing but micro-history, in the same way as I would not recommend a person to do women's history and nothing else. Ideally, an individual historian should try at some point to work in different modes as a way to see what the stakes are, the relations beween the local and the general frame. In the case of Martin Guerre, for example, his story does not make any sense without the judicial apparatus of the early modern French state and widespread hopes of social mobility. Historians must keep a dialogue going on between these sharply focused studies and larger ones, developing the dialogue fully in all its implications. In a way, it's the task of teaching to promote the dialogues that make those connections and put things together. In fact, in teaching we are always doing this when we use this and that book, one type of study alongside another type, and so on.

And going back to Elliott's remark about Martin Guerre and Martin Luther, I would say that it was essentially a warning rather than a statement, because, to be fair, Guerre's name is not better known than Luther's. My book is often assigned in courses, but as collateral reading, and Martin Guerre's trial is not part of the official curriculum. It's true that people are having more fun with his story, especially since the film made about it, and are perhaps chatting about him more than about Luther. But that is a superficial short-range thing. What I hope has changed now is that the Martin Luthers are no longer taught without reference or relation to the Martin Guerres. What I would hope for is that German micro-studies will present a new and more interesting Luther, taking into account all the new findings of Bob Scribner, Lyndal Roper and other interesting German studies.

Historical film-making is one of your great and long-lasting interests (as a student, as you confessed, you had a plan to make documentary films), and after co-operating in the making of The Return of Martin Guerre *you've said that 'good historical films have much more than authentic costumes or props: they must suggest something truthful about the past and be the visual equivalent of a written truth statement'. How would you then reply to Hayden White's assertion that historical film and historical writing share the same limitations in relation to the attainment of truth, and that, therefore, the 'fictionality' of the film and of the historian's discourse are equivalent?*

Hayden White and others have done us a great service in pointing out some of the literary features of historical prose that affect our narrative. There is no doubt that making us sensitive to that was excellent.

Nevertheless, as a total view of the meaning of historical writing his position has its limits, because it neglects the efforts the historians make and the rules of evidence they follow in order to argue their case. In my view the two things operate simultaneously. By focusing on the question of the literary genre which historians adopt, Hayden White does not take into consideration the conventions in prose writing that were developed in the two thousand years of writing history we have behind us, which allow our readers to know when we are speaking with assurance, when we are doubtful about an argument, or when there are multiple points of view. And there is much more that can be done with these conventions. So Hayden White's discussion of the fictionality of historical writing based on narrative genres ignores the many possibilities opened up by the conventions of prose, and the fact that history stands both in the world of literary organization and in the world of proof. For instance, two of my former colleagues at Princeton, Tony Grafton and Lionel Gossman, have discussed footnotes beautifully both as a literary genre and as a proof genre. And this is just one of the many possibilities.

As for historical films, the cinema has a long way to go before its visual and dramatic conventions begin to catch up with the rules of evidence and the ways they are stated in historical prose. I'm thinking, for instance, of the cinematic techniques that might one day express the equivalent of phrases like 'maybe' or 'there are several ways to interpret this'. The problem is that we have all this language that we know how to use when we write, but we don't yet have as many dramatic or visual ways to express cinematically what we want and to deal successfully there with the question of authenticity. So there is lots of room for improvement in historical film-making, including the need for more research, preferably carried out by cinematic people who, if they are not historians themselves, might seek the advice of historians orientated toward visual media. There may be a limit to the ways in which a story can be told in a film, and I'm sure there are areas in which prose tellings are going to excel visual ones, as well as others in which the situation inverts. Cinema, for instance, may have some of the advantages of micro-history, given its capacity to show performance. It forces you to imagine features of how something happened that you might not have bothered to think about if you were just writing in prose. I've already given the example of Elizabeth, but the same is true of Martin Guerre, which has made me think about how history has been enacted, in ways that historical writing never did. Cinema might show the role of contingency in the past as well as the role of general forces that you might never have suspected were there; forces that only surface when you actually watch a scene develop, and to which diaries and newspapers give only faint clues. In short, cinema should perhaps be viewed primarily as a lab experiment, a thought experiment and not as truth-telling.

Your Fiction in the Archives *gives a vivid illustration of the way in which narrative traditions are active in the so-called factual documentation of the past. So would you support the theory which blurs the distinction between history and fiction?*

Historical writing and historical research include an element of imagination. So there is this overlap between the two genres in the ways that we both think and write. But, on the other hand, historians are supposed to have evidence to support every statement that they make. Or if they don't have such clear evidence they use the prose conventions of saying, 'must have been', for instance, or 'it probably was'. As it came up yesterday in my conversation with the novelist Beryl Gilroy,[8] this is the deep and important difference between the two genres. The writer working on fiction may well decide that he or she is not going to go back to a text in order to do some checking, but is just going to let things happen as the plot seems to unroll. Well, historians can't do that. This is just not allowable if you are going to stick by the rules of the historian. We have as an imperative not to consult our minds alone but also something external to ourselves, documents or manuscripts, or pictures or some trace from the past. And I must say that I like submitting to something external to myself.

For many years you've worked mainly on France, and especially on Lyons. Would you say that your Women on the Margins, *with its concern with so many parts of the world, is a change of intellectual direction, or a natural development from your earlier researches?*

I felt it was a change, although it is not unrelated to my previous works. In fact, I felt that I was building on what I had done before. But I could have stayed with France and so choosing a topic with such geographical range made me feel very different as a historian of Europe. I'm seeing things with a European eye and also with a non-European eye, and this made me start to situate myself differently in regard to the world. I like to have some sense of solidarity with people from other parts of the world, and that was a way of having it. So now, when I hear about European projects, if they don't also have a concern with the wider world, they seem odd to me. I'd never have been opposed to anybody working on those lines before.

When I decided to work on non-Western, non-European things, that was really strange to me because it meant going far beyond the Catholic–

---

8   Beryl Gilroy, educationalist and novelist who migrated from British Guiana to England. Her books include *Black Teacher* (London, Bogle-L'Ouverture, 1976), *In Bed* (London, Macmillan, 1977) and *Granpa's Footsteps* (London, Macmillan, 1978). She is one of the four twentieth-century figures studied by Davis in her project on cultural mixture.

Protestant contrast which was where I began. The first move was to decide that I could do research on non-Christians, on Jews, as opposed to simply bringing them into a chorus, or reading a text on them with my students. And that was a big change because it involved a whole new set of research materials. I had read many things in English and French translation, but I had never worked on Jewish documents or archives. Another change is that I had to learn about the seventeenth century when I did *Women on the Margins*. I knew something about it, enough to teach, but I had to immerse myself in a lot of new material, including material about millenarian movements, which I needed to do in order to understand the utopian thread that went through the lives of the women I was studying. And to be able to work on Africans in Surinam I had to acquire a new scholarly apparatus, which was lots of fun. Of course, all these changes involved a huge amount of work, but I am at a stage in my life when I don't mind that at all.

Of all these new experiences, I would say that one of the most important things they taught me was to realize the relevance of the place where the historian comes from and to remember that history is being done in many different places. The meeting of the Association of Caribbean Historians in Paramaribo, which I attended last spring, was particularly revealing. I had never been at a conference where the agenda was so clearly defined by what I would call non-Western, non-European concerns. Even the International Congress for Historical Sciences, which I have often been to, does not do this in the same way. The meeting was totally organized around things that they felt were important, but which, to my eyes, didn't always seem important. I was just fascinated by it, and happy too. I was thrilled to be able to share what I had been doing on Surinam, to tell them about what I had been finding and to get their reaction. I chose the Jewish paper, and the fact is that it dealt with issues that were rather different from the ones they cared about. History is being done differently in various places. To me this is at least as important as the Hayden White discoveries and in some ways more important. He brought to our attention the importance of thinking about how people write, but to see how history is written in different parts of the world is also extremely relevant. Here I am, a European, so to speak, writing about Africans. Well, it is important to know how they would write about us.

How important for the understanding of the past is the comparative approach? Would you agree with Jack Goody that comparison is one of the few things that we can do in the historical and social sciences to perform the kind of experiments the scientists do?

I agree with him that it is extraordinarily important, and I think versions of micro-history and also, in some ways, films are experiments too, because through them, if we've done well, we try to imagine how things actually happened in the day to day, and that's fascinating. In my 1998 article 'Beyond Evolution: Comparative History and its Goals', I argue that almost every statement that we make involves comparison, although we talk consciously about it only when we are comparing things spatially separated enough or different enough. There are three kinds of comparisons we can make, each with its own problematic. One is the kind that I tried to make in *Women on the Margins*, where I take people who are, in fact, in the same society but who belong to groups which were either neglected or haven't been treated comparatively. In this case, they are Catholic, Protestant and Jewish people who come from a similar sort of middle class of artisans or traders and lead an urban life. In this kind of comparison there is a lot more that can be done. A comparison of Jews and Christians in regard to the persecution of witches might, for example, be very illuminating. Because the question that remains unanswered is, why didn't the Jews persecute witches like the Christians? Our hypotheses about what stimulates witchcraft persecution imply that the Jews would be very prone to it. They were themselves persecuted from without as ritual murderers or magicians and they have great concern about the Evil Eye, in fact, they're just obsessed with the Evil Eye, and they were worried about possession by dead souls. So they have the ideology that might have generated a witch-hunt, and yet it didn't happen.

The second type compares societies that are spatially and temporally separated from each other. In this case I think that the questions that we ask should not be generated exclusively by our own historical preoccupations but also by those of the society with which the comparison is being made. If the comparison is just between England and Germany, for instance, then the questions might not be that different. But if the comparison is between Japan and France – as in a case on which I chose to comment in that article – the problem is much clearer. An otherwise very interesting book on Edo [Tokyo] and Paris makes the mistake of framing all the questions in terms of interests generated in American universities.[9] Ideally, if you really want the method to work, some questions should have come out of Japanese historiography. Funnily enough, about a third of the authors are from Japan and there is a Japanese co-editor, and yet certain things weren't even considered.

The third kind of comparison is the one in which you compare not things that are strictly analogous, like France and Japan, but something that isn't at all the same, like the Jesuits from France meeting Amerindian culture in Quebec in the seventeenth century. One of the challenges of this

9   J. L. McClain, J. M. Merriman, U. Kaoru (eds), *Edo and Paris: Urban Life and the State in the Early Modern Era* (Ithaca, Cornell University Press, 1994).

comparison, as the Dutch anthropologist Johannes Fabian pointed out so well, is to write about societies that live at the same time without taking one as though it was the forebear of the other. And that is not easy to do, because when you're dealing with societies that are so different in their technological systems, communication systems, it is extremely tempting to say 'well, these people aren't really contemporaneous'. In short, to make fruitful comparisons is very difficult, but it is well worth the effort.

You are working now on cultural mixture and seem to be optimistic about the positive implications of such studies, because, as you say: 'they warn us away from the impure altars of nationalism and race, they urge us to think beyond boundaries, they remind us to look for the métis *within ourselves'. What would you say, then, to a historian who finds in cultural mixture examples of discord and not of understanding, of the grip of an intolerant tradition and the narcissism of small differences instead of human compassion?*

I do not deny that there is a negative side as well, and that under some circumstances the émigré can be resentful. One of the examples I deal with in my new book is that of a Jewish-Romanian émigré to France who lived in the late nineteenth and early twentieth century. He was a very interesting and creative philologist, a specialist on Rabelais who produced really important work on him, which we still read today. Well, the background he brought from Romania was essential, I think, to the innovations he brought to Rabelais studies, but the sad thing is that he ended up totally embittered and isolated. Going through the records of the Linguistic Society of Paris, which was a vanguard institution, you can see the curve of his life in it, and how he just turned more and more sour as he never felt himself really accepted. But I'm still not going to tell this story and others which involved a lot of human cruelty and sorrow (like the ones that deal with slavery) in a totally sombre way, because within that situation there are some mechanisms by which a shred of human solidarity emerges. This becomes very clear in the case of the African slaves of Surinam who became Jews. Although there were prejudices against them by virtue of the fact that they had been slaves (and it's conceivable that the Jews also had a distaste for their colour), once freed they took part in the prayer service, they intermarried and were, on the whole, part of the Jewish community. I'm not saying that this was the result of simple human love or compassion. At the moment, my argument is that Judaism is a religion of the law, and one of the things that the law says is that if you're Jewish you're Jewish, and you can't make that go away. And if you're a Jewish man, you have a right to be part of the prayer service. This might not be a story of full human compassion and empathy, but it is surely a story of a certain kind of solidarity.

So the points I'm trying to make in this study of cultural mixture are three: first, that against those who are always seeking for a false authenticity, cultural mixture exists; secondly, that we need to have better descriptive tools and some typologies to tackle this phenomenon, in the same way as we need a more precise vocabulary to describe complicity, which I've mentioned before; and thirdly, that cultural mixture can have some unfortunate features, but it can also have very positive ones.

'My best general reader', you once confessed, is 'my husband Chandler Davis, mathematician and writer.' But when you are at work is there anyone else you imagine as looking over your shoulder, criticizing or discussing it with you?

As I tried to show in the prologue to *Women on the Margins*, when I imagined a conversation between me and Glikl bas Judah Leib, Marie de l'Incarnation and Maria Sybilla Merian (the three protagonists of the book), I often think of the people I'm writing about as reading my words and try to guess what they would say about and feel about them. That's a good way to think, because it reminds you of your responsibility to them as persons who once lived and died as well as to the evidence about them. I also have other interlocutors in my own day, but they are just shifting all the time. According to what I'm writing I wonder what X would think of this approach, or whether Y would enjoy this, and so on. Often I'm so engrossed in my dialogue with the sources that I just think about them and forget about interlocutors until after the book is published. As to my husband Chan, I love to show my work to him while I'm doing it in order to be sure that what I write is clear, accessible and makes sense.

You do not like to be identified as a professional historian associated with specialization and careerism, and have already been described as a 'radical historian'. Do you like this description or is there any other identification you prefer?

I don't mind being loyal to the profession or craft in circumstances where teaching or professional issues are at stake and which require a kind of political solidarity or loyalty. But it's true that I don't like to think of myself as a professional historian, because the term 'professional' seems to carry with it the exclusion of other ways of telling about the past that I want to listen to and attend to. Would I call myself a radical? No, because I think it also implies limits and excludes many directions. I would like to choose the word 'critical', instead of 'radical', to describe myself, because I like to think that I'm working in a critical mode, which is wider and allows for working in multiple directions.

Your work has created a whole school of followers and has also caused controversy and attracted criticisms. Have any criticisms of your work helped you with the development or reformulation of your ideas?

Very early, when I published my first essay, 'On the Protestantism of Benoît Rigaut', a friend of mine told me it was pedantic and that I hadn't told his story in a way which would reveal all its human interest. I was just a graduate student then, committed to the notion that I wasn't just writing to please other professors, and my friend's criticism and suggestions were very helpful in making me think about how to say things better. More recently I learned from Robert Finlay's comments on *The Return of Martin Guerre* how to respond to criticism, using it as an occasion for discussing and clarifying my work. As you may know, his review was rather aggressive (and somewhat rude in the original version that was sent to me) but I decided that, no matter what happened, I would not take this personally. So I used my response to his review, which was published together with his piece in the *American Historical Review*, as an occasion to elaborate on ideas that had had to be more compressed in the book. It's interesting that the two articles together are used in methodology courses all over America, and maybe even in England, and I've heard that some students agree with Finlay, and not with me. But that is fine, because the main thing about writing is that you want your readers to read, to debate and to think about it; and they might make your writing their own in a totally different way from yours.

My *Women on the Margins* was criticized for my use of the word 'margins', as well as for my failure to bring the three stories sufficiently together. More than anything, these criticisms have taught me that you have to be much more repetitive and say things over and over again in order to be understood. I had approached these issues in the prologue and thought I had made myself clear. In any case, the thing that I most wanted to achieve with this book, I did achieve. Through these three women, I wanted people today to experience a seventeenth-century life, and to realize that there was more than one model for it. And considering that this book is being used in undergraduate and graduate courses in America, and has been published in several foreign languages, I think that my main message is getting through.

May I ask you the same questions you once put in relation to Marc Bloch and Eileen Power, two innovative historians like yourself: 'How do you relate to your teachers? Whom do you define as co-reformers? What kind of heirs do you expect?'

I respect and learned a great deal from the scholars of the past and from my university teachers, but they don't have a special weight for me. I really do think of myself as being totally free to do whatever I want to do. And that comes, in part, from belonging to a political generation that had a sense of freedom and also didn't feel any 'anxiety of influence', to use Harold Bloom's phrase. I, for instance, didn't feel that I had to be so individual that I couldn't say anything like those scholars had said. I neither felt bad about revolting against them nor felt desperate when I was not totally original. I just didn't see that as a problem. Maybe this attitude is also somewhat related to my gender, to my being a woman. I wasn't a son worried about a father-figure, and my mother-mentors – few in those early days – were more like older sisters.

As to the future, to my heirs, I like my students to pay attention to my advice about how they should work, but I also like them to be independent. When I feel that they are going in a direction that is definitely critical of what I've done, I like them to be fair to what I've written, not twisting my views, but then go on to make their own argument. Here, again, there may be a gender characteristic that I've sometimes noted about reviews by women. They often try very hard in their reviews to make extremely accurate and careful summaries, even if they are going on to attack afterwards. And finally, a last point I'd like to add about students who are independent and break away from you concerns their getting ideas from you but not recognizing the genealogy. What to do about that? Of course I'd like to have my authorship acknowledged, but if it is not, I always remember a great line in one of Woody Allen's movies, *Manhattan*. Remembering his boyhood, he recalls his father and mother arguing about the black maid who was stealing. The mother says she is going to fire her, to which the father answers: 'but whom else is she going to steal from?' And that is the way I try to feel in relation to those students: what was I there for except to give them ideas? So let it go, since what is important is the advancement of thought. And it would be interesting to reflect on whether this attitude is more common among women than among men. It's possible that women are more used to see children growing up and more willing to launch them into independence.

As to the people I think of as my co-reformers, among many people I could mention Carlo Ginzburg whom I feel very, very close to, fighting more or less for the same cause, even if we don't always agree. Emmanuel Le Roy Ladurie would be another, especially in his books *Montaillou, Les Paysans de Languedoc* and *The Carnival of Romans*.[10] Maurice Agulhon, whom I discovered at a time when I was working in considerable isolation, was also extremely important to the anthropological route that I took. In fact, when I read his *Sociabilité méridionale* I remember feeling a

10   E. Le Roy Ladurie, *Montaillou*, London, Scolar, 1978; *The Peasants of Langue-doc*, Urbana, University of Illinois Press, 1974; *Carnival*, London, Scolar, 1980.

great affinity between his interests and mine.[11] As for Edward Thompson, besides admiring his work, I was astonished at the coincidence of his turning to 'rough music' and I to charivaris at exactly the same time. He wrote to me about this and we savoured the joint path we'd taken. When I began to work on the history of women and gender, I was very close to Jill Conway – a real pioneer – and also felt that Louise Tilly, Joan Scott and I were good allies.

The recognition you've received from the scholarly world includes no fewer than thirty prizes and honorary degrees and the translation of your books into more than ten languages. Looking back on your successful career, what achievement are you most proud of?

I think these prizes are wonderful but when I get honours I see them as fundamentally a social event that might have more meaning for others, and not just for me, in the sense that they might be helpful and stimulating for the careers of young people. If I consider my work, though, I couldn't think of any one that makes me specially proud – I don't have any special favourites among my writings. I would be happy to imagine that my books could sometimes bring some enjoyment, insight and hope to people's lives – to scholars and to the wider public both. As to the achievement that makes me most proud, I can't think of anything more important to bequeath to the future than my children and my grandchildren. I can't put anything above that.

London, November 1998

11   M. Agulhon, *Pénitents et franc-maçons: sociabilité méridionale*, 1968; not translated into English.

SELECT BIBLIOGRAPHY

Society and Culture in Early Modern France (Stanford, Stanford University Press, 1975); translated into German, Spanish, French, Italian, Japanese, Portuguese.

'Anthropology and History in the 1980s: The Possibilities of the Past', *Journal of Interdisciplinary History*, 12/2 (autumn 1981), 267–75.

The Return of Martin Guerre (Cambridge, Mass., Harvard University Press, 1983); translated into German, Spanish, French, Dutch, Italian, Japanese, Swedish, Portuguese, Russian.

Fiction in the Archives: Pardon Tales and their Tellers in Sixteenth-Century France (Stanford, Stanford University Press, 1987); translated into German, French, Italian, Japanese.

'Censorship, Silence and Resistance: The *Annales* during the German Occupation of France', *Literaria Pragensia: Studies in Literature and Culture*, 1 (1991), 13–23.

'Women and the World of the *Annales*', *History Workshop Journal*, 33 (1992), 121–37.

ed., with Arlette Farge, *A History of Women*, vol. 3: *Renaissance and Enlightenment Paradoxes* (Cambridge, Mass., Harvard University Press, 1993); translated into German, Spanish, Italian, French, Dutch, Japanese.

Women on the Margins: Three Seventeenth-Century Lives (Cambridge, Mass., Harvard University Press, 1995); translated into German, Finnish, French, Italian, Portuguese, Swedish.

The Gift in Sixteenth-Century France (Oxford University Press, 2000).

Slaves on Screen: Film and Historical Vision (Toronto, Vintage, 2000).

4

Keith Thomas

Keith Thomas, or Sir Keith as he is formally known, is one of the most eminent and innovative historians in Great Britain today. Beginning his career at a time when most historians still focused on narrative political history, Thomas made a brilliant contribution to a new field: the social-cultural study of past societies. The book that made him famous – and earned him the prestigious Wolfson Prize – was *Religion and the Decline of Magic* (1971), best-known for its discussions about the reasons why people accused their neighbours of witchcraft. It became a best-seller almost overnight, was displayed in bookshops specializing in the occult and is sure to have been consulted not just by students but by clairvoyants as well. In 1994 this book achieved even greater prestige when a panel of eminent intellectuals included it in the list of the 100 books that had most influenced public discourse in the West since 1945. Another book, which consolidated his fame as an innovator, was *Man and the Natural World* (1983), in which Thomas dealt with the change in attitude towards animals and nature during the sixteenth, seventeenth and eighteenth centuries, making pioneering use of literary sources as historical evidence. Enthusiastic reviewers like Christopher Hill considered that this work would lead to a rethinking of the nature of history and its methods. Translated into several languages, these two books have placed Keith Thomas in the forefront of what has become known as 'historical anthropology', a position he shares with Emmanuel Le Roy Ladurie and Carlo Ginzburg, two of the present-day historians he most admires and who, like him, approach the past as if it were a foreign country. A great admirer of the anthropologist Sir Edward Evans-Pritchard, a Welshman like himself, whom he met at Oxford, Thomas was inspired by his work on witchcraft, oracles and magic among the Azande of Central Africa to develop his own studies on English culture and society in the seventeenth century.

Not so well-known internationally but equally important are Thomas's many articles, keynote lectures and essays, which are scattered in journals and newspapers but have never yet been collected into a book. Two of these articles, written in the 1950s, dealt with women's history long before this form of history became respectable, let alone fashionable. Others, inspired by the works of social theorists such as Mikhail Bakhtin, Norbert Elias and Bronislaw Malinowski – not to mention Sigmund Freud, to whom Thomas's work owes much more than it might seem at first sight – cover a wide variety of themes, including the history of attitudes to laughter, cleanliness and godliness, health, the social function of the past, children, intergenerational relationships, literacy, school discipline and indiscipline, etc.

As a young man Keith Thomas caused an uproar with the biting criticism he made of his more conservative colleagues who refused to see any use for the social sciences in the study of history. Now much more moderate and appreciative of tradition, Thomas is cautious and sceptical about the possibility of great changes in historical method. Nevertheless, he is still basically a radical historian in his approach, or as he has been described, 'a quiet revolutionary' who does not like to boast about his innovations.

If Quentin Skinner can be described as essentially a Cambridge man, Keith Thomas is quintessentially an Oxford man. He is extremely happy and proud to have lived and worked in Oxford for almost fifty years and regards this city of 200,000 inhabitants as a real metropolis in comparison with his native Welsh village. London is not to his taste, and when a few years ago he was invited to lecture at the University of São Paulo, his first question was, 'How big is São Paulo?' Naturally, he declined the invitation!

After studying at Balliol (the most prestigious Oxford college at the time) in the 1950s, he began his career – without needing a doctorate – as a fellow of All Souls. From there he went to St John's College, where for nearly thirty years he gave twelve tutorials plus two lectures a week on English history and the history of political thought. Finally, in 1986, Thomas gave this up and moved to the other side of the High Street on his election as President of Corpus Christi, a post which he held till his retirement in 2000.

In the last decade or so Thomas has been awarded two of the greatest honours that a British intellectual can covet: he has been knighted by the Queen for his 'services to history', and he has served as President of the British Academy (where his annual speeches are remembered for their brilliance and wit). A tall, thin man with dark hair and a winning smile, looking much younger than his years, Keith Thomas received us in his study at Corpus Christi. His rooms, located in the 'new' wing of the college (built in the eighteenth century), have all the charm and elegance of the age of the Enlightenment: high ceilings, large windows opening onto beautiful gardens, antique furniture and paintings, and bookcases full of books, many of them seventeenth-century editions. Occasionally getting up from his comfortable armchair to pick out a book to illustrate what he was saying, Keith Thomas conversed for several hours in a friendly yet unemphatic tone which often made his customary irony almost imperceptible. He talked at length about his intellectual trajectory, his interests and his experiences.

MARIA LÚCIA PALLARES-BURKE   *You grew up on a Welsh farm, in an environment not much in tune with intellectual life. What made you spend your life in the study of the past?*

KEITH THOMAS   Yes, I grew up on a farm and the only non-farmer in the family is me. The farming world is very self-sufficient, not introspective, and has a pretty considerable respect for money. People, in its view, tend to be divided into two categories, farmers and non-farmers, and the academic world is seen as parasitic. But my mother, who had read English at the University of Cardiff and had been a schoolteacher, encouraged me when I turned out to be a rather bookish child. On the other hand, my younger brother reacted against that and became a farmer, a very successful one in the end, much richer than I am as a result!

As a child I read a great number of historical novels (works which are now mostly forgotten, I suppose), by people such as Harrison Ainsworth and Walter Scott. I also read lots of books for children about history by Dorothy Margaret Stuart. However, I don't think that that had anything very much to do with my choice of subject. As a schoolboy I was quite good at all subjects, and it was a pure accident that I did history for the Higher School Certificate, as they called A levels in those days. I intended to do English, Latin and French, which would have been disastrous; because Latin would not be enough to do classics, French would not be enough for foreign languages, and English, I don't know... But there was a newish history master in my school who was a very good teacher and I just happened to meet him by accident on my way to the place where the students had to declare their choices. And he said, 'You are going to do history, aren't you?' and I replied, 'Well, I don't know, but I suppose I am if you say so.' I always do what the last person I meet tells me to do.

So then I did history in the sixth form, and that is when history rapidly became my main subject. I owe a lot to this young Welsh left-wing teacher, whose name was Teifion Phillips. He not only made me read Tawney's *Religion and the Rise of Capitalism*, but insisted that I should try for Oxford, although the headmaster thought that that was a ridiculous idea, because boys from my school were not meant for that! But, anyway, I did go to Balliol and also won the Brackenbury scholarship, the top one at the time. I did that largely, I think, on the basis of the essays on Luther, Calvin and associated subjects, which were a mixture of Tawney's book and Phillips's lessons. By then I was completely hooked on history.

I must also say at this point that there was a strong historical tradition in the grammar school I went to in Wales, the Barry County School. From it came Glyn Daniel, who was quite a celebrated Cambridge archaeologist; H. J. Habakkuk, who became professor of economic history and Principal of Jesus College Oxford; David Joslin, who became professor of economic history at Cambridge, and who died young; and after my time Martin Daunton, who is now professor of economic history at Cambridge. Well, that is already three professors of economic history. I doubt whether there are many schools which can begin to equal that. And there was also David Williams, a very good Welsh historian, who had taught there as well. So there was definitely quite a strong intellectual tradition in my grammar school.

How important was Oxford and your familiarity with Christopher Hill in shaping your attitudes and interests?

When I arrived at Balliol I had already heard of Christopher Hill and knew who he was. In fact, I had read him in a Marxist journal called the *Modern Quarterly*, and also in a booklet he wrote called *The English Revolution of 1640*. But I first met him on the day of my examination and interview at Balliol. I was sitting with another candidate in this miserable room after the interview and Christopher Hill, to my amazement, appeared and called me out, indicating that I had done quite well. The real purpose of his calling me out, I think, was to say that he didn't think I needed to go on with the Higher School Certificate if I got a scholarship to Balliol. Technically, it was not required to get a grant, he explained, and I'd better spend more time on my languages. Well, I suppose the effect of this was that Christopher Hill was much imprinted on my consciousness.

I must say that although I sat the scholarship exam in history, it was with a view to reading law and becoming a civil servant or a lawyer. It was only after coming back from my two years' service in the army (an experience that I initially hated) that I started my undergraduate course and decided, at a certain point, that I wanted to be an academic. And I think that I gave up law only when the history tutors said, 'You don't want to read law, do you?' To which I replied, 'No, of course not.' I'm very weak, and really blown around in the wind.

My first real experience of historical research must also have helped in this decision. It was the essay I wrote on Anthony Wood for a university prize, the Stanhope Essay. I had never heard of A. Wood, the prescribed subject of the prize, and I suppose you haven't either. He was a seventeenth-century antiquarian who lived in Oxford, by a curious irony two doors down from where I live now. He wrote a biographical dictionary of all the people who were at Oxford, the *Athenae Oxonienses*, and also a history of the university and other works on the city of Oxford. He kept an extensive diary which was very well edited at the beginning of this century, and all his manuscripts are kept in the Bodleian Library. His handwriting was very neat and pretty, and totally legible, so it was quite easy for an undergraduate to read this manuscript material. Well, I think the experience of sitting in the library reading these manuscripts written hundreds of years before about places I knew, and totally accessible to me, was really quite strong and enjoyable.

During the course I tended to choose the subjects which Christopher Hill taught, although there were other equally distinguished tutors available at Balliol to whom I became closer later in life. There was, for instance, Hugh Stretton, a nineteenth-century historian from Australia, a very clever man who used to set very sophisticated essay questions, like 'Which is the better portrait of Mr Asquith, the one in the hall or the one in the senior common room?' There was also Dick Southern, a medievalist with whom I made friends later. Anyway, I suppose I became a historian of the early modern period through the experience of doing the prize essay on Anthony Wood (which I won!) and also because that was what Christopher Hill was.

Did you come to share Christopher Hill's political attitudes?

I was struck by Christopher Hill more as a person than as a Marxist, I think. He was a very undidactic tutor; that is to say, when you finished reading your essay he wouldn't say anything. You would then think of something else to say, and that was followed by a long pause, and you'd think of something else to say, and so on. So the idea of Christopher Hill pushing Marxism at his pupils is just ludicrous. There really wasn't much Marxism around and I don't think we spent very much time even discussing it. He didn't push Marxism or indeed anything. He didn't even tell you what to write on, and normally you had to choose your own subject for the essay. You were thought to be rather feeble if you couldn't think out what you were going to write by yourself! But he was definitely very good at getting across the idea that only the highest standards would do.

However, a lot of my contemporaries at Balliol were Marxists in a serious way. In fact, one necessarily became much aware of Marxism because a lot of the intellectual undergraduates around the place were actual Marxists. I was, for example, an exact contemporary of Raphael Samuel and of Charles Taylor, who was perhaps a Catholic Marxist, certainly very much on the left on those days; there were also others of whom, although prominent Marxists, you wouldn't have heard because they didn't become academics. I myself was associated with the Past and Present Society, which had been the Karl Marx Society, though since its speakers included Hugh Seton-Watson, it wasn't necessarily very Marxist in practice.

I suppose I can say that I was, to a considerable extent, a sort of vulgar Marxist, in the sense that my order of historical priorities, if I had been asked to define it, would have started with material circumstances, and then gone on to social and political structures, and then you'd have had some sort of culture and ideas at the end as a sort of superstructure. So I suppose I shared the underlying assumptions of Marxism. In those days, Marxism seemed to me the only alternative to an almost mindless political empiricism. There wasn't any anthropology, sociology or political science in evidence, at least not to me. So it was either Marxism or one damn thing after another.

But did not the Annales *school provide an alternative at that time?*

I must confess that I never read an article in the *Annales* when I was an undergraduate. I knew that Richard Southern (the greatest living English historian of the Middle Ages) did not have a particularly high opinion of Marc Bloch, probably because he thought that Bloch was too secular a historian, I guess. But Braudel did make some impression on me, although he wasn't very much help with the syllabus. The second half of that great book on Philip II was far too detailed to be of any help for anything much; and the first half, in which he developed his ideas of geographical determinism, did not fit into anything very much either. So, in spite of the fact that it was conventional to say that Braudel's book was a great book, in fact, it was rather an indigestible one. And, as in the case of Bloch or Febvre, Braudel didn't really impinge on me at that time.

How did you react to the political crisis of 1956, which divided the English?

I suppose the sad thing is that I wasn't passionately engaged by either the Suez Canal crisis or the invasion of Hungary, as I should have been. I could easily pretend to have been, retrospectively, but I wasn't, really. The thing is that I was more interested in the past than in the present at that particular stage of my life, and therefore wasn't passionately interested in contemporary politics. But, considering my background, my political views have changed a lot since my undergraduate time at Oxford. My parents, being farmers, were strongly conservative and I remember the 1945 election, when the results of the election came and Cardiff had elected three Labour MPs. That was a really bad day in my house. So that was how I was brought up. By the time I became a voter, though, I was a Labour voter, but not a Marxist one.

And how do you see Marxism today? Do you reject it en bloc, *or do you think that it can still contribute to the understanding of the past and present?*

No, I don't reject Marxism *en bloc*. I think that there are social classes, whose interests, up to a point, conflict, and that those interests find some reflection in art, religion and thought, as well as in politics. I also think that Marx was right about the tendency of capitalism to lead to monopoly. But I don't think that Marxism has any predictive power otherwise; and I certainly don't think that cultural life is determined by class relations; on the contrary, cultural assumptions will affect the way in which class relations are conceived of.

Who are or have been your intellectual heroes?

It depends on what time we're talking about. I came to think very highly indeed of Marc Bloch and to be very much taken by the programme of Lucien Febvre, but as an undergraduate the historians I thought of as very good were Gardiner and Firth, whom I read when I did a special subject on the Commonwealth and the Protectorate. I was terribly impressed by what these two people had written on the subject, fifty years before, in Firth's case, and seventy years before in Gardiner's case. They had produced extremely detailed and by no means exclusively political narratives on which it was very difficult to improve – and still is, for that matter. So that was the thing I was impressed by then. It doesn't hang together at all, does it?

But I developed other enthusiasms later. Another important encounter I had as an undergraduate was with John Prestwich, who was one of the best historians I met at that time. His work on secular medieval history was of a very high order, very original, but he hardly published anything.

Long before the women's movement led in the 1970s to an ever-greater interest in the role of women in history, you were already writing pioneering articles on the subject. What prompted you to do that?

I'm not quite sure actually. But maybe a kind of long retrospective of how everything started will help me to answer this. After I graduated I was going to do a doctorate related to the great intellectual issue at the time, the so-called 'gentry controversy', that is, the rise of the gentry, in which prominent figures were involved: Trevor-Roper, Lawrence Stone, Tawney in the background and Christopher Hill a little bit. The great question was the relative importance of land and office as the foundation of the authority of the English landed classes. And I was initially going to do a doctorate on Robert Cecil, who was an Elizabethan-Jacobean politician, whose fiscal activities impinged on all this. My supervisor, who was going to be the late J. P. Cooper, wrote to Joel Hurstfield (an expert on Cecil) in London, who wrote back saying he was about to publish the definitive life of Cecil, so I shouldn't do that. Well, he never did publish any life of Cecil, definitive or otherwise!

So I shifted slightly and was going to do the court of James I, looking particularly at office-holders, discussing who they were, what the profits of the office were, and so forth; something that would have been very close to what Gerald Aylmer did on the office-holders of Charles I, and subsequently on the Protectorate, and then on Charles II. But then I was elected to All Souls, and as soon as that happened it was generally indicated to me that doing a doctorate was terribly *infra dig* and that I could use that time to read more widely. And that is exactly what I did. And because I was doing quite a bit of teaching at the time, my interests were generated by whatever I happened to be teaching that week, that is, they were totally unstructured. First, I did a certain amount of work on the antiquarian movement of the seventeenth century, which goes back to Anthony Wood, but then, because I was working on religious toleration in the 1640s, I read what was a prominent book of the time, Thomas Edwards's *Gangraena*.

Edwards was a Presbyterian and the book he published in 1646 was an attack on the idea of religious toleration and on the religious sects. His great argument was that you couldn't allow toleration because that would break up the family, since it would mean that wives would pursue a religion different from their husbands' and children from their parents'. So I explored that in what ultimately turned out to be an article entitled 'Women and the Civil War Sects', which I read as a paper to the Stubbs Society, and which Christopher Hill suggested that I offer to *Past and Present*. What I argued there was that some of the Civil War sects, by allowing women freedom of speech, freedom to preach, to discuss religion and also to enjoy a certain amount of equality in the government of congregations, provided a form of female emancipation. It was from that article that I was led on to the history of women more generally.

The next stage after that was an article on the double standard, which was on sexual morality, an article I was advised not to mention when I applied in 1957 for a fellowship at St John's, because it would not make a good impression. The double standard topic was actually just one of a set of half a dozen lectures which I gave after I got to St John's in 1957. The title of the series – which I had to announce the year before – was something like 'The Relations between the Sexes in England from the Reformation to the First World War'. Well, about five people came to the lectures!

There was a very fatuous debate in the *New York Review of Books* quite recently, which arose out of a review somebody wrote about Olwen Hufton's book on women. Somehow Olwen had taken the fact that hardly anybody came to my lectures as an indication that in the fifties nobody was interested in women's history. Well, it was observed that the reason was not that there was no interest in women, but that no one had heard about that obscure don at St John's, so why should they go to his lectures? Anyway, both explanations were wrong in a way, because when this 'obscure don' chose next to lecture on Aristotle, Hobbes and Rousseau, which was a compulsory paper, he had to move to the Examination Schools because there was not enough room in St John's for all the students who came. And they came not because I was a particularly notable lecturer, but because that was part of the curriculum. So the reason people didn't go to the lectures on women is because that subject was not on the curriculum, and the examination is the only reason undergraduates ever go to lectures.

I haven't quite explained why I was interested in this subject of women. Well, I don't really know, but I suppose that it struck me as quite central, women being half of the human race; and yet this topic, although central, seemed to be inadequately explored. Once I embarked on it I did read books that impressed me. Simone de Beauvoir's *Second Sex* was a book which certainly made an impression on me at the time, and I think that that was probably the nearest thing to doctrine I read on the subject. And I read a lot, and collected a lot of nineteenth-century tracts on women. And it was because there was absolutely no interest in the subject at all that I moved away – very foolishly – from it.

Your list of publications impresses by the great number of articles that, since the 1950s, you have written on education and women in history. Would you say that these interests have the same roots?

I suppose all these things are actually related. I think that my underlying approach when studying the history of women was that human nature and human attitudes are pretty plastic and malleable, and shaped by social, cultural and intellectual pressures of one kind or another. And, of these pressures, formal education was the most obviously formative and didactic. So that's what linked it all. The educational values of a period are very instructive because not only do they influence what sort of people are created in that period, but they also tell us a lot about its values.

I didn't deny that there were innate differences between male and female, but I suppose I thought that most things were the product of society. Nowadays, I think that slightly less and realize that certainly lots of things are, but not everything. Perhaps I'm not putting it very well, but

I suppose that at the beginning I was inspired by a sort of psychology like that of John Locke, which was really rather unsophisticated, I fear. You must appreciate, though, that I, like most of my contemporaries, were not educated in anything really, except history. There was no sort of instruction in psychology, in any of the social sciences, or the natural sciences for that matter. So the assumptions one made in order to understand historical action were a mixture of what people call common sense – that is to say, the prejudices of the age – plus the books one happened to have come across.

Another book, which influenced me a lot, though in fact in almost the opposite direction, was Freud's *Civilization and its Discontents*. That was a favourite book of mine in the fifties, which illustrated the way society involves the inhibition of human emotions of one sort or another.

In one of your most incisive articles you have shown that in the increasing literate world of the seventeenth century the illiterates did not live in 'mental darkness'. On the contrary, they were often successful in business and were in the forefront of religious and political upheaval. Could this have a lesson for those who still believe in education as a panacea? Would you agree, then, with those critics (like Jack Goody), who doubt that formal education necessarily leads to an improvement, that educating the people in Ghana, for instance, makes them more unsatisfied?

I would say that literacy means something different now: the literacy of the computer is what matters at present. If you are illiterate in computing terms, I don't think you can do anything very much; you couldn't be very successful in business nor could you govern or rule.

As to formal education, I suppose I'm old-fashioned in this respect. An author I do approve of on this is John Stuart Mill, which means that, like him, I believe in education, I think that it widens horizons. Although I've spent a good deal of my life studying popular culture in one form or another, I do not wish to romanticize that. I think, therefore, that the notion of some people living in darkness is by no means totally ridiculous. If we think, for instance, about the geographical knowledge of the average person in the United States, it is very slight indeed. Ordinary people there wouldn't really know if Oxford, say, is east or west of Constantinople. And I find ignorance of that kind an obstacle to understanding things. So I do believe in education, I do believe that there is such a thing as knowledge and that it is good to have it. All the same, I don't deny that totally illiterate people, uneducated people can live in a world which is as symbolically rich as ours, and that they can have a meaningful life and all that. But I still think that they are losing a lot!

*In 1989 you urged historians to study the vital subject of the history of
children in a proper way, since, according to you, until then they had written
not the history of children, but the history of adult attitudes to children. Has
the subject developed since?*

Well, I suppose a little bit but not very much. In anthropology in the
1970s there is the study of Charlotte Hardman, who worked on the
anthropology of children in contemporary society. She studied children
in Oxfordshire playgrounds in the tradition of Iona Opie, but was slightly
more sophisticated. But in history remarkably little has been done.

A good deal more is known about the sort of physical circumstances in
which children lived. It is possible, as was shown by the American
historian Barbara Hanawalt, for example, to make inferences about the
differences between being a very little girl and a very little boy, from
looking at inquests on accidental deaths, and finding that whereas the
little girls might be more likely to have boiling water from cooking pots
falling on them, the small boys might be further away, falling into ponds
or off trees. In other words, you can show that there were gender differences in the lives of very small children. But, since the culture of children
is essentially oral, it is very difficult to study it other than in action. But,
nevertheless, I still think that more effort could be made.

The trouble about children's diaries, for instance, is that they are the
least spontaneous of all activities – unless you are an unusually gifted
child – and are deeply influenced, first of all, by other literary models, and
also probably by the reaction of adults. I have read a certain number of
children's diaries, and some of them are, incidentally, quite interesting;
but I still don't think they are a very direct route into the minds of
children. They provide mainly incidental information. I myself kept a
diary as a child, which reveals that when I was thirteen, I think, I was
given what I thought was a very luxurious present, a Biro pen, and it
really was at that time. This documents quite well a moment when the
Biro was still a luxury, but does not tell you anything about children.

*In 1961 you gave a lecture entitled 'History and Anthropology', the mere
title of which was enough to intrigue the academic community. In a period in
which hardly any historian took anthropology seriously, what made you
interested in this discipline?*

I think everything started when I was the editor of the *Oxford Magazine*
for the year and a pamphlet by Evans-Pritchard called *Anthropology and
History* was sent by the publisher. As soon as I read it I was much taken
by it and wrote an article on this theme in June '61.

I think that at that time I was still smarting a little at people thinking
that the study of women's history, which I was doing, was ridiculous, not
real history. I suppose I was immediately smitten by the notion Evans-

Pritchard conveyed in that text, that in other parts of the world the concentration on everyday life was perfectly normal, and even central, rather than incidental and peripheral. This discovery coincided with a moment in which I knew that I was interested in making sense of all dimensions of human experience, rather than just the conventional political one. I suppose that underneath that, my guiding assumption was that we should begin by thinking that we know nothing about people in the past, and that we should not attribute to them emotions, beliefs or reactions which are ours, just because they seem to us natural, human and normal. Ever since then I've oscillated between the two opposed views, that people in the past were quite different from us, and that people in the past were just the same. And, in fact, there is a lot to be said for both points of view! But I still think there is greater intellectual integrity to the view that you must build up your picture of the people from the past from what you can actually find out about them, rather than assuming that they must be like us and, therefore, this is how we would have behaved in those circumstances.

So, going back to my discovery of Evans-Pritchard's pamphlet, it was in the wake of my review of it in the *Oxford Magazine* that Lawrence Stone, who was running a sort of small seminar, asked me to give a paper on anthropology and history. I did a lot of reading for it in the Anthropology Institute, and after hearing the paper Stone suggested that I publish it in *Past and Present*.

I must confess, though, that I didn't lose interest in conventional history. I went on teaching and being perfectly interested in that. But henceforth, and possibly even earlier, my own intellectual activities and my teaching went off in different directions. I even think that it's true to say that I virtually never in my life set an essay – and Peter Burke, as my ex-student, may contradict this – on a topic which I've worked on. So I was a bit schizophrenic in that way!

Would you say that your experiences as a national serviceman in Jamaica had prepared you to be interested in anthropology and regard the Englishmen and women of the sixteenth and seventeenth centuries as foreigners?

Well, it was my first experience abroad, and after the initial shock I learned to appreciate this opportunity of living and travelling extensively for eighteen months in Jamaica. I did do a bit of fieldwork there, in the sense that on leave I went with some others into the Cockpit country, which is an area inhabited by the Maroons (the descendants of escaped slaves who had set up what was a self-governing, quasi-independent republic). Well, we rather blundered into this and were, in a sort of polite way, arrested by the Maroons and put on trial. I remember this very vividly. The trial happened in a large barn lit by kerosene lamps, and the question was whether, under the treaty of 1730 or so, it was appropriate for British soldiers to be in a Maroon country. We had with us a small Jamaican youth with a donkey, who was helping us with the luggage. Well, he was taken away in the middle of the night by somebody else, who cut his wrist and did some kind of voodoo magic.

I might say that at that stage I became interested in all these things, but it isn't true. It was an exciting experience but, to my mind, it didn't have the slightest impact on my later interest in anthropology. This is the trouble really; people's lives, mine at least, are much messier than they ought to be!

Which anthropology attracts you? Malinowski, Evans-Pritchard, Lévi-Strauss and Geertz are all cited somewhere in your footnotes, although their intellectual styles are very different. How do you choose between them, or do you think choice unnecessary?

I suppose you are asking how on earth I can believe in all these people when they don't believe in each other. I suppose that when reading anthropology I was never looking for a system or a key to all mythologies, or a way of opening all doors. All I was really looking for was stimuli to the historical imagination and, in their different ways, all those authors have stimulated my historical imagination. This might be a weak answer, but the fact is that, in the end, I don't have a carefully worked-out, well-defended and defined intellectual position. I'm sort of blown around and tend to believe the last book I read!

It might be interesting to tell you that when I sent a copy of that article on history and anthropology, which appeared in *Past and Present*, to Evans-Pritchard, whom I knew a bit, he wrote a marvellous sardonic letter back saying more or less this: 'Thank you very much. You've read far more anthropologists than I have. I find most of them totally turgid and jargon-ridden, unreadable, I fear.' Broadly speaking I also found later anthropology less immediately accessible and I agree with him in finding the lucidity of traditional British social anthropology much preferable to the more inflated pretensions of what came later.

I must explain that the period when I did most of my reading in anthropology was in the early sixties, which means that I didn't read people like Lévi-Strauss then. The books and articles on the shelves at that time had been written in the fifties and possibly the forties. Therefore most of it was British social anthropology of a primarily functionalist, or structural-functional type, as it was sometimes called. So by the time I was reading this, proper students of the subject were talking about Lévi-Strauss, which came a little late for me, as it happens. I did find sympathetic the underlying assumptions of that kind of structuralist anthropology, and yet I somehow found it harder to relate it to historical writing. And, no doubt, that is a defect of *Religion and the Decline of Magic*. I should have done more in that direction.

You were described in the early seventies as one of the greatest enthusiasts for a new history, who as early as 1966 wrote a manifesto calling for a 'more systematic indoctrination' of historians 'in social sciences'. Are you still such an enthusiast?

'The Tools and the Job' was an article that certainly caused a lot of pain. If you look at a very interesting volume of letters by the great medievalist K. B. McFarlane to his pupils, you'll see that in his last letter, just before he died, there is a denunciation of my piece in the *TLS*. The problem was that it [my piece] was couched in very arrogant terms, the arrogance of youth, I suppose. It said that history, in the twentieth century, had gone totally in the wrong direction, implying, in an unjustifiable way really, that all this distinguished work done by 'conventional historians' had been a waste of time, which is not true at all.

Frankly, that was not a topic to which I had given much thought before I got an invitation from the editor of the *TLS* saying simply: 'Would you write an article on history and the social sciences?' They were doing a series of special supplements on 'new ways in history', and I'm not sure who the advisers behind that invitation were. I suspect that Barraclough was one, and Hobsbawm and Finley were also closely connected with it. Anyway, I warmed to the theme and it became a rather aggressive article. I just sat down to write and it was as if my pen ran away with me.

I stand by some aspects of that article more than others. That was the time when there was a temporary infatuation with quantitative history, econometric history, which was suddenly going to be the answer to everything. And I was all for that, although I never practised it myself, because I thought that that type of history was based on counter-factuals, and it would be able to work out and quantify questions like, how different would the world be if there hadn't been railways? Most history is counter-factual really, that is, concerned with finding out how much difference something makes. And quantitative history suddenly seemed to be the way of producing the answers to such questions. But it wasn't, in the end. So the enthusiasms on that side were short-lived. On the other hand, I was implying in that article that there were a lot of sciences out there from which you could learn systematically. If today I don't think that things are quite so scientific as I thought then, I still believe in historians reading as widely as possible because, in the end, history only is what the historians bring to it; and if the historian is narrow in his or her assumptions, cultural range of reference and so forth, the results will be narrow too.

How important has Norbert Elias been for your thinking about history?

I knew Norbert Elias and even wrote a review of his great work when it was first published in English in 1978. As you know, his *Civilizing Process* was published in German in 1939, and rather sank without trace for decades (it is known that he was very finicky about translations, and several that were planned failed to materialize). I was greatly taken by his study of manners, but his overall theory, designed to explain the ever-mounting degree of inhibition, I found crudely evolutionary and not really plausible. I met him in Princeton, and even had lunch with him once. He was extremely pleasant, a remarkable figure, really. By then quite old, he gave on this occasion a lecture that was very impressive, but I suppose that although his subject matter interested me a lot, his approach to it did not. In a sense, Elias was a mixture of Freud and Weber, even if he had ideas of his own.

Everyone talks about your interest in anthropology, but few people comment on the references which recur in your work to psychology and psychologists, especially the social and developmental psychologists. Do you think it possible to write psychohistory?

In the past I was somewhat infatuated with this approach and was extremely interested in the work of C. R. Hallpike, an anthropologist who may not have had as much recognition as he deserves. In his *Foundations of Primitive Thought*, which is an attempt to apply a sort of developmental-psychological approach to the study of simpler societies, he has some very comic passages that come out from the Russian developmental psychologist Luria on how peasants can't grasp the concept of a syllogism. Luria, who, no doubt, is more important than Hallpike, had done experiments among illiterate peasants, the Uzbeks, in Central Asia and had recorded the following conversation. The questioner says: 'There are no camels in Germany; the city of Berlin is in Germany; are there camels in Berlin?' The peasant answers: 'I don't know, I've never been to Germany.' So they try again, the questioner repeating: 'There are no camels in Germany; the city of Berlin is in Germany; are there camels in Berlin?' To which the peasant answers: 'Yes, probably there are camels there.' And after another go, the peasant says: 'Because it is a large city there are probably some camels there, since there should be camels in large cities.' And the questioner argues: 'But I'm saying that there are no camels in Germany and this city is in Germany.' Anyway, it goes on and on because the peasants can't grasp the idea of a syllogism. Or at least this is what Luria was trying to prove.

One can understand the appeal of this kind of psychological approach. If one is viewing the past as a foreign country and the people as having reasoning and beliefs which are different from ours, superficially anyway, the psychological approach seems valuable. But I think that, in the end, it doesn't work. I'm slightly at a loss to explain how Luria had conversations like those, but I think that it is probably better to assume that people's cognitive equipment (at least in the historical period we are concerned with) is like ours rather than unlike ours. Of course, this creates a problem for historians confronted by institutions like the ordeal and the belief in miracles, and so on. How does one deal with that? One way is to say that people just reasoned differently because they were at a different phase of psychological development. But this is not convincing at all.

How important to your intellectual development was the British empiricist tradition in which you were brought up? Is there any tension between this tradition and your interest in theory?

Well, I suppose that, although I've written against the British empiricist approach, in the end I'm more a product of it than not. But it all depends on what you mean by empirical tradition. I'm certainly not in agreement with Geoffrey Elton, who said that there is no need to find a problem. You just have to go into the archives and wait and see. I'm not an empiricist to that extent. I do think that going into the archives can suggest new questions to you, but you really have to be asking something; otherwise, which points do you take note of? To me all knowledge advances by formulating hypotheses and then testing them, rather than just accumulating facts and somehow expecting something to come out of that. On the other hand, having formulated some questions, I would expect progress to be made by producing evidence of a moderately conventional kind, rather than invoking a theory. In a sense, then, although I see a tension between the theoretical and the empiricist approaches, I would say that my working methods and modes of argument are probably pretty unadventurous. The subject matter may be very different, but the modes of argument are not so very different from those employed by the 'benighted generation' of historians in the first half of the twentieth century!

There is, no doubt, an element in British culture which makes it difficult for us to adopt more theoretical approaches, like the French, for instance. This is well illustrated by the reaction of two British publishers to Le Roy Ladurie's *Montaillou*. I read it in French galley proofs for CUP and Penguin, who were considering a translation, and neither would take it. In each case I told them that I was really impressed by it, that it was a brilliant and remarkable book, and in each case they said, 'Yes, but it is about an early fourteenth-century village, isn't it?' At that stage it hadn't appeared in France, but when it came out and François Mitterand was seen clutching it on the first day, it became a world best-seller! No need to say that Penguin had to buy it later at a vast price!

Montaillou, by the way, certainly had several defects on the empirical side – some medievalists have pointed out that Le Roy Ladurie was somewhat slipshod in his use of the evidence – and yet it illustrates a terrific way of writing history. It uses documents, which were compiled for one purpose, to illuminate something else, and it sets about to recreate the physical and the mental world of a community which one would have thought was absolutely lost forever. I think that it is really a wonderful book, and even if Le Roy Ladurie went too fast and did it in a somewhat sloppy way, his assumptions about what historians should do are just the ones I share myself.

Do you share in any degree the concern of John Elliott about micro-historical studies, which he put in this dramatic way: 'there is surely something amiss when the name of Martin Guerre becomes as well or better known than that of Martin Luther'?

I'd like to have said that! I certainly don't lie awake worrying about it, but I think a little micro-history goes a long way. Carlo Ginzburg's *The Cheese and the Worms* and Le Roy Ladurie's *Montaillou* are wonderful books, but I think I'd stop there in the list of micro-histories that I think of as very important. I may have forgotten some good ones, and of course there's nothing wrong with doing them as long as they don't drive everything else out. Contrary to what you might think, I'm all for pluralism in historical activity, all for people doing different things. As a fashion, I don't think it very attractive. First of all, to do it well you need a slight touch of genius, really. It's not the sort of thing to be done mechanically. It may seem easy to do, but it certainly is not. There are very good subjects for this type of work, but for the most part you don't have the source materials that you would need. When I read Pepys's diaries, which I've done several times, I think that a micro-history of Pepys would be deeply illuminating for wider issues in the seventeenth century. And yet, I've read some very boring studies along these lines. Even leaving aside the need for a touch of genius, not all topics and not all people are equally interesting for this kind of history!

In your article 'History and Anthropology' in Past and Present *you suggested new and interesting topics for a social cultural history, such as the history of dreams, the history of the attitudes to pain, the history of drinking habits, etc. Given such a variety of topics, why did you choose to invest so much effort in writing a large book on the decline of magic, which cost you many years of work?*

Well, I think that since then different historians have developed most of the topics I suggested. As for my *Religion and the Decline of Magic* –

which, contrary to what you might think, didn't take that long at all, since I wrote it in about one year – it all started accidentally. I was teaching the Commonwealth and Protectorate special subject with John Cooper, which we both took very seriously, no doubt in a mildly competitive way. That meant that each one of us worked pretty hard on a topic each week. One topic of mine was the Levellers, and as I was looking around the Bodleian Library to see whether there were any manuscripts related to them, I came across a reference in the Ashmolean manuscripts to a note by Richard Overton. Now, Overton was the most rational of the Levellers, who wrote a book called *Man's Mortality* and, generally speaking, was thought to anticipate the secularism of modern ages. Well, this manuscript turned out to be a tiny scrap of paper addressed to the astrologer William Lilly, basically saying: 'With your astrological knowledge, could you tell me if I should go on being a Leveller or not?' This was pinned inside one of the casebooks which Lilly maintained, recording consultations with his clients.

At first, I looked idly at this, but then realized that these casebooks, which had never been looked at since Ashmole collected them in the seventeenth century, were potentially the most wonderful source for investigating the fears, anxieties and hopes of people in the seventeenth century, because Lilly had a huge business and saw perhaps 2,000 people in a year! So the part of the book that was written first was the section on astrology. It was in the course of studying astrology that I came to see that among the problems that clients brought to the astrologer was the question of whether they had been bewitched or not. By then, through reading British social anthropology, Evans-Pritchard in particular, I was well aware that witchcraft was a large issue in anthropological studies. That's why I went on to study witchcraft, which I always meant to be part of a larger picture.

This book has often been discussed as a book about witchcraft, or the decline of witch-trials. Is this view of the 'Thomas thesis' fair?

From discussing witchcraft I went on to writing on more or less everything. I had chapters on prophecies, fairies, and so forth. I even wrote one about irrational panics, which I never included. So the book is not essentially about witchcraft, although this is the section – which in my view is no better or worse than the rest of it – which is endlessly discussed. In a way, *Religion and the Decline of Magic* has been the victim of its title. I'm hopeless with titles and I didn't have a title until the book was ready. And then I was just stuck with this one. And the title possibly implies a thesis that isn't entirely stated in the book. But, anyway, one of the weaknesses of the book, which has also turned out to be a strength, is that you can find something in it that will support almost any position. So it is true that one can still find plenty of magic around after 1700. All I said really was that the legal position changed emphatically, and that the attitude of most of the social and intellectual elite – the gentry and the upper clergy – changed. But I also said that at the lower social level things weren't very different.

How did you come to write about the relationship of man to nature? Was it a reaction to current preoccupations about the environment?

Well, it wasn't that at all, any more than *Religion and the Decline of Magic* indicated that I had some interest in the occult! I've never had the slightest interest in the occult, and try more or less to be rational in a very ordinary and boring sort of way. In fact, I'm not a bit spooky in taste and I was certainly not feeling particularly green when I wrote *Man and the Natural World*! I'm afraid that although I have some environmental sensibilities, they are no more developed than anybody else's. It all happened because I was asked to give the Trevelyan Lectures (from which the book emerged), and while working out a theme for this set of lectures, I discovered that in my index of notes one of the fattest envelopes was the one called 'animals'.

So I suppose the question now is why did I have an envelope devoted to that topic. Well, I suppose because I was making notes on virtually everything, really. You've heard of Sir Charles Oman's marvellous account of Lord Acton's study in his country house in Shropshire? Well, in order to write his great work on freedom, Acton took notes on absolutely everything, including the vanity of human learning. This voracious reader of course never finished his great work on liberty, or indeed on anything else!

I'm not quite like him, but I suppose that my ambition has really been to do a sort of all-round ethnography of early modern England. So I was interested in all dimensions, including politics. And I couldn't help coming across animals. That's how it happened. It didn't come consciously out of the preoccupations of the day, I'm afraid, although by the sheerest irony it seems to have mirrored them quite closely. But not self-consciously at all; and with no axe to grind. I wasn't thinking about what was going to be the flavour of the 1980s! I really wasn't. I was just thinking, what on earth have I got left to lecture on!

Your work on the relationship of men with the natural world has been criticized for not being comparative and, consequently, for contributing to the academic tradition of ethnocentrism, which claims the uniqueness of the West. How would you reply to this criticism?

Actually, everything one does, including works by anthropologists, is ethnocentric. But isn't it extraordinary? You engage with a very ambitious subject, and then you are criticized for not being comparative enough! If I had been writing a book on the 1832 Reform Act, nobody would say something like, 'I'm very surprised to see that you're not considering that the Brazilians...'. It's a hard life, really. The more ambitious the subject, the more they expect you to have wide horizons. The answer is that I didn't envisage the scale of the book as worldwide; the scope of the work was not intended to be comparative. I was more concerned to identify the main lineaments of the British, or rather English, situation than anything else. And having said that, *Man and the Natural World* is not entirely devoid of non-British, European, or extra-European references.

I agree that the comparative approach is interesting, but it depends on what your objective is. If you are trying to identify what is distinctive about any period or place, then obviously it has to be done by implicit or explicit comparison. The problem is that, even without comparing, it is laborious and difficult enough to establish what the state of affairs was in some particular context. Because if we are going to compare, what data am I going to compare with what? There are not very many *Man and the Natural World*s on all the other countries for you to look up and see how England compares! You'd have to do the work yourself.

How important have the criticisms of your work been to the development of your ideas?

I suppose that because my tendency has been to move on all the time to another topic, I haven't really been able to absorb and do sufficient justice to the criticisms I receive. However, if I were to rewrite *Religion and the Decline of Magic* to do some mammoth second edition, I would take many of the criticisms on board. The essay by Jonathan Barry in his book *Witchcraft and Early Modern Europe*, which was actually conceived as a sort of twentieth birthday celebration of my book, is full of criticisms that have a lot to be said for them. I must confess, though, that on the whole I don't think I feel particularly vindicated or refuted by later researches on the topic. But it's true that *Religion and the Decline of Magic* was a book of its time. It reflects what in those days were tolerably up-to-date assumptions, which have changed a bit. I can say that if I was doing it all again, it wouldn't be done the same way. And I think that in particular the vocabulary I employed would be different. And I would probably devote more systematic attention to the categories employed by contemporaries, as opposed to the labels stuck on these activities by later people. However, when I say this I'm not thinking of magic, because, in fact, 'magic' is a contemporary term, a word thrown around very extensively in sixteenth-century polemic. There is nothing, therefore, particularly anachronistic about it – people knew perfectly well what they were talking about.

As for *Man and the Natural World*, I wouldn't call it that these days. 'Man' wasn't meant to be a gender-laden concept, but it's become unacceptable, politically incorrect, in the same way as the word 'Negro' has become unacceptable. But I suppose I should say that I'm not a functionalist any more, in the way that I suppose I was in the sixties. Of course, my views have changed, simply through living the last fifteen years! I'm much more interested in cultural history, a concept which I wouldn't have recognized the existence of at the time. I'm more interested in mental assumptions than in material circumstances, or at least much more than I used to be. I just happen to find this much more interesting now, not necessarily any more important. I don't think that the entire world is a construction, and that there's no reality, and all that. I'm not at all postmodernist!

You often use literary sources as well as archival ones. What can they offer that the 'documents' cannot?

That sounds more like a question for the tripos! Well, they cover a wider range of experiences essentially, and clearly they present serious problems of interpretation, but no more serious than those which the traditional documents did. I mean, a play or a poem is a certain literary genre, is subject to certain conventions, and is influenced by certain models, and therefore you must be careful with what you are quoting. But if that is true, the same points can be made with equal force about anything in the Public Record Office. The documents there also need interpretation and sensitive handling. What, then, do the literary sources tell us? Well, they are concerned with human emotions and values and sensibilities, and they are often very important for the life they show in them.

Arguing, in 1988, that the distinction between fact and fiction is a matter of prevailing convention, you've urged, against powerful current trends, in favour of the reconciliation of history and literature. Would you say that in the last ten years this has gone too far?

Yes, I do think it has gone too far. I believe that there is a difference between fact and fiction and that, no doubt, dates me. For me it's true, and not fiction, that we are sitting here on this Thursday, the 28th of July. So I certainly think that the tendency to blur the genres is unhelpful. As to the new historicism, I welcome it to an extent, but their history, their historical dimension doesn't strike me as very rigorous.

I found most of the writings of Hayden White, La Capra and others ultimately a little disappointing because they don't get to grips with the sort of historians we actually read. I mean, I don't want to be told what particular tropes Michelet employs, for example, because I don't use Michelet. But if they really got to work on the latest numbers of *Past and Present* and said something about the tropes there, then I would find that much more illuminating. The case with these writers reminds me a bit of the analytical philosophers writing on history. What they discussed was always far away from what historians actually did.

You once stated that 'even the most scrupulous historian is busy myth-making, whether or not he realizes it'. Isn't there a way to train ourselves not to manipulate 'our genealogies to meet new social needs' (using your own expressions)?

There are many degrees of myth-making, but the most effective one is of a kind so subtle that I think it's very difficult to proscribe. Clearly, when people set out to find genealogies for modern feminism, or for lesbianism, or for whatever -ism it is, they are constructing bits in a rather crude way, which is not very different from the way the Tudors claimed to be descended from Brutus and the Trojans. There is also the fact that academic syllabuses and curricula are always being revised to establish new genealogies, so that they'll catch up, for instance, with the latest immigrant community by having it in the syllabus, and so on. But the sort of myth-making that I think is more subtle, more interesting and more difficult – indeed, to a certain degree impossible – to eradicate is really the kind that appears in all the sentences we write about human activities in the past. They inevitably contain implicit assumptions about how people behave, very often about how people ought to behave, about what is reasonable and about what is unreasonable, what is puzzling and what is not puzzling, and all the time this is reinforcing whatever the contemporary version of common sense is. In other words, when you write history or novels, you cannot but employ a vast number of working assumptions about human behaviour and human values, causation, priorities, and so forth, which you don't have time to discuss; and you're possibly barely even aware of them yourself.

So the fundamental myth-making I'm talking about is the way the cant of the age gets into the literary and historical prose. That's why whenever we open a history book written in 1840 or 1740 it hits us in the eye. And what we are writing in the 1990s will hit people in the eye in just the same way, and we'll be a foreign country to them.

What do you think of the New Labour ideal of a New Britain? Is it any less of a myth than Mrs Thatcher's return to Victorian values?

I'm pretty disappointed by New Labour, and the aspect which disappoints me most is, I suppose, that it represents the triumph of democracy in the cultural sphere in the worst way, that is to say, in exactly the way which Tocqueville or Mill thought might happen in the worst possible scenario. As an example, a photograph appeared in the national press of the Prime Minister and the Chancellor of the Exchequer, jackets off, lagers in their hands, watching football on the television. I'm sure that as soon as the photograph was taken, they went back to business. That this should be the sort of image which it was thought right to project depresses me a lot. It so happens that I've never been interested in football, and most of its associations, like the chauvinism and the violence, I find quite repugnant. But that's just an aspect of it.

New Labour has not, as far as I can see, involved any sort of commitment to scientific, academic, intellectual, literary or artistic activity, but it has involved embracing the world of popular culture, international sport and the media at the lower end. No doubt mine is an old-fashioned view, but I've always thought that the task of socialism was to raise people. Whereas now it seems to me that the Victorian notion of improvement is completely abandoned for one, not so much of pleasure, but of a sort of low-level hedonism. In short, it's pushpin rather than poetry.

What adds to my disappointment is that one was expecting a great change from the previous situation. One of the depressing things of the Thatcher period was, of course, that there was no interest in intellectual, academic things, which seemed to contrast very much with, say, France, where intermittently there was much more public recognition. And one had hoped that with the change of government this would make a difference. I spend a lot of time in public administrative things these days and I have noticed that the British Library is running down at the most tremendous rate. There has been a real cut in the new British Library for acquisitions and for conservation, so that they've reached the point now that they have seriously to consider whether to abandon collecting non-British books. They've hardly taken any new series, any new journals, and yet publication over the world is increasing at a terrific rate. Well, the British Library has a tradition, and it was one of the world's great libraries; it's now in danger of ranking about twentieth by American standards, let alone any others!

That rejection of the inheritance of the past is what I find most appalling; and I think that politically too it is an enormous mistake. Britain is possibly not very important internationally, but it is, for various historical reasons, almost uniquely fortunate in its ability to have preserved a lot of the physical and literary inheritance of the past. And I hate to see all that neglected. This is, in fact, closely related to the personal interests or lack of interests of the leading politicians of the period. Talking about Blair, for example, someone was telling me that when he visited the British Library it looked as if he had not set foot in a library before, which cannot be true because, after all, though I was not aware of him, he was at St John's when I was a tutor there; but still . . . So, the New Britain seems to involve the neglect of what I regard as some of the best aspects of the old one. All this, I think, is very, very shocking.

What other projects do you have in mind for the future? Have you ever thought of changing fields?

I prefer not to talk about ambitions for publication. I've got a lot of unfinished projects, and the life I've been leading in the last few years has allowed me no time to stop and look at them properly and see which are the ones to go on with. But when I retire in two years' time, I'll be completely free. At the moment my main preoccupation is to decide which of these make six suitable lectures for the Ford Lectures.

As to possible changes in period, there are times when I really wonder if it's the early modern period that I should be doing. I do confess to some doubts on that score. I was talking to an American historian of that period not too long ago who said he had stopped writing about that period because there was nothing new to say. I mean, there is a finite number of sources and it's very hard to find something surprising to say about this period, whereas the eighteenth, nineteenth and twentieth centuries are terrifically rich. You can go anywhere and do tremendous things. The early modern period, though, for several decades really took the cream of British and also possibly American and European talent. Look at the *Annales* school, in which an incredible concentration of talent crawled over the early modern period.

What have we got today? I find most articles and journals dealing with this period pretty dispiriting – people not of the second, not of the third, but possibly of the fourth generation trying to find something wrong with what was said by the third generation, and producing some new detail or spuriously trying to make something look new. That is not what was happening fifty years ago. It is the problem of the professionalization of historical scholarship. The field has got terrifically crowded, and also very specialized. Typically, the historians find something new, and then build their defences around it, and that becomes their area, their dominion. I'm quite sure that if I started again I wouldn't do the early modern period!

In 1988 you were knighted by the Queen. What does this title mean to you?

I was honoured and flattered to be offered a knighthood for services to history, since I know that these things come from committees made up of academics rather than politicians. I don't disapprove of honours, though I'd prefer it if they came after people's names rather than before, as I don't much like titles (and they certainly bring the worst out of some of the people one encounters!). But so long as there are knighthoods, then

I think that it is splendid that historians should get them as well as politicians and businessmen. I think that the academic profession does benefit from this kind of public recognition, even if it is not necessarily the right people within that profession who get the titles.

Among the books in your area of interest, which are the ones you would have liked to have written?

Let me think. I don't want to be like Geoffrey Elton who, when the *Times Literary Supplement* had a series in which people were asked to mention books which they thought had been overrated and books which had been underrated, said he could easily think of three books which had been overrated, but not one which had been underrated! But I do admire lots of books. I'd like to have written (at the time they were written, not now of course) Marc Bloch's *Feudal Society*; or, in a different way, Tawney's *Religion and the Rise of Capitalism*. I also admire Thompson's *The Making of the Working Class*, although I find it a rather loose, baggy monster. Lawrence Stone's *The Crisis of Aristocracy* could also be mentioned, because he's a wonderful writer. Coming closer to the present, Orlando Figes's book on the Russian Revolution, *The People's Tragedy*, is also pretty good. The same could be said of Robert Bartlett's new book on twelfth-century England. But if I go back chronologically, I could mention the great works by Burckhardt and Huizinga.

Oxford, July 1998

SELECT BIBLIOGRAPHY

'The Double Standard', *Journal of the History of Ideas*, 20 (1959), 195–215.

'History and Anthropology', *Past and Present*, 24 (1963), 3–24.

Religion and the Decline of Magic: Studies in Popular Beliefs in Sixteenth- and Seventeenth-Century England (London, Weidenfeld and Nicolson, 1971); translated into Dutch, Italian, Japanese, Portuguese.

Rule and Misrule in the Schools of Early Modern England (Stenton Lecture, University of Reading, 1976).

'The Place of Laughter in Tudor and Stuart England', *Times Literary Supplement*, 21 January 1977, 77–81.

Man and the Natural World: Changing Attitudes in England, 1500–1800 (London, Allen Lane, 1983); translated into French, Dutch, Japanese, Portuguese, Swedish.

'Ways of Doing Cultural History', in Rik Sanders et al. (eds), *De Verleiding van de Overvloed. Reflecties oop de Eigenheid van de Cultuurgeschiedenis*, (Amsterdam, Rodopi, 1991), pp. 65–81.

'Cleanliness and Godliness in Early Modern England', in Anthony Fletcher and Peter Roberts (eds), *Religion, Culture and Society in Early Modern Britain: Essays in Honour of Patrick Collinson* (Cambridge, Cambridge University Press, 1994), pp. 56–83.

'English Protestantism and Classical Art', in Lucy Gent (ed.), *Albion's Classicism: The Visual Arts in Britain, 1550–1660*, Studies in British Art, 2 (New Haven and London, Yale University Press, 1995), pp. 221–38.

'Health and Morality in Early Modern England', in Allan M. Brandt and Paul Rozin (eds), *Morality and Health* (London, Routledge, 1997), pp. 15–34.

ed., *The Oxford Book of Work* (Oxford, Oxford University Press, 1999).

5

Daniel Roche

Daniel Roche (b. 1935), a professor of the prestigious Collège de France, is one of today's most eminent French historians. An eighteenth-century specialist, Roche belongs to the third generation of the *Annales* group, the generation that according to Emmanuel Le Roy Ladurie transferred their interests 'from the basement to the attic', or in other words from economic history – the 'basis' of history in Marx's view – to cultural history, or the superstructure. Having been a student under the Marxist historian Ernest Labrousse, best-known for his pioneering study on the economic origins of the French Revolution, Daniel Roche distanced himself from his mentor by choosing to do his *Doctorat d'État* on a topic in cultural history: the role of the French provincial academies in the dissemination and production of Enlightenment discourse. In this massive study, examined in 1973 and published in 1978 in two volumes (one of them comprising just notes and references), Roche made a tactful but effective use of quantitative methods. While demonstrating shifts in interest and tendencies in the scholarship of the period, he produced a social history of culture which did not reduce it to the expression of economic and social forces or trends.

Since then his work has developed on three fronts: the history of the book and reading, the history of the city, and the history of material culture. The three themes together, he says, make up 'a broader way to propose a social reading of culture'. His study in popular culture, *Le Peuple de Paris* (1981; translated as *The People of Paris*, 1987), in which he proposed to 'reread the history of the popular behaviour of Parisians', was notable in several respects. Material culture, for instance, was taken very seriously, as shown by his examination of the food, clothing, houses and furniture of ordinary Parisians in the eighteenth century. Roche found the evidence for this material culture principally in thousands of inventories, basing his conclusions on the quantitative analysis of a mass of archive data collected in part by his students, who play an important part in most of his works. By contrasting his data with the image of the people found in eighteenth-century reformers and observers, Roche was able to present a view of the lower classes as being much more complex and dynamic than was usually imagined. Similarly, basing himself on the evolving relationship of people with their possessions, and noting the simultaneous increase in both poverty and wealth among the people of Paris, Roche showed that the Revolution was neither the child of misery, as Michelet claimed,[1] nor of prosperity, as suggested by Jaurès.[2] Upholding a mixed explanation, Roche argued that the increasing difficulties faced by the people were inseparable from the appearance of new demands, new values and new ambitions in life.

Among the material objects mentioned in the inventories there were also books, showing that the literacy rate among the craftsmen of Paris was relatively high. So *The People of Paris*, like the work of Roger Chartier (a former student of Roche's), made an important contribution to the history of reading and thus the history of mentalities, or what Roche, echoing Marc Bloch, sometimes calls 'modes of feeling and thought' (*façons de sentir et de penser*). His interest in the methodological problems of the sociology of the book and in the possibilities offered by the quantitative history of printed matter led him to collaborate with H.-J. Martin and R. Chartier in the *Histoire de l'édition française* (1984), in which he directed the volume on 'the book triumphant' and contributed ground-breaking articles on censorship, the book police and the great *Encyclopédie* of Diderot and d'Alembert.

While he was working on the popular culture of Paris, Daniel Roche made what he considers his most important discovery: the autobiography of Jacques-Louis Ménétra, a Parisian glassmaker who lived during the *Ancien Régime* and the Revolution. With this find, which Roche published in 1982 together with an interpretative essay on the man and his milieu, he was able to supplement his quantitative analysis of the popular culture of the time with a view from within, showing how an individual craftsman experienced his work, his leisure and also the French Revolution, since Ménétra took part in it as a popular militant, or *sans-culotte*. What Menocchio, the miller of Friuli, meant to Carlo Ginzburg, Ménétra meant to Daniel Roche. Both historians discovered documents that enabled them masterfully to reconstruct the lives of individuals from the popular classes, and through their experiences to paint a broad picture of popular culture under the *Ancien Régime*.

---

1 Jules Michelet (1798–1874), French historian, author of *Histoire de la France* (1835–67).
2 Jean Jaurès (1859–1914), French socialist politician.

Roche's most notable book is perhaps *The Culture of Clothing* (1989), a history of French dress and fashion during the eighteenth century, which gives a foretaste of another brilliant study of his published recently under the suggestive title *A History of Everyday Things* (1997). The culture of clothing project grew out of *The People of Paris*, since it is partly based on the inventories studied for that book, but it also discusses the dress of upper-class men and women at a time when French fashion was becoming internationally famous. What makes this book especially original is above all the way in which Roche uses clothing as evidence for the attitudes and values of those wearing it. Thus a history which at first sight seems only to be concerned with appearances turns out to be a means for investigating deeper structures of thinking and feeling.

Like Ménétra, Daniel Roche may be described as a master craftsman, practising what Marc Bloch has called 'the historian's craft' (*le métier d'historien*) with great finesse and managing a historical 'workshop' in which his students, like apprentices, make a visible contribution. Modesty, lucidity and balance all shine out among Roche's intellectual virtues. He has always been very open to the ideas of the social and cultural theorists from Marx to Baudrillard, but he carefully joins theory to thorough empirical research, just as he also joins an interest in 'high' culture to an interest in popular culture, and quantitative evidence with testimony of literary sources, from fashion magazines to autobiographies.

Daniel Roche received us at the famous École Normale in the Rue d'Ulm in Paris, where he has been the director of the Institute of Modern History for several years. Our meeting took place appropriately enough on the top floor, the 'attic', of the building, with a beautiful view of central Paris in the distance. He was relaxed and informal in manner, speaking slowly and deliberately, and his answers to our questions were direct, lucid and spiced with his customary wit.

MARIA LÚCIA PALLARES-BURKE   *How did you become a historian?*

DANIEL ROCHE   How did I become a historian? Well, I don't know, because I don't even know if I am one. I think I am first and foremost a teacher... I have a feeling that my story is not very different from that of many French historians. The route I took was, so to speak, highly traditional: I went to secondary school in Paris after the war; I went to the Sorbonne in 1954; I took the entrance examination for the École Normale Supérieure (where I studied from 1956 to 1960); and I became a secondary-school teacher. In those days you had to choose your subjects when you started university, and I chose history and geography. These two subjects were traditionally studied together, and you got a degree in history and geography at the same time. The fact that I studied both subjects together was very important, bearing in mind that the historical works in use at the time were the outcome of a very French tradition of regional history, in which the connection with geographical communities, cartography and the discovery of territorial space, for instance, were highly relevant.

How important was your family background in your choice of career?

I don't know whether this has any great intellectual interest, but I come from a middle-class family. My father, a First World War man, was first an officer and then devoted himself to administration; that is, his career was not at all intellectual. Unlike others, I am not from a university-educated family, a family of academics or anything like that. So, compared with my family and my siblings too, the path I followed was very individual. I was the person who always had to explain to everyone else what a historian or a professor actually did. But although not exactly intellectual, my family was well educated. There were lots of books around – we used to read a lot – but as far as I remember no history books. So I'd say that my specific interest in history was aroused under the influence of my secondary-school teachers. I particularly remember two or three of them who really knew their job well and gave marvellous lessons on the *Ancien Régime*: the origins of the French Revolution, the colonial conquests and the war in America, for example. Topics connected with the pre-Revolutionary and Revolutionary period were traditionally important in *lycée* education. I owe much of my interest in history to these teachers, then, rather than to reading any particular books.

I could have chosen to remain a history teacher in the *lycée*, which in the sixties was still an interesting and respected option, and in contrast to the violence you get nowadays the pupils were quieter and there were fewer of them. The idea of becoming a historian and not just a secondary-school teacher was due, again, to teachers I met; except this time it was the lecturers I had at the University of Paris and the École Normale.

Was it there that you met Labrousse and Braudel? Were they your principal mentors?

Before them, two other figures, Pierre Goubert and Jacques Le Goff, were very important to me. They were still very young, and obviously did not yet have the reputation they have today, but you could already see how innovative they were. Le Goff, for instance, was not yet at the École des Hautes Études but was still an assistant lecturer at the University of Lille. They used to come and give courses at the École Normale; they were representatives of what today we usually call the *École des Annales*, but in those days it was not called that. In fact the *École des Annales* is not something real; it is a fabrication of the eighties. There was, certainly, a movement around the journal, but it wasn't a school, I mean there was no desire to define very precise aims; on the contrary, it was all very open, and particularly open towards the social sciences. Now this openness was very different from what characterized the historical studies that were being carried out at the Sorbonne at that time, where there were great masters, like Pierre Renouvin, who represented the erudite, learned, positivist tradition. I remember taking courses that I found totally boring, tedious and even irritating – like Roland Mousnier's, for example. And I say boring and irritating because despite all the knowledge they had they were trying to be ideologically provocative, as if to say, 'I am not a Marxist and therefore I am going to demonstrate the opposite thesis.' Even though I had never signed up to a totally scientific ideology like dialectical materialism (unlike many other colleagues of my age or a little older, such as François Furet and Emmanuel Le Roy Ladurie), the attitude of these lecturers really annoyed me. I think I had avoided dialectical materialism partly because of my Catholic upbringing, which I wanted to escape from too, and I thought that subscribing to Marxism would be like leaving one church to join another!

My connection with Labrousse began in 1958, when I had to decide on the period, the field of study and the problem that I was going to work on for what today we would call an MA and at that time we called the 'diploma of higher education'. That was when Goubert told me I should work with Labrousse. At that time Labrousse was working on a large-scale study of the Western bourgeoisie, and he had the idea of having young students wade through the vast source material in what Pierre Goubert called *'les archives dormantes'*. His main ambition was to find an economic and social explanation for great uprisings, like the revolutionary phenomena of 1789, 1848 and the Paris Commune of 1871. And so he suggested I should work in the notarial archives of Paris under the more direct supervision of Furet, who taught me to read Tocqueville and Marx. Until then no one had told me to read them! My contact with Labrousse himself was rather distant and I seldom saw him. Another world, very different from today, when students don't hesitate to phone me at midnight to talk about a problem with their hard disk or the mouse on their Macintosh...

As for Braudel, I didn't meet him until later. He was in another world, a long way from the École Normale and the Sorbonne that I frequented. He belonged to Section 6 of the École Pratique des Hautes Études – which was to become the École des Hautes Études en Sciences Sociales only in the seventies. At that time it was a small establishment that held a few seminars, like those given by Labrousse and Braudel himself, but which I never attended. I discovered Braudel mainly through reading the first edition of *La Méditerranée*[3], and later from his contributions to the

3   1949; translated as *The Mediterranean and the Mediterranean World in the Age of Philip II*, 2 vols, London, Collins, 1972–3.

Annales journal – they were important papers because of their wider circulation. I met him in person only much later, in the late sixties or early seventies. His influence on me, then, was purely indirect and intellectual, not personal. I believe I can say, however, that if he had not written what he wrote, I wouldn't have done what I have done.

As a Parisian and an observer-participant in the famous events of May 1968, could you say what impact they had on you at that time? And how important do those events seem in hindsight? Would you say they affected your view of history, particularly the history of the French Revolution?

I must admit that it all took us by surprise. At that time I was already a *'maître de conférences'* or lecturer at the École Normale, and apart from a few militants, Trotskyists, Maoists and other third-world activists, the students were quite a long way from being as politically committed as many of us lecturers. In my case, for instance, I belonged to what is known as the SNES, the National Union of Higher Education, so I took part in their demonstrations and made the demands that the others made without realizing what the long-term consequences of our shouting might be. I also played a rather more specific role when the union asked me to look after the Sorbonne when it was taken over; I was to take charge of the running of this establishment, and look after the maintenance of the building. So in May and June 1968 I was the principal union member responsible for the occupation of the Sorbonne! That really was rather an unpleasant job, and it has only left me unhappy memories, because I soon started to be called 'the Sorbonne Beria'. It was essentially a night job, because during the day the occupation took the form of great discussions and highly conspicuous demonstrations; but at night there were violent demonstrations and I had to stop them degenerating into something more dramatic, both for the individuals themselves and for the buildings, facilities, libraries, etc. As you can imagine, it was a very difficult role to play, saving the Sorbonne . . . and it earned me the Légion d'Honneur!

If you want to know my opinion on the significance of those events, I would say that my attitude towards May 1968 is not like that of people who just talked their way through it all. I remember Michel de Certeau saying, 'On a pris la parole' ('We hold the floor'). I myself never held the floor, but I did try to stop people taking drugs in the Sorbonne basements, prevent female students getting attacked, and so on. So I have a nocturnal, sombre view of these events, which, compared with utopia, has the advantage of getting much closer to what things were really like and in particular seeing the way individuals are transformed when they take themselves too seriously as political leaders or something like that. I was never tempted to take up any political activity, so for me it was an interesting historical experience of how an event like that can use people and help transform them, and not always for the good.

So I would say that my concept of history as such was not deeply marked by that experience. What it did do was teach me to keep a number of things in proportion, like the great events of the French Revolution, for instance. When you can't sleep for two months, as was the case with the Comité de Salut Public (Committee of Public Safety), you end up very much on edge... What these events also showed was how difficult it is for change to come about in the French university system, and especially in historical studies within it. We had believed, at first, that the university would become more democratic, but in reality things just shifted and did not really change. There were a number of rather illusory transformations, which in fact prevented the French university establishment from directly facing up to the main problem, which was that all of society – those on the right as well as the left – wanted to create a truly democratic university. We believed this had been born in 1968, but the old institution is still there, more or less intact, together with its buildings and facilities. The thirtieth anniversary of these events in 1998 seems to have confirmed this, since university students were very little in evidence at the commemorations.

You belong to the generation that still had to write an enormous Doctorat d'État. *What made you choose the French provincial academies of the eighteenth century as the subject for your doctorate? Were you trying to take up the challenge posed by Daniel Mornet on the intellectual origins of the French Revolution?*

I would say it was the result of a combination of chance and intellectual encounters. I think it is almost always by chance that you discover what there is left to be done. Speaking particularly about the element of chance in one's choice, while I was still teaching at the *lycée* in Châlons-sur-Marne Labrousse said to me, 'Roche, the era of monographs is over, and... above all, don't study the countryside!' He meant that the great theses that until then had been regional could not be repeated indefinitely. And from the practical point of view, it was easier to find sources on the cities than on the countryside. I was persuaded to follow his advice, but I had not yet discovered a topic to work on. When I got my university job soon afterwards, however, I had to write my *Doctorat d'État*. At first I intended to write on the Sicilian nobility of the eighteenth and nineteenth centuries, because my wife had translated *The Leopard* into French, which gave me the idea of trying to understand its origins by working on Sicily. For that I needed to find funds to do my research in Italy, but I was unsuccessful. I remember approaching Ruggiero Romano – an Italian who was very important in Latin American studies and Braudel's right-hand man for Italian matters – to talk to him about my project. He received me warmly and listened, and in the end I asked him, 'How could I get to Sicily?' obviously wanting to know how to get a grant or some kind of financial assistance. To which he replied, 'You catch a plane!'

It was then that I decided to turn to a field of study that was situated between the history of the *Ancien Régime* and that of the Revolution. I thought of doing a study on the social and political role of the royal princes in both the *Ancien Régime* and the Revolution, following a few noble families from the court of Louis XIV through to their forced exile. I began working on this in the Chantilly archives and the British Library, but the research problems – which involved a pile of archives – were immense. In Chantilly, for example, the archives were open for only four hours a day and not every day of the week. I remember going to see Marcel Reinhard – a specialist in the history of the French Revolution, to whom Labrousse had referred me – to ask him to support my application to the CNRS [Conseil Nationale de Recherche Scientifique], which would allow me three or four years of research to finish the work. But he replied that it was impossible: I was too young for that, and anyway I should never forget the following rule: 'You should not try to adapt the researcher to the research, but rather make the research fit the researcher.' I still think this is a formula that one should always bear in mind. That was what made me change my topic, as I had found some files at the Academy in Châlons-sur-Marne while I was teaching at the *lycée* there a short time before, and I realized that it was very easy to work in provincial archives. I was encouraged to continue along this path by Furet, who confirmed my suspicion that intellectual sociability was a good topic as there was a lot still to be done in that field. And so I ended up being supervised by Alphonse Dupront, who was not at all demanding in his relations with students. In fourteen years I think I only saw him about three times, which made his supervision very agreeable! He would just ask me, 'Are you working?', and I would say, 'Yes, I'm making progress,' which I really was, as I was travelling all over the country studying the academies in the ninety *départements* of France.

Was it the aim of your thesis to write a history of intellectuals? Wouldn't you say, however, that such a term is anachronistic, and that it is not possible to write a history of intellectuals before the time of Dreyfus?

I agree that this term does not have the connotation of left-wing political involvement that it was to have after 1900, but I believe the aim of my thesis was part of what could be called a sociology of the dissemination of the Enlightenment. More than just a history of Enlightenment intellectuals, it sought to understand what limited the dissemination of those great ideas, as studied by my predecessors, both from the viewpoint of the history of philosophy or ideas in the style of Paul Hazard, and from the viewpoint of the intellectual origins of the French Revolution à la Daniel Mornet.

Would it be fair to describe the method used in your thesis as an example of what Pierre Chaunu has described as 'third-level serial history', in other words, as quantitative history applied to the superstructure, to culture?

What I was attempting was precisely to bring the human sciences and sociology together, on the assumption that statistical models can be transferred. I am of the belief that statistical studies only present obstacles to those who are only looking for obstacles. In my view, what is regrettable is that we don't know how to do more statistics, or that we can't apply statistics to everything. It is from this viewpoint that this type of study should be looked at, and Labrousse was fascinated by its possibilities. Every time I saw him he would ask me, 'Are you going to show us at last that the bourgeoisie made the Enlightenment?' And unfortunately every time I saw him I had to say, 'It wasn't the bourgeoisie that made the Enlightenment, and it certainly wasn't the bourgeoisie that consumed it.' Such a result is not at all irrelevant, because I think it changed the way in which we see the Enlightenment. From what we now know about the provincial academies, we can no longer say that the Enlightenment was what was being done in Paris by great names like Voltaire, Montesquieu or Rousseau. The Enlightenment is something much vaster and more complicated, demanding that we should investigate its most complex relations with the rest of society and its values. So I would say that my thesis may be seen as fitting in between two models: on one side the purely Marxist model of explanation based on social classes, and on the other the purely ideal model, in which the ideas work by themselves and only relate internally to each other.

After studying elite culture, you turned to popular culture with The People of Paris. *What made you change direction? Were you following the new historiographic trends of urban history and the history of popular culture?*

Well, this brings us to 1980, when I had become a university lecturer, which really changes one's working conditions. It was six hours teaching per week, plus the CNRS, the École des Hautes Études, since I did not wish to lose contact with the research in progress there, which demanded a minimum of participation in various seminars. So there was a lot of preparation involved and you still had to get the students to work. Now, a question of immediate policy was how to interest the students at a university (Paris VII) where the student intake was mostly left-wing, on account of the university's origins. There were people there like Le Roy

Ladurie, Denis Richet, Michelle Perrot, Jean Chesneaux, and several others much further to the left than I was. To interest these groups of students, who only believed in having a revolution there and then, it occurred to me that I should make them comprehend the idea of the people, popular culture, the working masses, and things like that. Partly this meant a return for me to Labroussian social history and the history of Paris, because the idea was to make them work in the Paris archives. The central objective was to comprehend this world which was not integrated through ownership of economic or cultural capital. We were trying to understand whether this large part of the population of the largest city in France had benefited to some extent from the economic transformations of the eighteenth century or whether it had got poorer, a victim of these economic transformations. Hence the systematic use of notarial archives to try to grasp the originality of this milieu through consumption of all kinds, both material and intellectual. This did not involve a limited definition of popular culture, a definition *a priori* by social categories, but rather a very open definition leaving room for what I termed appropriation. By the way, I think I was one of the first to talk about appropriation.

As for urban history, this is one of the areas where most progress has been made and where there has been plenty of reflection, especially since the research done by Jean-Claude Perrot and Marcel Roncayolo, with whom I kept in close contact. In fact I have been working with Perrot all the time, ever since the late seventies when I was elected to Pierre Goubert's chair at the Sorbonne. We have done joint seminars for twenty-five years, and I don't know if I have taught him much; I, however, have certainly learned a lot from him, through our discussions. There was also an urban history group at the Maison des Sciences de l'Homme that I am still connected with, though now more as some kind of ancestor.

What is your opinion of Chartier's critique of the history of popular culture and the emphasis it puts on uses and practices instead of texts and other objects?

You may not know this, but Chartier was one of my students at the École Normale and worked with me until the early eighties. He did his *maîtrise* on the Academy in Lyons with me, and it was because of that that he began to study the history of the book. In the matter of popular culture, he was attacking the concept put forward by Robert Mandrou in his study on the *Bibliothèque Bleue*, from which, on the basis of a rather brief analysis, he had extracted an extremely limited definition of popular culture. Chartier's challenge came from that, from the question of whether one should derive such a precise definition on the basis of those representations alone and not a whole range of practices. In connection with this debate, an attentive reader will notice that the Parisians in *The People of Paris* contributed many relevant points.

Your change in topic seems to have been accompanied by a change in method, in that teamwork has become very important in your work. Could you talk about this at greater length?

There is more than one way of conceiving group work in the historiography of the 1960s to 1980s. One is the way that was predominant in institutions like the École des Hautes Études or the CNRS – in which I took part sometimes as a player and sometimes as an adviser – whereby lecturers and researchers working on related topics get together; this can at times result in important publications, like *Livre et Société* under Furet's direction. This was the publication that finally allowed the history of the book to take off and led to a reorientation of the history of reading, the history of literacy, etc. Another kind of group work – and I believe I was a pioneer in this – is the sort where a lecturer mobilizes students to work on joint topics, and arranges visits with them to archives, defines the protocols for document analysis, determines what they are to do, and in the end gathers it all together. The lecturer in this case is acting as an architect, an organizer, or if you like a site manager who organizes and publishes the results. As I see it, in this kind of work everybody gains, both the students and the lecturer, who learns a lot from this type of contact. In most of the books I have published there is a long list of students, showing that I couldn't have written *The People of Paris*, for instance, or *The Culture of Clothing* without their co-operation. I would certainly have taken about fifteen years to write *The People of Paris* if I had not had the collaboration of ten students or so.

In The Culture of Clothing *you show that the study of apparel is not at all superficial. Does this book represent a new direction in your studies or is it a continuation of your work on material culture?*

This book is directly linked to the early results of *The People of Paris*, since from the analysis of popular consumption the phenomenon that stands out as having changed most in the eighteenth century is spending on clothes. When you look at the result of this consumption (because what the documentation reveals is not the consumption *per se*), this is the sector that changed the most, coming to top the list of people's possessions. I should mention here that this question, which was suggested to me by the very documentation we studied, was also inspired by the concerns described by scholars of English consumption, such as Plumb, McKendrick and Brewer. And so it was from this encounter between

English consumerism and French documentation that the idea came to me of reconstructing a global phenomenon, a 'global social fact', as Marcel Mauss would say, and drawing all possible implications from it. It is, therefore, a work on material culture, but a material culture that cannot be read just from a description of the objects. It has to be placed within a broader context and, in particular, related to the way in which contemporary people thought about the phenomena of consumption (especially the consumption of clothing), luxury or fashion. So it is a history of material culture that also has intellectual ambitions; in fact it tries not to separate these two domains. For me this is really necessary. Behind the apparel I believe you really can find mental structures, but ones which are not a direct product of social structures. I would like my work to be understood as an effort to comprehend different attitudes towards apparel, towards appearances, and not as an effort to demonstrate that the popular classes consumed more *robes à la française* than *manteaux*, as was the case with one American historian who did not understand anything that I was trying to say. According to her, what I discovered was no more than a semantic transformation because effectively a *manteau* is the same as a *robe*!

In the same book you put forward quite a bold idea when you juxtaposed 'liberté, égalité and frivolité'. Could you give a brief idea of how eighteenth-century fashion, especially women's fashion, had a liberating and levelling effect?

In studying the culture of appearances, trying to recover the history of clothing and relate it to social and cultural changes, what I was in fact trying to do was to understand how social consumption operated in general and not just women's consumption. If I had wanted to be successful in the United States I would have associated myself clearly with gender history, women's history, but I did not do that. Instead I left it all sort of French, in a republican-universalist way, wide open to criticism for being politically incorrect. But I am ready to admit that women pioneered this kind of consumption in the early eighteenth century and were still in the forefront at the end of the century, pushing forward a whole economic movement and a whole transformation through the acquisition of new habits – a transformation that paved the way for new types of liberty. In the thirty years leading up to the French Revolution there were feminists and a whole feminist press pushing new demands and urging women to read and join the cultured class. While they were showing them new fashions and new objects, at the same time they were also exposing them to new writings and a whole raft of new ideas. Hence, therefore, this connection that I see between equality, fraternity and frivolity.

Considering that what you call the 'clothes revolution' was a revolution made especially by women with the support of the women's press, wouldn't you say, therefore, that the role of women in the Enlightenment and the French Revolution needs to be reconsidered?

Without a doubt, because it would be a way of verifying the hypothesis that material things and intellectual things are inseparable, and that they need to be considered in interaction. It would also be a way of getting to understand even older organizations. One cannot imagine that women in the French Revolution came out of nowhere or that their rise was simply the result of events. There is no doubt that they were the result of this series of changes in material culture and a slow transformation in material relations within the family, as Arlette Farge, for instance, has shown. Studying the role of women in the Enlightenment is something much broader in scope than studying the role of women in the famous *salons*, which is very limited. And even the studies on this small circle of women focus only on those *salonnières* with certain intellectual pretensions, leaving aside the majority of them, whose only pretension in the *salons* was to pass around the tea and chocolate.

Together with Robert Darnton, you edited a book entitled Revolution in Print,[4] *in which you argue that without the press the revolutionaries could have taken the Bastille but not overthrown the* Ancien Régime. *What was more important in undermining the old order: the 'revolution in print' or the 'revolution in clothing'?*

For some things it was certainly the press, but the transformation in the consumption of clothing also had a profound effect on other things. I firmly believe that when we take this transformation into account our horizons open out considerably. The aim of the work I did with Bob Darnton was to think about what made wider access to printed matter possible in French society. Bob has a very precise theory on this: for him it was a specific type of literature – what he calls political pornography – that was at the root of the desacralization of the image of royal power. This literature was the main cause, according to him, of the transformation of society's relations with authority and more specifically the sacred authority of the king. I think that as in all theories of this kind there is an element of truth in it, but for me and for Chartier too the problem is knowing how it was possible for this to come about, how these writings won over the people and were able to transform their feelings, their souls and their ideas. In other words, the main question as I see it is to find out

---

4   R. Darnton and D. Roche (eds), *Revolution in Print: The Press in France, 1775–1800*, Berkeley and Los Angeles, University of California Press, 1989.

whether this literature was effective because it encountered a land ready for change. Darnton's thesis may still be valid, but within the broader framework of a discussion on what made the appropriation of new ideas by the various social categories possible. That is why the transformations in material culture, including the 'revolution in clothing', are important. I see it operating in the same way as what I call 'the facts of Diderot's *robe de chambre*'. As you may remember, Diderot changed his *robe de chambre* and after that nothing around him matched any more. Consequently then he had to change his furniture, his books, his prints and so on because none of it gave him any pleasure any more because it had fallen into disharmony. So everything had to be changed because of his new *robe de chambre*. It is the historian's job, as I see it, to try to understand how sudden changes or the possibilities of change arise, that is, how a whole system will change little by little.

In your observations on the press in general and the periodical press in particular, you try to show that the press does not just record events but can also create them, that is, it can be an important ingredient in the events it is reporting. Could you say something about the difficulties of using the media as a historical source?

In fact it would be more honest to say that I am more a historian of books and the dissemination of books than a historian of the periodical press as such. But I have had students like Caroline Rimbaud doing work on the feminist press which meshed in with my own interests in fashion, clothes and phenomena of material consumption. There was also Gilles Feyel, who has analysed the whole system of the early modern periodical press. But in general the press has interested me because I see it as one of the means of change, of incitement to change. But using the press as a historical source is only apparently simple. You have to be aware of the traps and that it is a very complicated matter to understand how the authorities, editors and the public are constantly adjusting their positions relative to each other. In the case of the French press in the eighteenth century – unlike the English – things are even more complicated because of the censorship that existed.

In 1997 you published a history of everyday things in which you explore the idea that there was a revolution in consumption in the eighteenth century. What motivated you to write such a book?

In part I wanted to distinguish myself from the fashionable trend that fundamentally concerns itself with everyday life in a way that is very *événementielle* and non-analytical, as represented by the collection of historical studies which has adopted the attractive title of *Vie Quotidienne*

– 'Everyday Life'. I considered I needed to reactivate the spirit of the studies by Fernand Braudel and the inspiration of Lucien Febvre and Robert Mandrou (especially in his *Introduction à la France moderne*) in order to understand the interaction between the world of consumption and consumers, and to write a history of consumption that tried to capture more effectively that kind of temporal imbrication that according to Braudel exists between long-term and short-term phenomena and the event. In other words, I wanted to analyse the place of the object and artefacts in Western civilization, breaking with the tradition which since Rousseau and Marx has seen the relationship between societies and things from an alienating viewpoint. The history of everyday things, an aspect of material culture, must take into account the investigations of anthropologists and their analyses of the appropriation of objects in traditional societies. At the same time, the cognitive aspect of the consumption process must not be ignored. Supply and demand subsume processes of information provision, access to choices, resistances, etc. In short, the history of everyday things is the history of confrontation, which becomes illuminating, because in the eighteenth century the multiplication of things called everything into question, the whole of society, the whole of culture.

Ultimately, via the history of consumption, I also had a more theoretical concern: to try to understand what makes change possible in the material realm. The works of Brewer, Plumb and McKendrick on English consumption, which obviously inspired me, showed that the English had started consuming earlier because their colonial trade was far more intense than that of France. Here in France our development was more inward-looking, more complicated. The physiocrats, for instance, are French and not English. There are physiocratic readers but no physiocratic theorists in England.

Do you agree, then, with the idea first put forward in the early nineteenth century that in order to understand Enlightenment France it is first necessary to study English thought and culture? And to broaden the question, is it possible in your view to understand the history of France or of any other country without comparing it with others?

I fully agree that it is impossible to understand what happens in France and in England too without looking at what is happening next door. The difficulty is that we have nationalist histories because of the way we have been educated and also because it is easier to work in the archives of one's own country. That is why comparative history started in the field of the history of ideas. It is much easier to compare texts, without moving from where you are; you can have access to the whole production of the Scottish economists right here in Paris, for instance, without having to spend long periods abroad. In the case of France, there is a tradition of comparative history that gives great weight to French Anglomania as one of the factors of change, but I think things are much more complicated than that explanation would suggest. In my view, we have to study the real exchanges that occurred in the field of social relations, and not just the exchanges in the intellectual field. We still have a lot to learn about sociability, about the people English visitors met when they came to France, for example. There is still a lot to do in this area.

And what do you think of comparison at a distance, à la Marc Bloch? Can one compare France, for instance, with Japan, just as one compares France with England or Germany?

This scares me a little. I am not saying that comparisons with China or Japan are not instructive and interesting, but they run the risk of being artificial. The question that arises is: can we compare everything with everything else? In the case of the history of the nobility, which Marc Bloch proposed to work on comparatively, there was, so to speak, a single model that could be applied to both the Japanese nobility and the feudal German nobility of the thirteenth and fourteenth centuries. But I admit that for a number of other things I'm afraid it would be easy to fall into artificial comparisons. What I am trying to say is that although I think it is essential, comparative history presents procedural difficulties that to me seem difficult to resolve wisely.

But remembering what Jack Goody argued in his book The East in the West, *how can one understand the specificity of Europe without looking outside Europe?*

By not believing that we have the only rational model of civilization. Goody is primarily an anthropologist, and as such he can examine a behavioural model over the long-term, whereas the historian who specializes in a period will not be able to do exactly the same thing. It is extremely important to develop comparative studies in Europe, but when I see the way the European Science Foundation organizes its programmes – sponsoring meetings and publications and not research – I realize we are not making much progress in this direction. In my understanding, spending a lot of money on getting people to meet and discuss studies they have already done is not a good or productive formula. It would be better to spend less but have small groups doing the same kind of research in two or three places that could be compared. Otherwise we will carry on having these constantly artificial comparisons. We may learn something about readers in Göttingen in 1750 and something about French readers in the same year, but we won't have made the studies in the same way.

You refer to a variety of theorists like Freud, Elias, Barthes, etc. How do you select and combine them?

I am not a Freudian, even though I know that you can't work on clothing without reading a little psychoanalysis, which, however, is not at all easy. It makes me want to cry when I come across the absurd things people do in this field, talking about the 'fetishism of clothes' and things like that. The real problem is that of the historical utility of Freud's fundamental concepts, such as 'unconscious', 'complex' and 'neurosis'. But Elias, I think, is fundamental, and ever since 1974 (when his book on the civilizing process was translated into French) I have been recommending that my students should read him, although you have to be very well aware of the context of his reflections. For example, he was almost completely indifferent to economics in his study of courtly society. It is not a matter of criticizing him over this, but rather of being aware that he was trying to explain everything through the political need for creating hierarchies without seeing the political and economic implications. As for using theories, I am not one of those who are always saying things like 'I found my methodology in Elias', or 'I am going to use the concept of distinction to explain how shoemaking operates in the Marais district', etc. All that kind of thing is rather irritating, in my opinion. It is not through citing Bourdieu, de Certeau or Ricoeur that all historical problems will be solved. Furthermore, why cite just these and not others, like Simmel,[5] for example, who is just as important as Weber? Simply because, despite his importance, nobody knew about him before he was translated into French, belatedly and incompletely.

When we do not cling to a single model and we set about verifying explanatory hypotheses, comparing them with the documentation, reality, readings, and so on, we can be classed as theoretical eclectics. Now as I see it, a historian ought to be an eclectic, which is much better than continuing to say, as used to happen, that the economy dictates everything, or things like that. It is not something to be regretted if you don't have a global explanation.

What would you say about the impact Foucault has had on historians? Does he have any special relevance for your work?

I actually worked with Foucault for a couple of weeks in the Arsenal archives, when I was doing some research for Furet on everything relating to censorship. And Foucault was on the same project looking for every-

5   Georg Simmel (1858–1918), a German sociologist of the same generation as Max Weber, author of *Philosophie des Geldes* (1900; translated as *The Philosophy of Money*, London, Routledge, 1978).

thing about the authors and I don't know what else. I remember we used to go for a smoke together during the breaks and he would talk to me a little about his mother and his father, and one day he simply disappeared. I never saw him again. In those days, 1960, he wasn't the great Foucault, the theorist, the philosopher of *Les Mots et les Choses* [1966], which was published later, like his more historical work, *Surveiller et Punir* [1975].[6] Among French historians there has always been a certain distrust of phil-osophers who turn historian, which is rather a bad thing, of course. It would have been better to join in and have a dialogue with Foucault instead of simply saying that he had not studied the documents. Some historians, like Michelle Perrot and Arlette Farge, for instance, did join in and developed close ties with him. This did not happen in my case; I am not sure why. Perhaps because of my daily life, everyday things... And then there was that business of becoming a star, partly promoted by the media, which meant that he became rather inaccessible to anyone who had not known him very well beforehand. The French system has this rather irritating thing which means that our stars are exported to the United States. American film stars come to France, while our intellectual stars go to the US where they are idolized! This is a phenomenon worth studying: why people like Barthes, Foucault, Michel Serres and René Girard have turned into some sort of gurus in the United States.[7] And there are more concrete issues to think about, such as: what does 'une pratique descriptive' [descriptive practice] mean? I have read *Les Mots et les Choses* several times and I always wonder what this actually means. What happens, then, when ex-pressions like this are translated into English or Portuguese? This intellec-tual idolatry can perhaps be explained by the need people have to identify with very strong figures who are highly visible in the public arena.

Let us talk about your move from the basement to the attic, that is, from social to cultural history. What would your mentor Labrousse have to say about this?

I think that although I write cultural history I am still a social historian. I tell Chartier that I do socio-cultural history, while he tells me he does cultural-social history. In fact, the point is that we have given up explain-ing one level through the other. I think historians can be distinguished from one another like this: on the one hand there are those who give greater weight to the study of representations and how they are con-structed from texts and the practices by which texts are disseminated;

6 M. Foucault, *The Order of Things*, London, Routledge, 1970; *Discipline and Punish*, Harmondsworth, Penguin, 1979.
7 Michel Serres (b. 1930), French philosopher of science, author of *The North-West Passage* (Paris, Gallimard, 1980); René Girard (b. 1923), French thinker best known for his book *Violence and the Sacred* (Baltimore, Johns Hopkins University Press, 1974).

and on the other there are those who study how groups develop certain types of practice, customs, readings, dress habits, etc. The procedure, the path followed in these two cases is clearly not the same, but the method is still pretty much equivalent, because in both cases it is a dialogue between practices and representations.

What is the status of historical studies in France today? Would you say that the history of mentalities is still going strong?

First of all, who has done the history of mentalities? I only know of two people who have actually said that they did the history of mentalities: Philippe Ariès and Michel Vovelle. They were the ones who developed a very distinct theory about this kind of history. If for instance you read the entry by Georges Duby on this in the Pléiade encyclopaedia, you will see that Duby was a historian of the imaginary, more specifically the political imaginary – he wrote the history of collective representations in the Middle Ages – and not a historian of mentalities. Ariès, with great talent, did the history of mentalities in the long, very long-term, such as the history of death, for instance. And Michel Vovelle, in an extremely imaginative way, does the history of mentalities in the shorter term – very important, for sure, but it leaves a number of questions unanswered on how society functions. That is why I prefer to say that I do the social history of culture. That said, I think these types of history that have marked French production are now taking a serious beating, because the conditions under which history is produced in France are changing drastically. Not only has the *Doctorat d'État* been abolished, but library work is also becoming increasingly more difficult. Just look at the new Bibliothèque Nationale – it is a real national disaster. What we see happening is terrible, really alarming! Even more alarming is the cost of the operation: for the library to operate it needs an astronomical budget. We've been set back over sixty years with this madness. It is going to take a long time and vast sums of money to get everything working with some semblance of normality. In about 2050, perhaps, everything will be just right!

Is it time for a new political history to appear, or do you think that type of history is unnecessary?

I think in France there is always a bit of play-acting when people analyse historiography, as they say, for instance, that the *Annales* 'school' did not do political history. But in fact one of Braudel's concerns in the early *Annales* groups was to have people doing just that, political history. Marc Bloch not only wrote political history, he also gave courses in political history. Right now, in both the École des Hautes Études and the universities there are people trying to write another political history, following the American model of studying institutions through histories of rituals or festivals. Although I have never written political history, I myself have supervised very good work in this field. So I can safely say that political history has never disappeared in France. Most of it, true, was written according to very traditional criteria, dealing with the history of institutions, ideas and political figures. And what's more, I would also say that political history in the traditional sense has never disappeared from the curriculum in France, which I think is even a necessary thing. How, for instance, can you train students in eighteenth-century European history without starting with political institutions like the French monarchy, the English parliamentary monarchy, the empire, etc.? I agree, though, that only a few valuable contributions have been made in this area. They include the work of Christian Jouhaud and Robert Descimon on the early modern period, or H. Burstin on the Revolution. It would be important if something more was done. I am sure it will happen eventually, but I won't be the one writing it. I have already reached the end of the day, so to speak . . . and anyway, we can't be trained for everything!

How would you compare your work with that of Roger Chartier and Robert Darnton, historians of culture who deal with similar topics to yours?

We have many problems in common: the histories of printed matter, the public arena, the republic of letters, etc. But we can be distinguished by the way we deal with them. We do not always make the same choices and we also differ in our specialities. For example, my book *France in the Enlightenment* – which in France was a flop but was so well received in the United States that it would have turned my head, if it weren't so wooden! – was a different attempt, a global attempt, I would say, to answer common questions. Chartier is turning more and more just to texts. Now, for instance, he is working on Shakespeare, and doing an admirable job of it. He chose to avoid working in archives and to devote his research to the history of representations based on the ways books and reading are used. And in that work he is what we discussed earlier, an eclectic, since he does not have a mentor or a theory to guide him. There are, of course, theorists who become more important for his explanatory system as his work develops. At the moment, for instance, he is using Foucault to understand the evolution of the figure of the intellectual from the eighteenth century to the present.

As for Bob, I don't know what he is working on now, but he has a very strong interest in the social sciences, especially anthropology; in fact, he is the product of a certain relationship of history with anthropology, especially the anthropology of Clifford Geertz. Personally I am convinced of the importance of this relationship, but I cannot see very well how to put it into practice as a historian. We cannot do in history exactly what Geertz does as an ethnologist, because he can effectively go into the field and see how things are organized. I know Geertz inspires many micro-historians, and this thread can also be seen in Bob's work.

In your view, are the most innovative works in history the result of research-ers approaching the archives forearmed with imaginative questions, or is it the archives that suggest the questions?

First of all, I would like to say that I don't think one should necessarily distinguish people who work in archives from those who work with other kinds of documentation. It is a matter of taste: some like it, some don't. There are also those who are literally allergic, who can't stop sneezing. And the dust there can be in an archive of eighteenth-century parliamentary papers from Paris is unbelievable! Things that haven't been touched for over 200 years! But one must not forget that books or pictures, for instance, are another form of archive. And things like monuments, buildings, land-scapes or anything else can in fact be meaningful sources. But the question you have asked is whether the field upon which the historian is working raises the questions and elucidates itself more or less unaided, or whether in contrast it is basically up to the historian to suggest hypotheses, to present problems to the sources and to solve them. I see the question as follows: using one's imagination is very important when working with archives, because one needs to have a good nose to deal with documents. Just like gastronomy, history is a field where intuition is needed. The problem, then, is how to develop this intuition. The only way is by using the archives! The question is more or less as Ginzburg described in his fine article on clues. As in a jigsaw puzzle or a game of patience, intuition, a good nose and traces are all used to try to piece together other traces, and so on.

What advice would you give to young historians starting out on their careers?

Read a lot, and I mean a lot, on everything. Literature, philosophy, scientific literature if possible, everything you can imagine. Take note of everything that is happening in today's society so you can assess the importance of studying past societies in quite a comprehensive manner. And lastly, be modest!

What kind of contribution can the historian make in today's world?

I don't think we have any lesson to teach and I don't believe this is the role of the historian. It is very unusual for a historian to play a part in the political and spiritual organization of society. Our role, whatever the type of history we do, may just be to provide examples of critical reflection. I mean, it is the historian's job, as I see it, to show that things are always much more complicated than people think. Nationalism, for instance, is undeniably one of the most odious things that exist. So for anyone who wants to read it there has been plenty of good material written on this phenomenon since 1871.

You have just been elected to the prestigious Collège de France. Could you say something about the importance of this institution for French culture in general, and for French intellectuals in particular?

There is a kind of mythology about the Collège de France, because there have certainly been notable figures there with whom few people are able to identify. When I was in Germany a short time ago, somebody said to me, 'So you are Michelet's successor!' This remark made me blush. The Collège really has attracted some major intellectuals of the nineteenth and twentieth centuries, such as Michelet, Renan and a number of great scientists. When it recruits a Nobel prize-winner in nuclear physics, as happened two years ago, the institution obviously gains a lot of publicity. But there have also been many less well-known individuals on its staff, people whom no one today would remember if they were mentioned. So it is quite a complicated institution which has the great advantage of giving the members it elects plenty of freedom and good working conditions, as well as maintaining and developing certain disciplines that do not receive much support in the universities. This is the case, for example, of palaeography, Assyriology, Mesopotamian archaeology, etc.

As regards recruitment, in the sciences the criterion is quite clear and precise, as they choose people who are recognized authorities in the international scientific community. But in the field of human sciences it gets more complicated because, after all, what is a discovery in history? What is the equivalent of a discovery in the field of human sciences? There are, without any doubt, highly inspirational figures who have contributed significantly to philosophical thinking, such as Foucault, for instance, or others like Duby and Le Roy Ladurie who have played a significant role on the intellectual scene. But not all those recruited have the same stature. I myself, at least, have no pretension to be identified with these big names! I see my election to the Collège de France as recognition for my role in developing the group work I have done over the years in conjunction with my university students.

Could you tell us a little about your next book?

The book – another team effort – ... is one entitled *La Ville promise* [published in 2000], which studies the phenomenon of the attraction of

Paris life according to various parameters: how it worked, how it was managed by the police, the population, etc. In it I basically adopt the perspective of Felicity Heal, an English historian who has written a very nice book on hospitality, dealing with the subject in an English context. I take up the issue at the point where she left off, which is with the appearance of what might be called the hospitality economy, the hostel economy, which in Paris began in the seventeenth century. I am also writing another book which will deal with equestrian culture in the modern age. I think as I get older I am getting more solitary, as this book is much less of a team effort than the others.

Paris, May 1999

SELECT BIBLIOGRAPHY

Le Siècle des lumières en province: Académies et académiciens provinciaux, 1689–1789 (Paris and The Hague: Mouton, 1978).

The People of Paris: An Essay in Popular Culture in the Eighteenth Century (1981; English translation, Leamington Spa, Berg, 1987).

My Life by Jacques-Louis Ménétra; with an introduction and commentary by Daniel Roche (1982; English translation, New York, Columbia University Press, 1986); also translated into Italian.

'A chacun sa Révolution. Réflexions à propos du bicentenaire de la Révolution Française', *Études*, 369, 3 (1988), 197–210.

Les Républicains de lettres: Gens de culture et lumières au 18e siècle (Paris, Fayard, 1988).

The Culture of Clothing: Dress and Fashion in the 'Ancien Régime' (1989; English translation, Cambridge, Cambridge University Press, 1994); also translated into Italian.

France in the Enlightenment (1993; English translation, Cambridge, Mass. and London, Harvard University Press, 1998); also translated into Italian.

'Le Précepteur dans la noblesse française, instituteur privilégié ou domestique?', in R. Gruenter and B. Wolff Metternich, eds, *Studien zum achtzehnten Jahrhundert* (Hamburg, Felix Meiner Verlag, 1995), pp. 225–44.

A History of Everyday Things: The Birth of Consumption in France, 1600–1800 (1997; English translation, Cambridge, Cambridge University Press, 2000).

with E. Ferrone *Le Monde des Lumières* (Paris, Fayard, 1999).

ed., *La Ville promise* (Paris, Fayard, 2000).

6

Peter Burke

Peter Burke is known as a historian with wide-ranging interests, who has used many approaches to write on an immense variety of subjects: the Italian Renaissance, popular culture in early modern Europe, the urban elite in Venice and Amsterdam, the fabrication of the image of Louis XIV; the social histories of language, of dreams and of Carnival; questions of historiography, the relationship between history and social theories, etc. Despite the various kinds of history that he writes, however, he prefers to describe himself as a cultural historian. Unlike specialists, he says, the cultural historian strives to 'make connections between the various domains of a given culture, relating politics with art, science, popular culture, etc.' According to an article published in 2000 in *History Today*, this is precisely the 'clue' needed to understand Peter Burke's work: 'his indefatigable delight in seeking links . . . His passion is to build bridges – between languages, cultures, periods, places, methodologies, disciplines – and then stride across them, open-mindedly, to see what lies beyond.'

Born in London in 1937, Peter experienced cultural diversity at a very early age. With an Irish Catholic father and a Jewish mother of Polish and Lithuanian descent, his family brought together very different cultural traditions. He lived all his childhood and youth in a flat in the house of his maternal grandparents; every time he visited their quarters, he remembers, it was like crossing a cultural frontier. He was educated at a Jesuit school in north London – which prides itself on having had Alfred Hitchcock as a pupil – which Peter left at the age of seventeen to enter Oxford University, having won a keenly contested scholarship to St John's College. But before continuing his studies he had to do two years of compulsory military service, just before it was abolished in Britain. He was greatly disappointed, he recalls, when he received the news that he was not going to be accepted for the Russian course or be stationed in Germany, as he had requested (where the chance to learn German was attractive), but instead on the other side of the world, in Singapore, one of the last bastions of the rapidly crumbling British Empire. He soon discovered, however, that this was an unparalleled experience for the subject he was shortly to read at Oxford.

After his undergraduate course, during which he had the young Keith Thomas as a tutor, Peter embarked on a doctorate under the 'very loose' supervision of Hugh Trevor-Roper, who had recently been appointed Regius Professor of History at Oxford. His extremely ambitious initial topic was European historiographic trends over a 200-year period (1500–1700); as he admits, 'Only Trevor-Roper would have let me get away with this!' But before he completed this vast and (as he was to recognize later) 'probably impossible' thesis, an invitation that he could not refuse from the University of Sussex – recently created in the progressive wave of the 1960s – led him to abandon his formal studies and swell the ranks of the select number of British historians who have never done a Ph.D., such as Quentin Skinner, Keith Thomas, Christopher Hill, Eric Hobsbawm and a few others.

At Sussex, a university set up with the explicit purpose of 'redrawing the map of learning', Peter Burke was to find the environment he needed to break new ground in his teaching and research. His prolific production soon began, his first two books dealing with the Italian Renaissance, the period of history to which he was initially most attracted. Although the subject of these first works was what was conventionally considered elite culture, he was to shift the emphasis in *Popular Culture in Early Modern Europe* (1978). This was the work that established Peter Burke's international reputation, and was described by Christopher Hill as compulsory reading which 'frees us from our traditional national or West European short-sightedness'. His recent efforts to 'decentralize' the Renaissance and to approach it from both central and peripheral viewpoints – as he proposes in *The European Renaissance: Centres and Peripheries* – suggest that Hill's appraisal remains a valid description of other works by Peter Burke.

A few years ago, in a review of *The Fabrication of Louis XIV* published in the *Guardian*, Keith Thomas referred with his characteristic wit to the time when he tutored Peter Burke at Oxford in the late 1950s. Having only just begun his academic career, he was literally 'terrified' of this young student who created the major problem for him of how to fill the time during the tutorial. Normally the hour would be calmly taken up with the reading of the essay written by the student on a previously set topic and the tutor's critical comments on it. In Peter's case, however, Thomas recalls that his 'essays were written with limpid clarity and

Tacitean brevity. They said all there was to be said on the subject, but seldom lasted more than a few minutes. The tutor's problem was how to spin out the rest of the hour.'

In certain respects, Thomas's description of the young student is still echoed today in appraisals of the mature Peter Burke's style of writing. Whether it is seen as subtle, succinct and measured (by his admirers) or laconic and cool (by his critics), his work has attracted the attention and interest of a broad range of readers, as attested by the surprising number of languages (twenty-eight to date) into which his work has been translated – from Serbo-Croat and Belorussian to Chinese, Korean, Albanian and Kazakh. Alongside the sociologist Anthony Giddens, Peter Burke is recognized as one of the most translated English intellectuals of today.

I conducted the interview with Peter in a similar manner to the others – arranging certain days and times and making a recording face to face – so as to minimize, as much as possible, the effects of our natural proximity. On the other hand, I took advantage of our greater intimacy (which enabled me to 'demand' less concise answers) to allow the conversation to touch on notions expressed by some of the other interviewees, getting Peter to act as a kind of commentator, a role the others might have found sometimes awkward. Thus, in addition to talking about his intellectual trajectory, his interests, his books, his projects and his view of history, Peter reflected on Keith Thomas's reflections on history and myth, on Ginzburg's rather negative view of Foucault, and so on.

MARIA LÚCIA PALLARES-BURKE *Toynbee justified his effort of writing an autobiography by the fact that 'often when reading historians like Thucydides I have missed not having a record of their lives and training. Such a record would certainly have illuminated their works for me.' Do you agree with him and, if so, which aspects of your own life and training might illuminate your work?*

PETER BURKE Very much so. As E. H. Carr once wrote, in *What is History?* (1961), in a vigorous formulation which influenced me when I began teaching, 'Before you study history, study the historian.' If you know nothing of the purposes they had in writing and the point of view from which they looked at the past, it is easy to misunderstand the work of Thucydides, say, or Ranke, to fail to see both their weaknesses and their strengths.

Maybe I could begin with what hasn't happened to me. I have not lived through major crises such as wars or revolutions (I was too small a child during the Second World War to understand what was happening). I have spent almost a lifetime in educational institutions (1941–55 and 1957– now). I am not apolitical – I have been somewhere on the left ever since I was eighteen or so – but I have never been deeply involved in politics.

I vote but I never thought seriously about joining a political party. I feel that I have been extremely lucky to escape the conflict and suffering that so many people have undergone in my lifetime, but also that for a historian such luck may also be a limitation. If I had been born in Poland (say) rather than England, I imagine that I would have developed more of a nose for politics. If I had survived, that is.

On the positive side, from the age of eighteen onwards I have had many opportunities to leave my island and observe and participate in the life of other cultures, and this has probably made me less 'insular' or provincial in attitude than might otherwise have been the case. When I was at school, aged ten or eleven, I already wanted to be a historian but I also wrote poems and painted (mainly still life) and sketched (mainly buildings). But my critical powers were better developed than my creative powers, and so I stopped. Writing cultural history is in some sense a compensation for not being an artist or a poet.

Would you say that your interest in cultural encounters – or failures to meet – owes a lot to the fact that you come from a family of immigrants, and that you lived eighteen months among the Muslim Malays in Singapore?

I suppose I am not the right person to ask about this. There are some aspects of an individual's life which may be more visible to outsiders. But looking back, I am convinced that the two experiences you mention were crucial for me. In the first place, my family. I am only second-generation English. My father, although he was born in England, always spoke of 'the English' as if he did not belong to the group. I didn't and don't feel really Irish, since I have spent very few days in Ireland. I didn't feel Jewish, since I was brought up as a Catholic. I have ended up feeling something of an Englishman and rather more of a European.

As for the army, which I joined after leaving school (two years' military service was compulsory in Britain in those days), it educated me in all sorts of ways. First there were the three months of 'basic training' in England – marching, shooting, and learning how to be a clerk. But the real education was meeting working-class boys of my age (my grammar school was mainly middle-class). Then I was sent to Singapore. I had only spent a few weeks outside England (in Ireland, Belgium and France) until then, and always accompanied by my parents, and at the age of eighteen I was suddenly sent to the other end of the world to live there for a year and a half. This too was an educational experience. The regiment to which I was sent, as the pay clerk, was what would now be called 'multicultural'. The majority of the soldiers were Malays, but there were also some Chinese, some Indians and a few British. So there were four cookhouses serving different kinds of food: I was tempted by the Malay food and in theory I could have transferred to the Malay dining-room, but that would have meant eating with my hands (more exactly with my right hand, since the left hand is considered unclean), and that skill would not have been easy for me to learn! Another thing. I was an innocent schoolboy and I suddenly found myself in an environment in which British soldiers were expected to visit Chinese prostitutes (I didn't, but this was for lack of courage, not out of moral scruples), and in which the Indians and Chinese in particular were operating all sorts of rackets, selling equipment and so on. The officers didn't know about this. I could see it all but I kept my mouth shut. When I began to read books on anthropology, around 1962 (about five years later), I realized that I had been doing fieldwork without knowing it. I had been a spectator, and had kept a journal (now in the Imperial War Museum as a record of a 'National Serviceman's' experience of the end of the British Empire and the Malayan 'Emergency'). It was easy to be a spectator, not only because there were so many unfamiliar sights (like people doing the laundry by beating the wet shirts on a stone) but also because I didn't quite fit into any group. I hadn't chosen to go to Singapore, I was an ordinary soldier but white and relatively well-educated, and so I perceived myself and was perceived by others as on the margin of all the main groups.

Only recently did I begin to think that I had started this career of spectator and amateur anthropologist long before. From 1940 to 1955 I lived (with my mother and from 1945 my father as well), in my grandparents' house. The ground floor was divided into two parts, two apartments. On one side of the hall, my grandfather and grandmother ate Jewish food and spoke English mixed with Yiddish words. On the other side, we ate English food and spoke English like the English. When I visited my grandparents (most mornings of weekends and holidays), crossing the hall was like crossing a cultural frontier. I didn't think this at the time of course, but it meant that some awareness of cultural difference started early.

Talking about frontiers, your tutor in Oxford, Keith Thomas, was one of the pioneers in crossing the frontier between history and anthropology. Was his teaching decisive for the development of your own interest in anthropology?

As you know, Keith is very cautious and even secretive (like a typical Welshman, one might say). I didn't know he was interested in anthropology until I was a postgraduate student in 1961. He was a very young tutor when I went to St John's, and rather earnest, without much trace of the irony for which he is now well known. I remember that when he asked us to write essays on political history – which happened quite often, as the syllabus required – he expected us to look at politics from a social angle. He didn't say this in advance, but it was clear from his comments afterwards. Looking back, I have the impression that he had been echoing his own tutor, Christopher Hill. I expect that when I began teaching I did the same. Oral traditions remain important in universities!

Could you explain in which way the study of anthropology was beneficial to you? Do you think that one cannot become a good historian without studying this discipline?

I read a good deal of anthropology from the early sixties onwards, including many accounts of fieldwork in different parts of the world, Africa, India, the Mediterranean, etc. I enjoyed reading these descriptions partly for their own sake, like reading travel books, and partly because they demonstrated so clearly the variety of human ways of life and customs and attitudes or mentalities. I was also interested in the concepts the anthropologists used and the theories they tested, for example the structural-functional analysis which was still dominant in Britain and the USA when I began reading, or the structuralism of Claude Lévi-Strauss, which was still relatively new.

Some books were of course more inspiring than others. Like Keith Thomas, I was and remain a great admirer of Evans-Pritchard, especially his description of attitudes to time and space among the Nuer and his account of the belief system of the Azande (an account which consciously or unconsciously follows the model of Marc Bloch's great book on the royal touch, especially the central idea of a belief system being impervious to contradiction). Like Natalie Davis, I was inspired by Mary Douglas, above all her book *Purity and Danger*. In the academic year 1997–8 I organized a series of seminars on the history of purity, in which my share was the idea of purity in language. I have also been inspired by Jack Goody's work from the sixties onwards, for example by what he said about 'structural amnesia' in oral cultures, in other words, the way in which the past is remembered in a way which suits the needs of the present.

Like Bob Darnton – and many other historians – I have been impressed by Clifford Geertz, especially by the famous essay on the cockfight in Bali. Actually there's an interesting question of reception here. Geertz's interpretative anthropology is much closer to normal history than either structuralism or structural-functionalism, so there was a kind of circular tour involved in turning to him. I could easily add to this list. Malinowski, for example, especially his economic anthropology, his idea that some forms of trade take place for social rather than economic reasons, to reinforce social relationships. Or Marshall Sahlins, especially his reflections on the relation between events, social change, and what he calls the cultural order. Or Pierre Bourdieu, whether one calls him an anthropologist or a sociologist – his relatively detached analysis of his own society may be the result of his having done fieldwork in Algeria before writing about France.

So when, to come back to the last part of your question, I am talking to my students, I don't begin with a particular name. I try to suggest an anthropological study which deals with a theme close to the one on which they are working historically, to allow comparisons and contrasts. In any case, despite my admiration for Evans-Pritchard and the others, I think that it is what might be called 'everyday anthropology' which is most useful for historians – including the controversies of course, for there is no more consensus within the tribe of anthropologists than in the particular cultures they study.

Your tutor, Keith Thomas, confessed that he chose to read history in Oxford because a tutor had advised him to, and that he became a historian of the early modern period because that was what his mentor Christopher Hill was. What do you think made you turn to Renaissance history?

Remember that as a schoolboy I had tried to paint and that I loved the paintings on show at the National Gallery and other museums in London and also – like Quentin Skinner – visiting country houses. I found painting a more interesting activity to study than politics. So I thought briefly about becoming an art historian, but I believed, rightly or wrongly, that art historians were concerned simply with technique, brush-work, etc., which for me was interesting but too narrow. So I looked for an opportunity to study art inside a history course. Now at Oxford, when I was a student (just as had been the case in 1900, and as is still the case today, the university being a rather conservative place), there was a 'special subject' called 'The Italian Renaissance', with 'set books' which included Vasari's *Lives of the Artists* as well as Machiavelli's *Prince*. I decided that this was the subject for me. So I started to learn Italian (more precisely, to teach myself, buying two copies of *The Prince*, one in each language and reading the text a sentence at a time, first in English and then in Italian), and in 1958 I went to Italy for the first time (the college paid my expenses) and I loved the country and the people and the squares and streets and cafés at first sight. Maybe I was ready for this experience because at the age of seven, when my father was in Italy in the Intelligence Corps during the war, there was a map of Italy on the wall next to my bed so that I knew where he was (in Bari, Caserta, Cagliari and so on). The first foreigner I ever met, at the age of seven, was an Italian colonel whom my father brought back to England for interrogation. I remember sitting next to him on the bus, showing him my picture-book and finding him *simpatico*. Odd to think that my father never saw Italy again after 1945, while I have been going almost every year since 1958. Anyway, the Renaissance and my personal discovery of Italy are closely linked for me. A sip of strega (a favourite drink then, but too sweet for me now) might revive all sorts of memories like Proust's madeleine! As it happens, Italy isn't a bad place to begin to study cultural history.

In your most recent book on the Renaissance you speak of 'decentring' the Renaissance. What exactly do you mean by that?

The Renaissance is traditionally viewed as part of a Grand Narrative of the development of Western civilization from the ancient Greeks and Romans, through Christianity, the Renaissance, the Reformation, the Scientific Revolution, the Enlightenment and so on, in other words as the rise of modernity. The story is often told in such a way as to assume the superiority of the West over the rest of the world. Like some other historians I wanted to liberate the story of one cultural movement, the movement to revive classical art and learning, from the twin assumptions of the superiority of modernity and the West.

I don't assume the superiority of Renaissance art to medieval art: they are simply different. I don't think it useful to regard Renaissance culture as 'modern' if we mean by 'modern' similar to us. It was 'post-medieval' if you like, defined by contrast to the 'Middle Ages', a concept invented by the scholars of the Renaissance so that they could define themselves against it.

As for the West, the Western European revival of classical antiquity did not take place in a vacuum. It depended on other classical revivals, in Byzantium and Islam. And classical revivals belong to a larger group of cultural revivals in other parts of the world such as China. I also give a place in my account of the Renaissance to women and to ordinary people. This is not for reasons of political correctness, but because the participation of these groups in the movement, long ignored or given little emphasis, has been demonstrated by recent research. Women and ordinary people participated in the Renaissance more as consumers than as producers – but of course the distinction between production and consumption looks less sharp than it did before the rise of interest in creative reception.

In any case, in my view, historians are essentially translators, trying to make one period intelligible to another. In this book I was trying to make the Renaissance intelligible to readers in different parts of the globe in the early twenty-first century. I tried to keep this potential world audience in mind while writing.

Your book Popular Culture in Early Modern Europe *covered an immense geographic space over three centuries. What led you to such an ambitious enterprise?*

My first idea was to write something much more limited. I had written a book about elite culture in Renaissance Italy, and in the course of writing the book I kept asking myself what the culture of everyone else was like, the culture of the majority. When I began research I soon realized that 'Italy' was not the right unit of enquiry. It was either too wide or too narrow. People were conscious of belonging to a regional culture, to Tuscany or Lombardy, rather than to Italy. On the other hand, if one investigated practices or values or the heroes who embodied those values, it turned out that they could be found – with local variations of course – all over Europe. The choice was therefore between a regional and a continental study. Remember that one of my imaginary interlocutors is Braudel. Thinking of him I chose the 'global' option. When I had just finished I met Braudel, in 1977 I think, and told him that I had written about Europe from Gutenberg to the French Revolution, and he seemed to like the idea.

One of the fetishisms that the so-called 'new history' took on the task of counteracting was the 'fetishism of facts'. Would you say that this battle has already been won and that the 'fetishism of interpretation' is what now has to be counteracted in history?

In my view, in historiography as in history we see what is sometimes called the 'contemporaneity of the non-contemporary'. Take the eighteen-year-olds entering Cambridge to study history: some of them sound like Geoffrey Elton, 'just give us the facts', while others sound postmodern. The difference probably depends on the age of their teachers at school. After all, a teaching career lasts more than forty years and however the teachers may try to keep themselves up-to-date in precise ways, they probably don't revise fundamental assumptions about 'fact' and 'theory'. So the battle you describe may not be won completely. Especially in England. The Americans (North and South alike) seem to be more volatile, more ready to follow the latest intellectual fashion. The English, on the other hand, show much more resistance to change. I remember a conversation with Carlo Ginzburg about the new history, in which he was saying how he needed to argue against it because his Californian students accepted it uncritically, while I said that I had to support it because my students had not yet come to take the movement seriously!

But enough has happened to suggest that – as is usually the case in intellectual conflicts – a weakness is usually over-corrected, in other words replaced by the opposite weakness. First the pendulum swings one way, then the other. First the claim that written history is simply a matter of discovering the facts, and then the counter-claim that written history is simply a matter of construction.

Would you agree that postmodernism (at least in its most extreme form) is very much responsible for the scepticism about the possibility of attaining the truth? Could you say something about what you consider to be the positive and negative sides of postmodernism?

That's a difficult one! Let me begin by distinguishing postmodernism from postmodernity. By 'postmodernism' I mean a relatively self-conscious intellectual movement or cluster of movements led by architects and writers and of course by philosophers such as Foucault or Derrida, in both of whom the scepticism you mentioned is present in a Nietzschean – or neo-Nietzschean or perhaps a post-Nietzschean form. By 'postmodernity' I mean something more difficult to define, at the level of assumptions or 'mentality' rather than fully articulated thought. These assumptions may have been influenced by the philosophers, directly or indirectly, or the philosophers may be reflecting or, better, articulating the assumptions, or both.

To be more specific about the postmodern mentality, I would describe it as a sense of the multiplicity of points of view and the difficulty of establishing what happened in the present or the past. Also a sense of the softness, fluidity or fragility of structures (social classes, nations, etc.), replacing the opposite assumption of a generation or so ago that these structures were a kind of social bedrock. In other words a reaction not only against objectivity or the myth of objectivity but also against social determinism, Marxist or whatever, a reaction which became visible in 1968 (I'm thinking of Prague as well as of Paris in that famous year). Hence today's language of 'invention', 'imagination' and so on, book titles such as 'Imagined Communities', 'The Invention of Argentina', etc.

Remember that Frank Ankersmit spoke of the work of Carlo Ginzburg and Natalie Davis as postmodernist and that they both hotly denied this. But their work may be 'postmodern'. The authors should know whether or not they are postmodernist, but outsiders are able to say whether or not *Cheese and Worms* or *Martin Guerre* are postmodern. In their emphasis on the freedom of action of ordinary people these books are indeed of the seventies and eighties, they are part of a trend.

But you were asking me about positive and negative aspects. In the case of postmodernity, I think that the reaction against both determinism and the myth of objectivity was necessary and valuable. Take the case of historical writing. Historians, whether Marxian or Braudelian or disciples of quantitative history, 'cliometrics' as we used to call it, were too dismissive of events and of the actions of ordinary people and too confident that they saw everything clearly from on high. Now that confidence has gone. Historians are more humble, which is good, less reductionist, also good, but some have gone to the opposite extremes, moving from faith in facts to complete scepticism and from determinism to a romantic belief that we can shape our destinies.

I was never a proper Marxist, I don't like joining parties, but I still admire Marx and think that the old man had insights that are now being forgotten, as if the collapse of the Berlin wall had made his ideas irrelevant. Marx had a sharp sense of the limitations on human action. He may have exaggerated but now people are exaggerating in the other direction. It's more or less the same story about the reliability of historical knowledge. Too easily accepted by one generation, too easily dismissed by the next. The crucial thing, as I see it, is to make distinctions, to discriminate between relatively reliable statements and relatively unreliable ones. That was the solution proposed by Locke and others during the last crisis of historical knowledge, in the late seventeenth century, when the sceptics were already saying that the past could not be known. Actually I am writing an essay comparing and contrasting the two 'crises of historical consciousness' of the 1690s and the 1990s – I think that in this case as in others, historians can learn something useful from studying the past of their own discipline.

The notion of cultural relativism provokes passionate attacks and defences in many fields, including the historical one. Are you a relativist?

I am sure that it is necessary to distinguish kinds of relativism, hard versus soft, for example, perhaps also cultural relativism versus individualist relativism. A hard relativist, as I would define the term, is someone who assumes that all cultures are equal, as good as one another. My position is more sceptical. I am a soft cultural relativist. I don't think that we can know whether cultures are equal or not, so it might be wise to proceed as if every culture had something to teach every other culture! That is, I try to draw the consequences of the fact that if we try to compare and contrast cultures, there is nowhere for us to stand to view them except in a culture, one's own. From this position it appears to me that some cultures are strong in some domains, others in others. But I don't want to take these appearances too seriously. The point is that although we can try to be Olympian or to view the world from the standpoint of humanity, we should realize that this claim is a pretence or at best an aspiration.

Considering the importance that is given to archival research as a necessary condition for a well-founded historical interpretation, would you agree that the 'fetishism of facts' has, to a certain degree, replaced the 'fetishism of archives'?

In my view the two forms of fetishism have coexisted for quite a long time, since the age of Ranke in the early nineteenth century, if not before. There is the idea that a historian who works in libraries rather than archives is not a 'real' historian, for example. Like fieldwork in anthropology, a period in archives has become a rite of passage into the profession. But the relevance of archives depends on what one is studying. Much of the evidence for the answers to some kinds of historical question, such as 'What were Hitler's war aims?' is to be found in archives, while the evidence for answering other kinds of question, such as 'What was Machiavelli's intention in writing the *Prince*?' can be found in libraries. Working in archives is an exciting experience, somewhat different from other kinds of research. It allows a closer relation with the past, or at least the sense of a closer relationship with the past, than is usually possible in the case of libraries – reading letters which were not meant for us, for example, with some of the sand which was used to dry the ink still remaining in the envelope after 400 years. But the archive is not the universal panacea. Written history depends on evidence, but that evidence can take many forms.

Keith Thomas reminds us that even the most scrupulous historians are always constructing myths, whether they want to or not. Do you agree that objectivity is a chimera and that the greatest effort to achieve impartiality is bound to have an extremely limited effect?

I am not sure that the problem we are discussing should really be posed in terms of 'objectivity'. It often has been put that way because around 1900 historians liked to compare themselves to scientists. Personally, I would rather talk about 'fairness' or about 'detachment', because these are words describing humans reacting to humans. Some historians are fairer than others, making the attempt to understand everyone rather than to divide the world into heroes and villains.

And that brings me to 'myth' – a difficult term to define. By 'myth' I mean a story with a moral, a story following a stereotyped plot (as in Hayden White's examples of history 'emplotted' as tragedy or comedy), a story with heroes and villains, or a story about the past which is used to legitimate certain institutions in the present. Some historians produce myths of this kind, others try to 'demythologize' the past in the sense of exposing earlier stories as myths. However, it would be too simple to operate with a simple dichotomy between history and myth, and it would be all too easy to say what I write is history while what other historians write is myth. I would say instead that the boundary between history and myth is hard to define and that the distinction is a relative one. No one can escape myth altogether (consciously or unconsciously, we all need heroes and villains and stories about the triumph of good over evil). But some histories are freer from myth than others.

But what Keith Thomas wanted to say is that we cannot free ourselves from the subtlest myths, from the language and the assumptions of our culture which lie behind everything we, as historians, write about the past. This is the reason, he says, 'why whenever we open a history book written in 1840 or 1740 it hits us in the eye.'

Keith is absolutely right about the way in which an artefact made in a certain generation smells of the mentality of that generation, a historical text no less than a novel or a painting or a house. It is impossible to avoid this smell and perhaps we should not even try. After all, what are historians for? In my view, they exist in order to interpret the past to the present. As I said earlier, they are a kind of interpreter, in the sense of translator. Like other translators, they face the dilemma between being faithful to the text, that is the past, and being intelligible to the reader in the present. What might be described as a 'free translation' of the past is close to what Keith calls 'myth'. And since the present keeps changing, written history, like a translation, can become more or less obsolete, out of date. But only more or less. It is still possible to appreciate Montaigne's essays in their sixteenth-century English translation. We can still learn from great historians, from Burckhardt on the Renaissance, for example, although his book smells of the 1860s. Or from Charles Firth on the English Civil War, as Keith himself points out in his interview!

This can be related to the difficulties involved in the encounters between different cultures. Umberto Eco, for example, talks about 'the power of background books' which affects everybody (including great minds like Leibniz and Kircher) and which make us see the unknown through the known. Is there, in your view, a way to face this problem with any degree of success?

That's right, we are still talking about what I like to call 'cultural distance', whether it coincides with remoteness in space or in time. The central problem, in my view, is that we cannot understand either our own culture or another one without a more or less coherent system of concepts. When I spoke of the historian as a translator, I was thinking of him or her as describing the past (including its concepts) through the concepts of the present. Like other forms of translation, this enterprise is not easy and it requires finesse. There are 'false friends', attractive analogies which also mislead. In the age of Leibniz and Kircher, for example, some people assumed the equivalence of the Chinese concepts of Yin and Yang with Aristotle's concepts – still familiar in the seventeenth-century West – of matter and form. But these concepts are not altogether equivalent.

But you were asking me for a solution. I don't know whether finesse can be taught. But one can at least try to be conscious of the problem. We can try not to assume that apparent analogies are exactly equivalent, for example that the English word 'magic', central in Keith Thomas's book, had exactly the same meaning, uses, and associations in the seventeenth century as it has today.

As a representative of the so-called 'New Cultural History', would you say that the 'new historians' are necessarily the best ones?

Definitely not. To be a good historian, what is necessary is, above all, imagination, penetration and the gift for asking relevant questions and for knowing where to look for the answers. A historian might well possess all these qualities and still prefer to work in a traditional field – like political history in the narrow sense of the term – and in a traditional manner, writing narratives of events. I am no musician and the analogy I am going to draw may not be musically appropriate, but I believe that Bach was a much more traditional composer than his contemporary Telemann, which did not prevent him from being much better, much greater. You may be wondering why I have not said anything about originality. To be a good historian it is clearly necessary to be original, but this originality may be, let us say, 'local', asking new questions about Gladstone's foreign policy, for example, or giving old questions new answers.

In saying this I do not mean to say that I do not value the new approaches which have enriched historical writing. We all owe a great deal to Braudel, to Bloch, to Burckhardt, to Ranke (who was also a great innovator in his day), to Gibbon, to Guicciardini, and to other historians who have widened the range of choices available to their successors. The last generation has been a time of the multiplication of new approaches, a fascinating as well as a confusing time to be practising history. I am happy to have been working in this period and to have been able to participate in a collective movement of experiment and renewal. I believe that the new approaches were necessary and that in a certain sense they responded to the needs of our time, just as I believe that they will, in the long-term, enrich the practice of history, as the innovations of Gibbon or Ranke have done. But it is perfectly possible to be an enthusiast for the new history and at the same time a mediocre historian, just as it is possible to be the Bach of the historical profession, employing a traditional approach in a wonderful way.

Bertrand Russell said once: 'Oxford and Cambridge are the last medieval islands – all right for first-class people. But their security is harmful for second-class people – it makes them insular and gaga. This is why English academic life is creative for some but sterile for many.' Having spent most of your academic life in these two institutions, and having observed so many of your colleagues spending their entire adult life in these centres of excellence, could you comment on Russell's idea?

I'm not sure that Russell is right about the survival of the Middle Ages, but that isn't the real point. The point as I see it is the concentration of academic talent in two small towns, with the consequent sense, which

I can remember from Oxford student days, that one is living in the centre of the intellectual universe. But to believe that one is living in the centre of the universe is a virtually infallible sign of provincialism, or insularity, to use Russell's word. What is more, it even affects some first-class people. It isn't a uniquely English disease – the French suffer from it too. But it isn't quite so bad to be Paris-centred as it is to be Oxford- or Cambridge-centred, since Paris is after all a great city with much more to offer than the Sorbonne and the Collège de France!

In other ways, the environment of Cambridge is a wonderful one. I am thinking especially of the material conditions of intellectual production, but also of the opportunity to encounter people from different disciplines in the colleges and to exchange ideas. But the danger of provincialism remains serious. The only remedy is to get out, whether permanently or temporarily. I spent sixteen years teaching at the recently founded University of Sussex (1962–78), and since then frequent visits to other countries have kept me from becoming too insular – or do you think that this is just my illusion?

You are known as an author who writes in an accessible style, and the fact that you have been translated into a number of languages suggests that your work attracts interest in parts of the 'peripheral' world. Is the reception of your work by distant readers something that intrigues and disconcerts you, considering the multiple possibilities of appropriation? In other words, does the way that the Chinese, for example, might read your book on the construction of Louis XIV's image worry you?

As a historian of cultural reception I am fascinated and disturbed by the reception – or receptions in the plural – of my own work. I wonder whether a Chinese reader of my book on the image of Louis XIV keeps thinking of Mao Tse-Tung. Maybe the work was translated as a contribution to a process of 'demaofication' on the lines of 'destalinization', or what I called in my book 'delouisfication'. That creative application of my book wouldn't worry me at all.

What disturbs me is to read interpretations of my work in book reviews in which views are attributed to me that I don't hold. If this can easily happen in England, within my own culture, what is likely to happen elsewhere?

Although you have been formed in the British empiricist tradition, many of your British colleagues (though not your French ones), consider you a historian with distinctively theoretical preoccupations. How do you explain this concern? Is there a tension between your empirical and theoretical interests?

The French have a nice phrase, 'on est toujours le néapolitain de quelqu'un'. In that sense everything is relative. To be British and a historian is to have swallowed a double dose of empiricism, the local and the professional! Somehow I have emerged a bit less empiricist than many of my colleagues, so that they think that I don't have my feet on the ground. Maybe it was reading philosophy that started it – my Catholic school encouraged us to read Thomas Aquinas, at a time when many schools did not encourage philosophy at all. I discovered the linguistic philosophy of Alfred Ayer and Gilbert Ryle at the time of the scholarship exams for Oxford, and Wittgenstein when I was an undergraduate. Then I went on to sociology and anthropology.

I don't see any conflict in principle between theoretical and empirical approaches. Take the case of Max Weber, for example. He read widely in comparative history and built his theories on this foundation. All theory needs to be a theory of something, so information is essential to it. Conversely, as Karl Popper and others have shown, contrary to what extreme empiricists think, it is difficult if not impossible for scientists to make systematic observations without having at least a provisional theory (or hypothesis, or model) to test. (I am throwing in the terms 'hypothesis' and 'model' because I am not happy with the dichotomy between fact and theory, there are all sorts of nuances to put in.)

In similar fashion, one can't work usefully in an archive if one is not looking for something. If there are 100 kilometres of material in the Archivio di Stato in Venice, why read some documents and not others? So 'facts' and 'theories' are interdependent. Even the historians who think of themselves as pure empiricists ask questions and investigate problems in their daily work. We need to mix fact and theory to make a kind of cocktail. There remain problems, such as which theory should we choose and on what grounds? How large a dose of theory should go into the cocktail? There is plenty of room for tension here.

Are you saying that the historian has to choose a specific theory at a certain moment? Couldn't he make a cocktail of the various theories as well as mixing them with the facts?

I quite agree with you and I think that mixing such theoretical cocktails is exactly what I have been doing for much of my career, since I've never been a Marxist, a Weberian, a Durkheimian or a structuralist. Of course, you can't mix just anything with anything. Some ideas are simply not consistent with others. But that is the only restriction, as I see it, in constructing a model or a theory to test in a given historical situation. The purists, dogmatic Marxists, for example, denounce the cocktail-mixers (Carlo Ginzburg and Keith Thomas and Natalie Davis as well as me) as 'eclectics'. It is ironic, isn't it? Because Marx himself was an eclectic in precisely this sense. He built his theory out of elements from Hegel, Adam Smith and so on, the same way as Norbert Elias built his theory of the civilizing process out of fragments of Freud and Weber. But Marx was careful to maintain coherence and consistency, at any rate most of the time.

A historian as distinguished as E. P. Thompson once referred to Michel Foucault as a charlatan. Is there anything of value to historians in Foucault in your view?

In my view, the value of Foucault for historians – leaving on one side his possible achievements as a philosopher – is essentially negative. That is, he offered powerful criticisms of the conventional wisdom, of the idea, for example, that the rise of asylums for the insane and of a new kind of prison was the result of progress in a humanitarian sense. On the positive side, he reconceptualized debates about power and knowledge, and that is important too. But the interpretation of the rise of the asylum, the prison, the factory, the new kind of school, etc. which he offered in place of that conventional wisdom is itself open to criticism. His argument suffers from the fact that he was not prepared to do serious historical research (not to mention his tendency to generalize about Europe on the basis of the French experience, a tendency which is not, of course, confined to Foucault). To be more exact, the books in which he dealt with social practices, notably *Madness and Civilization* and *Discipline and Punish*, suffered from this limitation in a way that *The Order of Things* did not. Other people have been doing this research since his day and they have often needed to qualify Foucault's original conclusions. This example illustrates a point we were discussing before, the relevance of archives to written history.

But do you agree that Foucault is overestimated and that he is, in great part, a 'footnote to Nietzsche', as Ginzburg argued?

I am sure that Foucault is overestimated in some quarters, that there is a cult of his ideas in some places, although this is less the case in England than it appears to be in some other parts of the world. And Foucault obviously owes a lot to Nietzsche, including the concept of 'genealogy' so prominent in his historical work. In future histories of philosophy he may well be placed in a chapter on Nietzsche's followers. All the same, I think that he is more than a footnote to Nietzsche, just as I think (contrary to Whitehead) that Western philosophy is more than a series of footnotes to Plato. In his work on clinics, asylums, prisons and other institutions, Foucault adopted what might be called a Nietzschean approach, but he was not a mere disciple. He made his own precise and concrete criticisms of the traditional history of asylums and so on. In the series of books on the history of sexuality which Foucault wrote in his last years, his richest and most illuminating work in my view, he is at his most positive and original.

Marcel Granet, the French sinologist, once said that 'la méthode, c'est la route après qu'on l'a parcourue' ['Method is the approach after one has arrived']. This assertion seems, at the very least, to raise doubts about a priori prescriptions and to allude to the useless advice one often hears about approaching the archives with the relevant questions, with an open spirit, and so on. Could you comment on this?

I don't believe that there is *a* historical method in the sense of a procedure to follow in all cases. I would agree with Granet in many situations. But I also believe that there are certain methods – methods in the plural – which are worth following when one is trying to write certain kinds of history. For instance, when I was working on the history of elites in two successive books, I chose to follow the method of 'prosopography' or the 'collective biography' of a few hundred people, a method which had been used by some historians of ancient Rome and in England by Lewis Namier and Lawrence Stone when they wrote about the English ruling class. Prosopography has its dangers, and the discussion of these dangers forms part of the debate on methods. Not doing prosopography is still more dangerous, as it means generalizing about a group without having tried to study all its members individually.

Again, I think that Quentin Skinner has formulated a good method for approaching certain problems of intellectual history. *A* method not *the* method, because there is also great value in approaches to the same material following the method of the *histoire des mentalités* or the *Begriffsgeschichte* practised by Reinhart Koselleck and his disciples.

You have referred, with great optimism, to the 'steps forward' on the way to the histoire totale *advocated by Braudel. What would you say to the people who complain that the increasing fragmentation of history and the widening of its approaches and interests have not brought any deeper or wider understanding of the past? Do you agree that fragmentation is bad and that interdisciplinarity and dialogue among historians is much more of an ideal than a reality?*

Absolutely right. I do believe in Braudel's ideal of 'total history' in the sense of the attempt to see particular problems, groups, places or periods as part of a larger whole. All the same I do, regretfully, recognize the increasing fragmentation of historical studies, like the fragmentation of knowledge in general. Collectively, humans know more and more. Individually, it gets harder and harder to see the connection between one's own 'field' (a revealing metaphor to describe intellectual property), and the rest. The trend in this direction is an old one.

I have also to admit, with regret, that the rise of the so-called 'new history', a movement in which I have participated with enthusiasm from the 1960s onwards, has made matters worse in this respect. The price of extending the field of history to include everyone and all kinds of human activity, which was surely an enrichment, has been this fragmentation. The increasing interest among Europeans in the history of the rest of the world, an interest I welcome, has multiplied the kinds of history on offer, and so encouraged further fragmentation.

I've been trying to practise an interdisciplinary approach (concentrating on connections between the study of history, sociology, literature and anthropology), ever since I went to what was then the 'new' University of Sussex in 1962. Combining disciplines is a remedy for fragmentation, and it is always exciting to see students, who are more intellectually flexible than their elders, quickly learning to practise this approach.

But the remedy is only partial. What we see today more clearly than thirty years ago is the rise of different groups of historians with ties to specific other disciplines – philosophy in the case of intellectual historians, sociology in the case of social historians, anthropology in the case of some cultural historians. Each group talks more than before to people in another discipline. The trouble is that it talks less than before to other kinds of historian!

And yet I remain optimistic. Showing the connections between regions and social groups and intellectual disciplines is a way of fighting fragmentation. Apologists for specialization denounce a global approach as superficial and claim to study history in depth. Yet it is really possible to combine breadth with depth, for instance by showing the links between the local and the global.

The comparative approach seems to be a delicate theme to discuss with historians, precisely because in spite of being advocated since Bloch (or even earlier), it is not practised very much. Virtually no historian would deny nowadays that this approach is beneficial for the study of the past; but, when questioned about their own work, they seem to feel uncomfortable with the enormous difficulties involved. There are few scholars like Jack Goody, who really uses this approach and defends it as the means to counteract ethnocentrism and the distorted view of the 'other'. What is your view about this?

I was talking a moment ago about the problem of locating one's own research or speciality within a larger whole. Comparison is a systematic attempt to do exactly this. It is a remedy against the provincialism of specialists as well as against the ethnocentrism Jack Goody is rightly criticizing. Historians like to say that they are concerned with the particular, leaving generalizations to sociologists, economists and others. Many of them don't seem to realize that you cannot tell what is really specific to a place, period or social group without comparing and contrasting it to others! But to do this means reading outside one's own 'field' and some people are too timid or too lazy to do so.

Comparative history has long been an enthusiasm of mine. I once edited a series of volumes of comparative history – writing one of the volumes myself, *Venice and Amsterdam* – but the series came to an end in the 1970s because it was difficult to find authors. *Venice and Amsterdam* is a study in what Marc Bloch called 'neighbourly comparisons'. An even greater challenge is that of the distant comparisons on which Goody concentrates. Both the dangers and the rewards are greater. The dangers are greater because it takes a lot of time even to begin to understand another culture, and the danger of superficiality is a serious one (though one can always show one's work to specialists before publishing it – I have learned a lot from consulting historians of China and Japan). The rewards are greater because comparison is a way of approaching the goal of 'total history'.

In the last generation or so, a few scholars have practised comparative history on a grand scale. I'm thinking of Barrington Moore's *Democracy and Dictatorship,* for example, or the two volumes in which Perry Anderson wrote European history within a comparative framework, or his brother Ben's comparative study of nationalism, *Imagined Communities.*[1] My own ambitions have been rather more limited. I have tended to focus on a specific place and time, while trying to place the central problem in a wider framework. For example, my study of culture and society in Renaissance Italy ended with two comparisons, the neighbourly comparison with the Netherlands and the distant comparison with Japan. *The Fabrication of Louis XIV* made comparisons and contrasts with the fabrication of rulers in other periods, from Augustus to Mussolini and Margaret Thatcher.

Asked about the advice they would give to young historians, Carlo Ginzburg recommended the reading of fiction as the way to stimulate their 'moral imagination'; Robert Darnton advised them to work as reporters of murders and robberies in order to learn to respect the facts and to counteract the idea that everything is discourse; Quentin Skinner recommended the reading of intellectuals who are good 'philosophers of their practices', like Geertz and Foucault, from whom they could learn to put important and imaginative questions to the documents; Keith Thomas recommended the study of a wide spectrum of themes and disciplines 'because, in the end, history is what the historians bring to it'. As a regular reader of novels, would you say that Ginzburg's advice is the most effective?

1   B. Moore, *Democracy and Dictatorship*, Cambridge, Mass., Harvard University Press; P. Anderson, *Passages from Antiquity to Feudalism* and *Lineages of the Absolutist State*, both London, New Left Books, 1974; B. Anderson, *Imagined Communities*, London, Verso, 1983.

Actually I agree with all four pieces of advice and try to follow three of them (I've never been a reporter), but I'd like to begin by adding something else. For me, the study of the past is inseparable from its material culture. My enthusiasm for medieval history, when I was a child, was largely the result of having seen so many objects from this period, especially Gothic cathedrals, illustrated manuscripts, the furniture displayed in the Victoria and Albert Museum, and the armour and weapons exhibited in the Tower of London and elsewhere. To view these objects is an enormous stimulus to the historical imagination.

To come back to your question about novels. I read them primarily for their own sake, but I can't switch off being a historian when reading a novel any more than when travelling or whatever, so I find myself scribbling notes on the flyleaf, sometimes about the art of narrative, and sometimes about the culture of the period in which the novel was written. I scribble most when I read historical novels, at least those historical novels which are not just costume dramas in an exotic setting but stories about the historical process: *War and Peace*, *Waverley*, *I promessi sposi* and so on. There are also a few films that are really about history rather than being merely set in the past, like the Kurosawa films about the decline of the samurai after guns have been introduced to Japan.

Would you say that the critics of your work are your main interlocutors? Do they have any special role for the development of your ideas?

I haven't actually been very much involved in historical controversies in the way that, say, the leading British historians of Britain (Hill, Thompson, Stone, etc.) have been. When someone has objected to my views on Italian history, as has happened from time to time, it has often seemed to me that the objection was the result of a misunderstanding, that it was an objection to something I didn't say.

I am not suggesting that I am always right! But I prefer moderate positions to extreme interpretations. I could have stirred up controversy and drawn more attention to my books by making more extreme claims, but it doesn't come naturally to me to do this. Indeed, this would in my view have been intellectually dishonest.

What has happened somewhat more frequently, and is much more irritating, is to find my approach (comparative history, say, or the history of popular culture) dismissed by someone who claims not to see the point of it or is content to label it 'fashionable' and to say no more. I welcome a serious discussion of the advantages or disadvantages of different approaches, but I rather resent having my work dismissed without arguments being offered against it.

I have learned a good deal from some reviews of my books, usually but not always on points of detail. I have learned still more from people who have read my work in manuscript, or asked searching questions when I presented papers in seminars (sometimes I am still trying to respond weeks later). And most of all from historians and others whose work has in some respects at least been a model for my own. Braudel, especially for his ideal of *histoire totale*. Max Weber, for his comparative history on a world scale. Jacob Burckhardt and Johan Huizinga, for showing how cultural history might be written, and most of the people who appear in this book, for conversations which have lasted, on and off, for decades.

Are all these your mentors or your heroes – the ones who you imagine discussing your works with?

Right! Keith Thomas is my mentor in the literal sense, since he still writes references for me and since it is difficult to shake off a tutorial relationship, even after forty years! Christopher Hill, Lawrence Stone and Eric Hobsbawm, especially when I was a student or a young teacher in the sixties. And I must mention Raphael Samuel, the founder of History Workshop, who was a kind of elder brother for me. I've had both real and imaginary discussions of my work with all of them.

Braudel and Weber, Burckhardt and Huizinga are certainly among my heroes, along with Montaigne, Chekhov and others (I would adore to write history in the style of Chekhov but I don't know how to do it). But the people whom I imagine as reading what I write over my shoulder and making objections to it are more or less the same people who do read my work and do discuss it, whether they are historians or come from other disciplines such as anthropology or literature.

Considering, with Bacon, that some books are to be tasted, others to be swallowed and only a few to be digested, which are the ones you would recommend as a kind of compulsory reading for future historians?

I don't like the idea of compulsory reading because it is counter-productive. For a long time I disliked the novels of Charles Dickens because we were made to read *Bleak House* at school! In any case, I'm a historiographical pluralist in the sense that I think that there are many good ways of writing history, including styles of economic and political history which I don't practise myself.

But I do have some strong recommendations. Bloch's *Royal Touch*, for example. Braudel's *Mediterranean,* despite its length. Burckhardt and Huizinga, whom I already mentioned. Jonathan Spence's studies of China. Namier's penetrating essays on eighteenth-century England. All these are to be digested, though not necessarily, to vary the metaphor, taken as recipes for one's own work.

What is important for the making of a historian, as I see it, is to be aware of the variety of historical writing, the models available to follow, reject, adapt or whatever, so as to choose the approach which suits one's personality and also one's topic, and also, if possible, to reveal connections between one's own topic and others, helping to avoid that danger of fragmentation which we were discussing earlier.

You once confessed to being a great admirer of the passionate way in which Ginzburg writes history. On the other hand, commentators on your work often refer to your moderate style (verbally and emotionally) and to the distance from which you examine the subject. Would you say that your choice of synthesis and moderation is, fundamentally, a British cultural trait, or is it a matter of principle, the result of a conscious decision?

I think that the style of history which everyone writes can be explained in part in terms of the culture from which they come. Only in part. Edward Thompson, who wrote with such passion, and Eric Hobsbawm, who writes with remarkable detachment, came from the same culture, indeed the same sub-culture of English Marxism! Personality as well as culture is relevant here. And also the kind of history people are writing. Economic analysis is usually cooler than political narrative, and historians of Europe are likely to feel more distant from their vast subject than historians of a region or village. In my case, I think that I am something of a spectator by temperament, as I suggested earlier, talking about Singapore, and I also tend to see conflicts from more than one point of view. I would not argue that everyone should write history in my way, but I do think that what you call 'detached' history, especially history which tries to show the multiplicity of possible viewpoints on the past, has an important function. Too many people take up political positions without having considered the alternatives with sufficient care.

Your work deals with a great variety of themes and uses different approaches. Yet you seem not to have been seduced by women's history or by its more modern version, the history of gender. Why?

I was already interested in the role of women and the obstacles to their careers when I was writing my Renaissance culture and society book in the sixties and trying to answer the question why the famous artists and writers came from some social groups and not from others. In the eighties, when I was studying the censuses of Florence and Venice, I noticed how many occupations women were described as following, including even that of sailor ('Isabella marinera' and so on), and this led me to write a few pages on women's work which appeared in my *Historical Anthropology* book. In my book about the reception of Castiglione's *Courtier*, I placed considerable emphasis on women readers. Most recently, in *European Renaissance*, I talked about women as patrons. It's true that I've never devoted an entire study to women's history. My reluctance to write women's history may have something to do with the politics of the movement in England. Despite the association of history from below and women's history in the History Workshop group, in which I participated from the beginning, I had the impression that women did not want men to work on women.

You once admitted that each new book of yours is in part an attempt to compensate for what the previous one lacks. Should your present project on the social history of knowledge be understood in this way?

As I said before, the Braudelian idea of total history has been a permanent inspiration for me, even a kind of obsession. As it is obviously impossible to achieve such an ideal in a single project, I have tried on different occasions to explore what one might call 'varieties of historical experience'. Since my book on the Italian Renaissance was based on printed sources, for the next one, on Venice and Amsterdam, I went to the archives. After concentrating on the study of elites in two successive studies, I deliberately turned to the history of popular culture. In the same way, after publishing a number of books which had relatively little to say about politics, my project on Louis XIV presented a case study of the relation between politics and culture. My project on the social history of knowledge was a step in a new direction but in a sense it also echoes themes from a number of earlier works. It is a social history of culture, like *Culture and Society in Renaissance Italy*. It is concerned with 'knowledges' in the plural and with their interactions, like *Popular Culture*. Like *History and Social Theory*, it makes systematic use of theorists such as Mannheim on knowledge and society, Foucault on power and knowledge, the new 'anthropology of knowledge', and so on. I had already made a number of case studies of historical knowledge from the sixteenth to the eighteenth centuries, including one entitled 'The Social History of Social History'.

Robert Darnton once walked into what he called 'a historian's dream', that is, a treasury of untouched documents from the biggest Swiss publisher of the eighteenth century. Something similar happened to Keith Thomas, who discovered the notes taken by a seventeenth-century astrologer about his clients. Has something like this ever happened to you?

The closest I came to such an experience was in Rome in 1982. I was working in the Archivio di Stato and I began to look at cases which had come before the Tribunal of the Governor of Rome. I had recently developed an interest in the social history of language and there were about a hundred cases concerning insults in the catalogue of that archive, all cases from the late sixteenth or early seventeenth century. As in the case of many Italian archives, the researchers in Rome are rationed to three volumes (*buste*) a day. With an average of only one insult case in each volume I might be finished by lunchtime. The choice was between taking the afternoon off, which I did sometimes, and browsing in the rest of the volume, which might include as many as twenty cases of murder, fraud, or whatever. The system of interrogation was much like that of the inquisitors, so that one had the sense of listening to ordinary people talking. It was clear that some of them were frightened – there were instruments of torture on display in the interrogation room – and trying to guess what kind of answer was expected of them, which answer would pacify the interrogator and allow them to go home. Others, especially the neighbours of the accused, appeared to enjoy testifying, beginning with the ritual words 'I mind my own business' and then revealing all sorts of intimate details about the lives of people they had been observing through the window and overhearing through the wall. So I thought about extending my investigations to the history of the city. There were hundreds of relevant volumes, but I could easily have spent a month or two in Rome every year, gradually working through the cases and building up a picture of a great city at street level. In some ways this was a most appealing project. But in another sense, it was a bit unadventurous. The existence of the material was already known, though scholars tended to work on only one kind of case, as I had done with my insults. Hundreds of social historians, including urban historians, study judicial records in this way. I like to write different kinds of history, as you noted already, and also to take the broad view that many of my colleagues don't. So I ended up leaving Rome behind.

You have written a book on the Annales *school as both an observer and a participant. Would you explain how you distance yourself from it and to what extent you side with it?*

My discovery of *Annales* history, when I was a student at Oxford, around 1960, was a revelation. I identified with the heroes of the movement and their struggle against the dominance of a more traditional history, an identification assisted by the fact that the kind of history against which Bloch and Febvre had rebelled was still dominant at Oxford in 1960. I thought vaguely about going to study with Braudel in Paris, but I was enjoying the freedom of a graduate student at St Antony's College, Oxford, and didn't really want to move. My ideal was to write history in the *Annales* manner. I tried to do this in the book, written in the 1960s, on the Italian Renaissance, a topic which had not attracted historians in the *Annales* tradition. In this book I attempted to combine *histoire sérielle* with the German approach to cultural history associated with Burckhardt, Aby Warburg, and Erwin Panofsky.

So I was a sympathizer but not a member of the *Annales* group, without the slightest desire, I should say, to take part in their conflicts or enter their patronage system. I have met many leading members of the group, and we have friendly relations, but we are not close. I can feel that I am viewed as an outsider.

The history of mentalities, which was one of the most successful innovations of the last decades, has been under attack recently on the grounds that the notion of mentality is an inappropriate tool for historical analysis. Jack Goody, for instance, says that the use of this notion reveals a certain 'intellectual laziness' on the part of historians. What is your view of this debate?

In my view, intellectual laziness is endemic. That is, it affects us all the time, whatever concepts we use, whenever we start to take a given concept for granted instead of using it in inverted commas, if you like, with awareness of its limitations. Of course this can happen and has happened in the case of 'mentality'. It is easy to reify the concept, to speak as if mentalities 'really' existed, in the sense that stones and trees and people exist. So Jack Goody is right to complain, just as Geoffrey Lloyd is right to speak of the need for 'demystifying mentalities', the title of a fairly recent book of his.

There's another context for Jack's complaint, of course, and that is the Western stereotype of the 'oriental' mentality, which hinders the understanding of other cultures. We have come back to the problem of human difference that Keith Thomas was also talking about. Should we view the past as a foreign country or not? Come to that, how different from us are foreigners? If we assume that they are just like us, we make mistakes at a concrete and practical level. But if we assume that they are quite different from us, then we make equally big mistakes. It's a bit like the physicists' problem, if I understand it correctly, with their concepts of waves and particles. They have to try to understand the nature of light, for example, using two incompatible concepts simultaneously. We have to view other cultures as composed of people who are both like us and unlike us in their modes of thought.

So we come back to mentalities. We need some way of speaking about human assumptions, about what people take for granted in a given place and time, as well as about the ideas which they hold consciously. If we throw out one word, we are going to have to coin another to occupy this conceptual space. There isn't going to be one 'right' term – all concepts can be misused. The laziness is in us, not in the concepts. So I think that terms like 'mentality' and 'mode of thought' are still helpful, as they were in the seventeenth and eighteenth centuries when people such as Locke and Montesquieu began to use them. Provided that, as in the case of other concepts, we try not to forget those inverted commas!

For the countries that are on the 'periphery' or the 'semi-periphery' of the intellectual world, it seems that the centre does not show any real interest in what is produced outside its boundaries. Thinking about Brazil, for example, one can cite names of first-class intellectuals such as Florestan Fernandes[2] and Gilberto Freyre who, in spite of their innovative work, remain unknown in the intellectual centres, except among Brazilianists. Do you agree that the situation of relative indifference to the peripheral 'other' becomes an obstacle to intercultural understanding? What, in your view, could be done to help remedy this situation?

Unfortunately it seems to be the case that where one speaks is just as important as what one says. Braudel made the point very well once when he expressed his admiration for a Polish historian, Witold Kula. He said – I don't know how sincerely – that Kula was much more intelligent than he was, but that he, Braudel, had a 'French loudspeaker' which made it easier for people to hear him. On a personal level, it is possible to make an effort to learn more languages, to look out for interesting ideas, and when one finds them, to spread the word. I've tried to make more people aware of the importance of Freyre, of Kula, of the Cuban sociologist Fernando Ortiz, and others. More translations would help. But a large-scale problem needs large-scale action. As you know, academic 'exchange' usually means young people from the periphery spending a few years in the centre, while older people from the centre spend a few days in the periphery. If substantial numbers of young people from France or the USA were to spend a year in Cairo, say, or Lima and learn the local language, then the situation might change.

'What is the use of history?' Marc Bloch wrote a whole book trying to answer this simple question, put in all its simplicity by a child, because, as he said, it dealt with the important issue of the 'legitimacy of history'. How would you deal with this question?

If you'd like a short answer to this huge question, I would simply say that the use of the study of the past lies in helping us to orient ourselves in the world in which we live. A longer answer would involve making distinctions, between uses (more or less practical), and also between pasts (more or less remote).

Since the world is in constant change, it is impossible to understand it without trying to locate what is happening in broader trends over time, whether they are economic, cultural, or whatever. This is the essential justification for the study of the recent past. But the recent past is not

---

2   Florestan Fernandes (1920–1995), one of the most outstanding Brazilian sociologists of the twentieth century, author of *A organização social dos Tupinambá* (2nd edn, 1963), *Fundamentos empíricos da explicação sociológica* (2nd edn, 1967).

intelligible by itself. I sometimes think that we ought to teach history backwards, starting with current events. To understand current events we might go back a generation, to the sixties. To understand the sixties, we have to go back another generation, and so on. When could we stop?

Another use of history is to tell people about their 'roots', the cultures from which they and their families came. At a time when more and more people feel uprooted in a world which is changing faster and faster, and when many people have been physically uprooted, sometimes violently so, as in the case of the Albanians of Kosovo, this psychological function of the study of the past is an important one. It explains the increasing interest in local history in the last few years.

But to study our own past alone is dangerous. It encourages insularity and a sense of superiority over others, as in the case of the Balkans. So it is crucial to combine the study of 'us' with the study of others, more or less remote. I sometimes wonder what kind of history should be taught in schools to educate citizens of the world in the twenty-first century. There is a strong case for beginning with the outlines of world history, partly as a framework for more specific studies and partly as a way of understanding other cultures today. For example, non-Muslims need to know something about the culture of Islam.

But, considering the sad reality of what has been happening in Eastern Europe, wouldn't you say that the chances for peace and harmony among various groups of people would increase if, instead of knowing their roots, they ignored them? If forgetting was cultivated more than remembering?

Although my own background is as sectarian as anyone's (my father's family came from Galway and my great-grandmother carried guns for the IRA), I have a lot of sympathy with that idea. I was once invited to a conference in Northern Ireland. It was in 1969, when open conflict between Catholics and Protestants was still fairly recent. I was impressed by the number of political graffiti in Belfast and especially by the recurrent message, 'Remember 1690'! In other words, the battle of the Boyne, after which William III established control over Ireland. I remember being tempted to take a piece of chalk and to write on the walls, 'Forget 1690!'

But it isn't as easy as that. Maybe you should have asked Jack Goody that question; he is the one who wrote about 'structural amnesia'. Would he say that our problem is that writing preserves the past? But then, isn't it the case that small children who can't yet read have already been taught by their parents to hate Protestants or Serbs, that they are 'socialized' into conflict?

So what do we do? I shall probably sound more like an amateur psychoanalyst than a historian, but I want to suggest that deep memories (including collective memories and historical memories, at least in some cultures) can't just be forgotten. The only hope is to make them conscious and 'work them through', by discussing them in school, for example, so that children already have a chance to understand the other side's point of view and so come a step nearer to abandoning the idea of 'sides' altogether. I may sound too optimistic but I'm thinking, for example, of the case of Spain, which was torn apart by the Civil War in the thirties. Today Spaniards appear to have put all that behind them. It may even be that memory of the horrors of war encourages politicians to obey the rules of the democratic system. Might we say that unpleasant memories make for good politics?

Cambridge, May–June 1999

SELECT BIBLIOGRAPHY

Culture and Society in Renaissance Italy (London, Batsford, 1972); translated into German, Spanish, French, Dutch, Hungarian, Italian, Japanese, Polish, Czech.

Venice and Amsterdam: A Study of Seventeenth-Century Elites (London, Temple Smith, 1974); translated into Italian, Dutch, French, German, Portuguese, Spanish.

Popular Culture in Early Modern Europe (London, Temple Smith, 1978); translated into Albanian, German, Serbo-Croat, Dutch, Hungarian, Italian, Japanese, Portuguese, Spanish, Swedish, Polish, Estonian, Bulgarian.

Historical Anthropology of Early Modern Italy: Essays on Perception and Communication (Cambridge, Cambridge University Press, 1987); translated into German, Dutch, Italian.

The French Historical Revolution: The Annales *School, 1929–89* (Cambridge, Polity, 1990); translated into Chinese, German, Italian, Japanese, Portuguese, Slovene, Spanish, Swedish.

The Fabrication of Louis XIV (New Haven and London, Yale University Press, 1992); translated into Dutch, German, Italian, Portuguese, French, Spanish, Swedish, Chinese.

History and Social Theory (Cambridge, Polity, 1992); translated into Turkish, Korean, Italian, Serbian.

The Art of Conversation (Cambridge, Polity, 1993); translated into German, Italian, Portuguese, Spanish, Swedish.

Varieties of Cultural History (Cambridge, Polity, 1997); translated into German.

The European Renaissance: Centres and Peripheries (Oxford, Blackwell Publishers, 1998); translated into German, Italian, French, Spanish.

A Social History of Knowledge from Gutenberg to Diderot (Cambridge, Polity, 2000); translated into German, Italian, Spanish, Turkish.

7

Robert Darnton

Robert Darnton (b. 1939), the American historian who occupies the Shelby Cullom Davis chair of history at Princeton University, is one of the most important experts on France in the English-speaking world and a leading writer on the history of the book, or as he prefers to say, the history of reading. Darnton's own extremely original way of writing the history of France lies between the two main approaches used by other eminent contemporary historians. On one side there are the political and social historians, such as Richard Cobb and his disciples, who are particularly interested in the institutions and social classes of France under the *Ancien Régime* rather than books and ideas. On the other lie the so-called intellectual historians of European thought, such as Peter Gay, John Pocock and Quentin Skinner, who are basically interested in the books and ideas of great thinkers like Montesquieu, Rousseau and Machiavelli and leave aside the so-called 'lesser' and more popular works of the time.

Distancing himself from both groups, Darnton develops what he calls a social history of ideas, thus resembling French historians like Daniel Roche and Roger Chartier who, like him, study what they term 'cultural practices' or 'the history of collective mentalities'. His first book, *Mesmerism and the End of the Enlightenment in France* (1968), investigated a subject treated by historians ever since the end of the eighteenth century as unworthy of historical attention, the seductive power that certain medical ideas held over the French. With *The Business of Enlightenment* (1979) and other later studies such as *The Literary Underground of the Old Regime* (1982) and *The Forbidden Best-Sellers of Pre-Revolutionary France* (1995), Darnton turned to the history of publishing and reading, approaching the *Ancien Régime* through the system of censorship (and the anti-system of evading the censors) and demonstrating the links between pornography, philosophy and politics in France during the second half of the eighteenth century. The first of these works, on the publishing history of the so-called Bible of the Enlightenment, the *Encyclopédie* of Diderot and d'Alembert, marked a real turning-point in eighteenth-century history. The *Encyclopédie* was a book with subversive ideas which was intended, in Diderot's words, to 'change the way of thinking of the common man'. Unlike other scholars, who devoted themselves to analysing the radical ideas in this famous work, Darnton concentrated on the production history of the *Encyclopédie* after Diderot and on the dissemination of the ideas it contained through the issue of cheap editions with large print runs. With a keen detective's mind, he revealed the complex process by which the Enlightenment, until then accessible only to a limited audience, spread more widely in the decade preceding the French Revolution.

Darnton's subsequent publications on the best-sellers and clandestine literature of the *Ancien Régime* show that his interests go well beyond the great works of the Enlightenment to encompass the 'lesser works' as well, often wrongly considered uninteresting. Of little value by today's standards, perhaps, but not necessarily by the standards of the time, they may in Darnton's view have expressed and influenced the mentality of a past epoch far more than masterpieces by eminent authors ever did. In fact, much of Darnton's effort in writing the history of the eighteenth-century book, from the great *Encyclopédie* to the countless pornographic works of the time, has been devoted to a discussion of the role played by printed matter in the 1789 Revolution.

Darnton is a historian with many interests and a master of the difficult art of writing in depth yet in a clear, colloquial and concrete style. He has made significant contributions not only to the history of the book but also to other fields of cultural history. *The Great Cat Massacre and Other Episodes in French Cultural History* (1984) is a good illustration of his broad range of interests and the clarity and brilliance with which he deals with subjects as diverse as the mental worlds of revolutionary peasants and craftsmen in Paris, of the famous Encyclopaedists, of a Paris police inspector, of a Montpellier citizen, etc. Of all his books this is perhaps the best known and most controversial; it is also the one that most clearly reveals the great influence on his work of the American anthropologist Clifford Geertz. *The Great Cat Massacre* was in fact one of the most fruitful and ground-breaking results of the seminars that for many years Darnton conducted with Geertz at Princeton. From the way in which he approaches the various topics in the book it is evident that, although it is impossible to interview our ancestors as an anthropologist would, Darnton believes that much of their mental world could be recovered if we asked the right questions of the material available and if we started out with the idea that the past can be just as foreign to us as are the Javanese, Balinese or Moroccans.

The author of nearly a dozen books translated into more than twelve languages, Darnton enjoys enviable conditions of work due to an agreement he reached some years ago with Princeton (where he has taught since 1968): each year he teaches one semester at Princeton and spends the other at All Souls College, Oxford, where he holds the post originally created for Arnaldo Momigliano, one of the most eminent twentieth-century historians of antiquity. In this extremely refined environment, where he is free from any external obligations, Darnton has, in recent years, regularly spent the first semester, always accompanied by his wife Susan, his undergraduate classmate at Harvard whom he married in 1963. It was at his flat in the picturesque village of Iffley, near Oxford, that Darnton received me with warmth and humour to talk about his ideas, his projects, his intellectual trajectory, his interests, his family, etc.

MARIA LÚCIA PALLARES-BURKE   *Your father was a journalist and you yourself started a career as a journalist, which you then quit in order to be a university teacher. But, in a way, one might say that you have remained attached to journalism with your interest in the press and in what one could call 'minor works'. In what way has journalism left its mark on you?*

ROBERT DARNTON   Well, it certainly has left a mark but the exact way in which it has may be hard for me to explain and even to understand myself. Part of it may be psychological and emotional because my father was killed as a correspondent for the *New York Times* in the war and I was supposed to carry on where he had left off, which meant that I was expected to go into the *Times* and be a reporter. For me, to be a reporter – not an editor, not a columnist, but an honest shoe-leather man, as people used to say – was to be the person in the raincoat, with a cigarette and a hat, who was on the street actually seeing events as they happened. This was a romantic image of what I ought to do in life. Everyone in my family, in fact, did it: my father, my mother, my brother and myself. My mother, who joined the *New York Times* after my father died, even rose from a reporter to become its women's editor. My first 'article' for the *New York Times* was when I was four years old. I couldn't write, of course, but someone took down my baby talk and turned it into an article. For me it was as though I was predestined to be a reporter. So when I left this newspaper it was a traumatic moment. And I became the black sheep of the family because I was going to become this disgraceful thing, a college professor!

Well, why did I leave, then, this profession for which I seemed predestined? I left because I adore history. It's hard work, writing is always painful, but it is a deeply satisfying vocation. Yet there is a connection, obviously, between the journalism I did and the history I write. For one thing, I study journalism, the history of journalism, newspapers, reporters, and so on. But the second point is that when I worked for the *New York Times*, and even before, during the time I did my training as a reporter on a cheap crime sheet in Newark, the *Newark Star Ledger*, my speciality was crime. All my training as a journalist I got in police headquarters covering murders and robberies. First in Newark, which was a very tough city in New Jersey, and then in different parts of New York City, in Manhattan, Queens and Brooklyn. So, ever since I was at college I always worked on newspapers part-time (it was my summer work) and have written dozens and dozens of stories about crime. Even when I finished my BA degree at Harvard and got a scholarship to do my D.Phil. at Oxford I worked as a 'stringer' covering Oxford for the *New York Times*; and during the summers I was a substitute correspondent in London. Since I did not want to become a professor when I finished my D. Phil., I went back to New York and immediately joined the *Times* as a regular reporter; and sure enough, started again with rape, murder and armed robbery. So I spent a lot of time learning to write fast, learning to write clearly, I hope, and also learning to respect my reader, by not using jargon and by trying to write in a vivid and direct manner. And I still believe in that. I think that is, in fact, how Voltaire wrote, even though he never covered crime for the *New York Times*!

That's one important point. I think that every historian should have some time working on a newspaper covering rape, murder and armed robbery. For one thing, you have to get the facts right. We can be very sophisticated about facts, but you have to know the exact spelling of the name of the person murdered, you have to know how old he or she was; you just can't get it wrong. And you have to attribute everything; you have to prove what you write in a newspaper, because you might be sued if you get it wrong. Certainly your editor will give you a terrible scolding if you don't have all the information. So solid research and a respect for accuracy is crucial, but many graduate students think that history is all about discourse and the postmodernist construction of the other. I'm not saying that those are silly ideas but I think you really have to develop the artisanal side of historical research. That is the basis of it all. But in my case it also turned into fascination with public opinion and the media. Therefore, much of my work has been about not rarefied philosophers and ideas, but about this middle and lower level of intellectual exchange: about how ideas work into society, the way in which attitudes and values are developed. I'm not really terribly interested in the way philosophical systems are passed on from one philosopher to another. What I find interesting is how ordinary people make sense of the world and develop some strategy for finding their way through the difficulties, the circumstances surrounding them. To me, ordinary people are not intellectuals, but are certainly intelligent. So why not do an intellectual history of non-intellectuals? And this concern comes, I think, from working as a newspaper reporter, interviewing people, covering stories; and while covering stories, asking yourself: what is it to tell a story? Because I believe that what you read in the newspaper are stories, not what really happened. This narrative aspect of reporting is something that has never, I believe, been adequately studied, although it's something that goes to the heart of the history of the media. These are all areas that I try to develop.

And yet a third way that the experience of working in newspapers has been important to me has to do with the police. I spent so much time with the police covering crime that I found myself attracted almost without knowing it to police archives. I've spent years in the archives of the police who were covering literature in eighteenth-century France and I found real police reports on people like Rousseau, Diderot, Voltaire, and also on gossiping in the cafés. Now, that does not mean that I believe in everything I read in the police archives; quite the opposite. Having actually talked to the police I learned to distrust them; but I also feel that you can exploit them and make the most of the information they provide in order to understand the world of books, of letters, of the entertainment industries and so on.

My book on the *Encyclopédie* reveals the marks left by my experience as a police reporter. It is secretly a detective story inside a more general academic account of the way books were produced and diffused in France. I won't give you the details of the detective story but anyone who reads it can see what happens. So in all of these ways this background as a crime reporter has proved to be important for my role as an historian.

You abandoned journalism because, as you said, you 'just adore history'. How did this passion develop? Has any encounter with an author or the reading of a book been especially important?

'Adoring' may not be the best word to describe the experience, but I find something deeply satisfying about the study of the past, and I don't know quite what it is. I feel it most when I work in the archives. As the tenor of a life begins to emerge from the manuscripts and I see a story unfold from one document to another, I have the sensation of making contact with the human condition as it was experienced by someone in another world, centuries away from mine. It may be an illusion, and I may get it wrong. I may sound like a romantic. But the archives, in all their concreteness, provide a corrective to romantic interpretations. They keep the historian honest. Unlike literary scholars and philosophers, we must marshal evidence in order to sustain our arguments, and we cannot pull it out of our heads. We extract it from boxes in the archives. I realize, of course, that other disciplines have a rigour of their own and that we, too, have flights of the imagination. I acknowledge the arbitrary and literary aspects that go into the writing of history and I don't consider myself a positivist. But as I get older, I have less patience with the sophisticated depreciation of facts. To say that we cannot have any unmediated knowledge of the past is not to say that any version of it will do, or that one version cannot be better than another. We can enter imaginatively into other lives, roam around in other worlds, make contact with other realms of experience, and do so with rigour, not fantasies or fictions. I still feel respect for newspaper reporters. They, too, have to get the facts right and align them in a convincing narrative. But when I returned to America after completing my dissertation in Oxford, I lost the satisfaction that I once had enjoyed in chasing down 'stories'. I logged long hours in police headquarters. And to while away the time between murders and armed robberies, I read Burckhardt's *Civilization of the Renaissance in Italy*. I knew that I could not read it openly in front of the other reporters, so I hid it inside a copy of *Playboy*. And I still think it is the greatest history book that I have ever read.

Most of your work is on eighteenth-century France. How did this interest develop?

I actually don't know the answer to that question. It is strange that an American in the late twentieth century should be obsessed with France in the eighteenth century. However, France in the eighteenth century is a wonderful area in which to study general problems, which can be of interest even to people who couldn't care less about the old regime and the French Revolution. So I think my interest is not just in France itself, though I love France; it's an interest connected to the desire to understand problems such as the connection between ideas and revolution, or the way the media operate. France has not only a very rich historiographical literature – so that you can build on the work of wonderful historians who came before – but it also has fabulous archives, especially, as I said, police archives. We should remember that France was the first police state. Of course, the word police meant something different in the eighteenth century: it meant something like rational administration. But the fact is that there were police agents everywhere reporting on public opinion. I found the archives of police spies in cafés, about forty cafés in the 1720s, so that you can almost listen in to conversations in cafés thanks to this police state that was trying to inform itself about public opinion. Now, I'm straying a little bit away from your question, but the point is that once you step into an archive of eighteenth-century France you can't get out because it is so interesting. And it's interesting for problems and preoccupations that we have today, such as the connection between ideology and political movements. So, although my base is indeed the eighteenth-century, from there I have worked on other areas. The book I'm writing now is a study of censorship beginning with eighteenth-century France, but expanding from there to include censorship in nineteenth-century India and in communist East Germany. So the idea is to take a theme that I originally encountered while studying France under the old regime, and to see what it looks like in a completely different historical context.

Would you say that carrying out a comparative study on the large scale you just mentioned, something that has been praised ever since Marc Bloch but very little practised, allows you to see more clearly the strengths and weaknesses of the comparative approach?

As I haven't yet written my planned comparative history of censorships, I can't look back on it and come up with pronouncements about the difficulties and advantages of jumping around in space and time. Still, I have completed a lot of research and have published a preliminary study in a volume for Amnesty International; so I will hazard a few remarks. First, I feel confirmed in the idea that comparative history is more talked about than written. When you get down to the writing, you can feel paralysed by the complexities. In my case, having spent so much time in the company of certain anthropologists, I have come around to the view that cultural systems are particular. Each has an idiom of its own, along with all sorts of confusing dialects and fault lines, which make it difficult enough to generalize about that culture in itself. How, then, can a historian arrive at viable conclusions by crossing over from one culture to another? I have no general solution to this problem, but I found what I think is a workable procedure in the case of comparing censorships. I don't treat censorship as a thing-in-itself, which can be traced through any system, like a radioactive substance in a bloodstream. Instead, I try to define the distinguishing characteristics of literature as a cultural system in each of the three cases, then I look at the specific ways the state attempted to bring it under control. The result will not be variations on a single theme, such as repression, but rather a study of the different ways censors did their jobs and understood what they were doing. Their understanding varied remarkably from case to case. In eighteenth-century France they thought they were applying a royal stamp of approval. In nineteenth-century India they thought they were establishing a liberal variety of imperialism. And in twentieth-century East Germany they thought they were engaged in social engineering. Of course, their testimony must be measured against other kinds of evidence. But to make sense of it all, I think it crucial to understand each literary system on its own terms and from the viewpoint of the participants, rather than to hold it up against a common external measure of the sort favoured by economists.

A historian of the Ancien Régime *does not often have a chance to observe the fall of an old regime, as you had in 1989 in Germany. Has this experience affected, in any way, your perception of the French old regime?*

Watching the GDR collapse in 1989 has indeed changed my view of the fall of the old regime in France 200 years earlier – another instance of comparative history. In retrospect, the Soviet empire now looks so unstable that we are amazed that it held together for nearly half a century; and I am sure that future historians will find further arguments for overdetermination when they analyse its fall. But when I wandered into the midst of the events, I was impressed by contingency, unforeseen consequences, and the human capacity for mismanagement. Now when I lecture on 1789, I spend more time showing how events linked up in unpredictable patterns and how people in power precipitated their own downfall by blunders. The other ingredient of 1989 that especially impressed me was the power of public opinion, even in the face of modern weaponry. Although I did not participate in the key demonstrations in Leipzig and Berlin on 9 October and 4 November, I went to many demonstrations afterwards. I was impressed by all the external signs of opposition: the placards, posters, graffiti, slogans and talk. But what struck me most was the feeling in the air that the entire population was rising against the regime. Individuals did not count. Everyone became absorbed in a collective sense of 'us' against 'them'. I believe the French government was isolated in the same way during the so-called 'pre-revolution' of 1787–8. Then, too, the contemporary perception of events became an ingredient in the events themselves, and the sentiment of solidarity – 'la Nation' like 'Wir sind das Volk' – proved crucial. Once the system had collapsed, of course, fault lines opened up, and the revolutionary process gathered momentum. I had developed this kind of argument long ago, in my D.Phil. thesis at Oxford, where I attacked the conventional interpretation of a *révolte nobiliaire* as the precipitating factor in the destruction of the old regime. But the street-level experience of the fall of the GDR made me willing to stick my neck out further in arguing for the importance of collective perception and public opinion.

Several times in your work you have referred to your luck in having walked into 'a historian's dream', that is, a treasury of documents waiting to be discovered. In your case, this was the finding of untouched papers in the archives of the Société Typographique de Neuchâtel, the largest publishing house in Switzerland. As you have confessed many times, a lot of your work on the Enlightenment came out of this wonderfully rich source. Have you

*ever speculated about what would have happened if you had not found this
'historian's dream'?*

Well, it's hard to speculate about non-events and certainly it would be
true to say that much of my scholarly life has been a response to exposure
to this incredibly rich unread archive: 50,000 letters and account books
and other kinds of documents, all in impeccable condition, waiting for a
reader. My whole sense of the past has been influenced by this total
immersion in the manuscripts of this unusual source. Now, if that had
not happened, I'm not sure what direction my life would have taken. I
had published a work before on mesmerism, a book on the history
of popular science. So it was a first attempt to do something like the
history of mentalities, even though I had never heard of that approach,
which was being developed in Paris. Anyway, since this book had to do
with how the people saw the world, I used the strange vogue for popular
science – animal magnetism or mesmerism – as an example of a world
view that actually spread very widely in pre-revolutionary France
and then became coloured with a kind of radical politics. So it could be
that I would have gone on and developed more of the history of mentalities. In fact, the book I wrote called *The Great Cat Massacre* continued
that line. And that has nothing to do with the history of the books and
the manuscripts in Neuchâtel. So I'd not have become a historian
of the book; that is clear. I always dreamed of writing about the
world of newspaper reporters in New York, in the 1920s and in
the 1930s, so I might have done that. And maybe some day I'll get around
to doing it.

How did you discover this amazing archive?

I was working on my D.Phil. thesis in Oxford in 1963 and I saw a
footnote at the bottom of a page in a Swiss book that suggested that
maybe there were some original letters by a man called Jacques Pierre
Brissot. I was interested in him because he was one of the French who
were fascinated by America and the American Revolution. Together with
other Americanophiles he had founded a club in Paris called the Gallo-
American Society, and followed Jefferson around Paris. He later became
one of the leaders of the French Revolution. So I was, so to speak, trailing
Brissot, and this note suggested that there might be some letters by him in
this tiny little town of Neuchâtel. So I wrote to the library, asking: 'do you
conceivably have any letters by Jacques Pierre Brissot?' The director of
the library replied: 'yes, we have 119 letters by Brissot, and here is a
photocopy of one of them.' And the photocopy was of a letter Brissot
wrote to his publisher just after being released from the Bastille, in which
he told the story of his life trying to explain why he couldn't pay his bills.
Well, I was amazed at this and decided that as soon as I had an oppor-

tunity I'd go to Neuchâtel and read these letters by Brissot. When I was back in New York, having joined the *New York Times*, Harvard University offered me a wonderful research position: a three-year appointment to do nothing but research. So I took that, quit the *Times* and, as soon as I could, went to Neuchâtel, where I found, sure enough, not only the 119 letters by Brissot, but also 50,000 letters by hundreds and hundreds of people that I had never heard of: people who had to do with books, either as printers, papermakers, smugglers, booksellers, publishers, people who made the ink, people who made the type, bankers, authors, everything imaginable. And they were all in impeccable condition and beautifully catalogued by a retired chemist who had devoted the last years of his life to this. So nothing could be easier than to use them. My first reaction was that I must write a biography of Brissot, which I did. I wrote 500 pages of a first draft, which has never been published and is sitting in a drawer back in Princeton. I stopped because I thought that more important than to write the biography of a man was to write the biography of a book. And that is exactly what my work on the *Encyclopédie* is. In the course of going through the archive of Neuchâtel I ran into many manuscripts showing the inside history of how the *Encyclopédie* came into being, and I began following this. Before long it turned into a fascinating detective story (so we are back into crime reporting, so to speak) involving a major swindle. That's when I stopped and said to myself: 'Wait a minute, this is the most important book in the eighteenth century, the great *Encyclopédie* by Diderot and d'Alembert. I would like to write the biography of a book, not of a person, and try to explain how books happened, how they were produced, how they were diffused, how they were read, in so far as that is possible. And in the middle of the narrative I want to tell a detective story.'

What are your links with the 'Annales *school*'? *Do you consider yourself a practitioner of the 'new history'?*

The *Annales* school has taken out a patent on the phrase New History, so they identify themselves with the new history and I'm very happy to be viewed as a fellow traveller. Many of my friends come from the *Annales* school and have written for the book called *The New History*. I think though, that as a non-French person, as an American, I don't totally identify with *Annales*. I did my graduate work at Oxford and I must say I probably became infected with British empiricism; by that I mean that I was encouraged to do archival research and to respect what the British call facts. Now, I know that facts don't really exist, that they are constructed and so on. But nevertheless there is a lot to be said for the artisanal side of historical research, for going into the archives, discovering new things, and then trying to make sense of them. This is, in a sense, different from the *Annales* school, which begins with very grand concepts, such as *structure* and *conjoncture* – at least that used to be what they began with. Now there is a much greater interest in anthropological history and I share that. So I'd say that, yes, I do feel close to the *Annales* school and, if you like, the new history. But this closeness doesn't mean that I sacrifice a perspective that would be more Anglo-American.

What are the main authors and books that have influenced your own intellectual history?

It's difficult to say. I have my heroes in the way historians do in general, and if I have to choose among historians, certainly for me it would be Burckhardt, and, if you like, Huizinga, the two writing almost about the same subject, each in a way that could be called anthropological, and yet each of them steeped in the subject, so that they have the subject in their pores, as part of them. They combine erudition with conceptual brilliance. But for anyone working on French history our god is, of course, Marc Bloch. Partly for political reasons, for his courage in fighting against fascism, but also because he was a very great and original historian, even greater than his colleague Lucien Febvre, in my opinion. Books like *The Royal Touch* now seem much more original than perhaps they did ten years ago. So those are my heroes. There's nothing original in choosing them. But I do also work closely with Clifford Geertz, for example, at the Institute of Advanced Studies in Princeton. As you know, he and I have taught a seminar on history and anthropology now for about twenty, twenty-five years, and I'd say that among social scientists his influence has been very strong. Among sociologists Robert Merton, whom I've also known well, has meant a lot to me. I could go on listing other heroes, but those would be the obvious choices.

You've described yourself not as a plain historian of ideas, but as a social historian of ideas, a phrase Karl Marx would have liked. Do you still think that Marx has something of value to teach historians?

There are many Karl Marxes, and he wrote on so many subjects that to claim one can learn nothing from him would be the height of pretentiousness. I admit, however, that I don't reread him constantly or search through his works for a key that will unlock a particular problem. In my view, inadequate as it is, dialectical materialism has little to offer us today. It is a general philosophy of history, which does not stand up, at least not to my own reading of the past. But Marx's more political and polemical works still provide insights, many of them surprising and rather non-Marxist in their implications. The Marx that speaks most to me right now is the Marx of *The Class Struggles in France*.

How would you compare your work with another well-known historian of the book, Roger Chartier?

People often ask me, 'why are you having such a war with Roger Chartier?' In fact, we are very close friends. But I think on the outside it's thought that we have a kind of running battle. We review one another's books and we do enjoy disagreeing; so it is quite true that I write a book, he writes some criticism of it; I respond in the next book or article while criticizing him; he responds, and we have a kind of conversation going on. But the criticism is really very minor by comparison with the areas in which we agree. So what I think we are doing is working out a very healthy collaboration in which there is agreement on the fundamentals: we both want to understand the power of print and the printed word – or just any words, including the spoken and sung word, but basically the printed book – as a force in history. And that means incorporating it into a very broad sort of social and cultural history, instead of simply treating the history of the book as something for erudition in which you identify watermarks and find out whether compositor C really did the work on *Antony and Cleopatra* for Shakespeare. This kind of trivial question has fascinated bibliographers for a long time, but Roger and I are interested in approaching the history of the book from a much larger perspective, discussing the central question of how print enters into the everyday life of ordinary people. So what does set us apart? Well, Roger is actually smarter than I am; I mean, he just gives off sparks of intelligence in every phrase and has wonderful bright ideas that come out of him as if from a machine gun. To read him is extremely enjoyable because in his work there is a density of original thought that you rarely find in historians. I tend to be slower and even phlegmatic; that is to say, I go into the archives and get my hands dirty doing research. This is related to my notion that part of the job of the historian is very humble, modest and even artisanal. Roger never does archival research, but he does not need to because he has so many ideas! I think he's an essayist, and why not? That's an excellent type of historian to be. Sometimes I feel that Roger takes my research and then uses his ideas and comes out with a very original variation. This, I think, is fun for everyone. For him, for me and for the readers, because they can, if they are interested, follow this kind of running dialogue.

My own style, though, is rather different, because I want to explore new material in a more systematic way. This may be part of that British empiricism that I already mentioned. It is also a matter of taste. I love to do research because you never know what you'll find when you open a new dossier and start reading through letters, account books or whatever it might be. I think that intellectually it's also invigorating, even though in my manner of describing it it may sound as if the historian's task is digging a ditch. The reason for it's being invigorating is that you go to the archives with conceptions, patterns and hypotheses, having, so to speak, a picture of what you think the past was like. And then, you find some strange letter that doesn't correspond to the picture at all. So what is happening is a dialogue between your preconceptions and your general way of envisaging a field, on the one hand, and on the other hand, this raw material that you dig out and that often does not fit into the picture. So the picture changes, and you go back and forth between the specific empirical research and the more general conceptualization.

The history of the diffusion of the Encyclopédie *reveals that, after being a very dangerous and prohibited book, which put Diderot in prison and threatened the Catholics who owned it with excommunication, it became a 'legalized illegal book'. As you showed in a lively and convincing way, what was once seen as part of a conspiracy to destroy religion and undermine the state was a few years later an approved best-seller backed up by the same* Ancien Régime *which had once banished it. Was this an exceptional case in the Enlightenment, or was it a common feature of an age rich in ambiguities and paradoxes?*

Well, I certainly agree that it was an age rich in ambiguities and para-doxes, but maybe you're overemphasizing the legal character of all that. The *Encyclopédie* was a quasi-legal illegal book, which is a notion some-what difficult to explain because today we think that things are either legal or illegal. Now, the history of mentalities as taught by the *Annales* school informs us that our categories may not coincide with the categories that existed in other periods. In the eighteenth century there was no clear dividing line between the legal and the illegal, especially in the world of books. There were things called, for example, tacit permissions, and others called simple tolerances. I could give you a long list of technical terms that describe this grey in-between area in which things weren't legal, but they weren't really illegal either. In these cases the police simply looked the other way when the books were being sold. But then, if they offended someone, especially someone in power, they could be confis-cated. Often, however, the police informed the bookseller a few hours before they raided his bookstore. That is to say, there was complicity at many different levels of the old regime. A wonderfully revealing example we find in the attitude of Malesherbes, the man who was in charge of the book trade from 1750 to 1763. Well, this top man believed in effect in the freedom of the press, even though he was in charge of a system of censorship. He believed that there should be an open debate about issues, so he secretly protected the *Encyclopédie* and even hid the copies of the first edition in his own house when the bishops and the king's council condemned it. So Malesherbes's help was crucial for the publication of this huge work, which turned into the Bible of the Enlightenment. However, at that time this work was published in a relatively small number of copies, and it didn't reach the general public in France at all. Most of the copies were actually sold outside France to princes and great aristocrats who wanted to have this fabulous book in their library (and this I know because I found other manuscript sources that told me where most of the copies went). The interesting part of the story comes afterwards when the book is reduced in size – from a folio to a quarto and finally an octavo format – and also in price. The price was slashed and the books were, so to speak, mass-produced. That's when a kind of war breaks out among the competing printers of the *Encyclopédie*, all of them attempting to satisfy the growing demand from a large reading public. It is at this stage of the history of the *Encyclopédie* – the 1770s and 1780s – that the government's permission to publish it is even more revealing of the complicity of the old regime that I mentioned before. So it is fair to say that a book that was officially banned was allowed by the state to reach a wider public. And even more than that, the government not only helped one particular enterprising French publisher, Panckoucke, to print the book outside France and to sell it (by looking the other way when copies were brought into the country), but also gave him ample support in the spectacular commercial war which broke out between the different publishers who wanted to profit from this great public demand. It's fascinating to follow this war and to see the power of the French State being used to keep the foreigners out of the competition. I could go on and on because the whole story became very complicated and intriguing, and also very comical. I must say, though, that the history of the *Encyclopédie* is not at all exceptional in eighteenth-century France, and I could mention other books which were also tolerated because they fell into that intriguing category of quasi-legal books.

How far would your pioneer study of the Encyclopédie *be different, if you were writing it now, twenty years later?*

This is a long book, with more than 600 pages, but I don't think I'd make it shorter, though I agree with the general argument that any book can be made better by being made shorter. I think, however, that I'd have spent more time on the text. I originally tried to maximize the aspect that I thought was most original, and when I wrote, a long time ago, there was no information at all about how publishers operated behind the scenes. So I tried to maximize what I found in the archives and talk about the Enlightenment as an economic and social phenomenon. Today, however, I think I would spend more time on the text of the *Encyclopédie*, showing how the different editions included significant changes, and I'd also speak more about the readers, since I have a bit of information about the readership of the *Encyclopédie*. So the study would have been more literary and less economic. That is the main change I'd have made. Beyond that I'd have kept it as it is.

You announced that The Business of Enlightenment *was the first instalment in your project of writing about the book as a force in eighteenth-century Europe. Are you still pursuing this project?*

I've taken the next step and published the second instalment, *The Forbidden Best-Sellers of Pre-Revolutionary France* in 1995, in which I tried to isolate the books that really were considered dangerous – because they openly attacked the authority of the king, or preached real atheism, or were really pornographic – from books, like the *Encyclopédie*, which represented a more moderate Enlightenment and fell, therefore, into the category of the quasi-legal. Well, many books attacked religion, the monarchy and public morality at the same time. Those are the ones I like most. There was, for example, the case of the *Private Life of Louis XV*, which is irreligious, seditious, and quasi-pornographic all at once. And these books were the real best-sellers in the eighteenth century, which I can be more or less sure about because I did market research, so to speak, and came out with statistics to prove it. So that one can actually follow different aspects of the book trade: the quasi-legal, the perfectly legal, and the perfectly illegal. My idea at this stage was to recreate the entire literary culture, and to know what books really reached readers, what the actual literary demand was. And in this sense, again, I'm talking about empirical research in the archives, dirtying my hands and proving the case with a great deal of evidence. And then there are lots of other questions, more difficult ones such as how do people read the books, how do they make sense of them; and even – still more difficult – how did that influence the mysterious thing we call 'public opinion'. And there's even a further step: how did public opinion influence events? So I think that book history opens into very large classic questions such as: why did France have a revolution in 1789? What is the connection between Enlightenment and Revolution? What was public opinion? These questions won't have some final simple answer, but I do feel that this kind of study of book history in all its detail and with a lot of research can give you a much richer understanding of, ultimately, the explosion of Revolution. But to get from book history to 1789 and the collapse of the old regime is a very problematic thing. That will be the next thing I concentrate on.

The third instalment will be a study of the inside workings of the publishing house, that is, how publishers made decisions, how they thought, how they did market research – which they actually did. I'll give you an example. They sent a man on a horse throughout France for five months. He went to virtually every bookstore in southern and central

France to find out what people were reading, to make contact with the booksellers, to develop a market, trying to know what the literary demand was. And there were other aspects, like the question of how they transported books and about the smuggling industry. It is, in fact, a lot of fun to understand how smuggling worked, and the way smugglers understood their jobs. They didn't call themselves smugglers, they called themselves insurers, and smuggling was an insurance industry. All of this is really fascinating and I want to write a third book more about the way the publishing industry operated. I've done essays about this here and there but I want to bring it together into a general overview, and that will be the third and last part of this series of studies. However, I probably won't write this third book for a while because I have other things I want to do first.

A more or less common view of the Enlightenment is that it was a huge educational enterprise, that is, a period in which the various members of the Republic of Letters (including journalists, philosophers, novelists, etc.), were devoted to the task of educating the public. Your book on the Encyclopédie *reveals this central educational text of the Enlightenment as part of a huge economic enterprise more devoted to making money and gaining power than to spreading enlightenment. How far does this involvement with trade wars, shares, profit-making, partnership, lobbying, peddling, alliances, rivalries, quarrelling, intriguing and bribery diminish the age which so proudly named itself the* Siècle des Lumières? *Could this relation of the Enlightenment to profits and business be seen as one of the dark aspects of the age, or do you think that such a view is naïve and romantic, part of the myth of the Enlightenment?*

Well, there is a myth of the Enlightenment and the *philosophes* created this myth; they presented themselves as warriors labouring for the cause of humanity in a totally selfless way. In fact, I believe there's a lot of truth to that myth. Certainly someone like Voltaire believed in the campaign to crush *l'infâme*, the infamous thing, which really meant the Catholic Church. Voltaire rarely made money from his books; he was really not interested in profit from their sales because he had made money in other ways. He even collaborated with the pirates who pirated him because that was a way to spread more light! So it's certainly true to say that there was a selfless quality, a real dedication to a cause at the heart of the Enlightenment. I'd definitely say that Diderot, Rousseau and Voltaire were men motivated by dedication to the cause of liberating humanity; liberating it from prejudices, from the control of the Church and even from the repressive authority of the State. So I don't mean to depreciate this genuinely idealistic commitment. In fact, I think the Enlightenment is the age when this animal that we call the intellectual was born. And the intellectual as a social type is someone who is *engagé*, who is committed to a cause.

However, even intellectuals have to eat, and sometimes there is *Madame* intellectual. What about her? You know, some of these *philosophes* did not follow the common precept that a philosopher should never marry, and had wives and children to feed. It's all right to have a family if you're an aristocrat with a set income, but Rousseau, for example, was the son of a watchmaker and Diderot the son of a knife maker. Intellectuals like them shouldn't have got married; but they did and that meant that they had to earn money; and to earn money . . . well, they sometimes did some hack writing. One of the subjects that has fascinated me is the hack writer, I mean, the writer who is forced to write to make a living and support a family, or just to get through life himself. In other words, I'm saying that along with the idealism there was a social reality and an economic reality in which the writers had to live.

And if you look at the publishers, we should remember that publishing is a business, and it's quite wrong for us to assume that publishers did it for truth and beauty. I do think that, of course, some of them had values and believed in truth and beauty and were outstanding people, but they had to make their business work. They had to return a profit; if they didn't, they could go under. And in the eighteenth century there was no limited liability, that is to say, when you went bankrupt you lost everything: your house, all of your property, and even your freedom, since there was a debtor's prison. I've seen many letters following the affairs of a bookseller as they get worse and worse; he doesn't pay his bills and in the end a neighbour or a bill collector writes: 'he left the keys under the door', 'he enrolled in the army', 'he's gone to fight in the American Revolution', 'he's left for Russia', 'his wife and children are begging at the doors of the church'. So when these people lost, they lost everything and they just disappeared. It was a very raw and brutal kind of capitalism. Those who won often won big, and made a lot of money; but if you're a publisher you're not a gentleman, you are a businessman; and the publishers of this famous book, the *Encyclopédie*, were people who basically had to make money. I've been criticized for taking a too brutally economic view of the Enlightenment and the book trade, but I've read so many letters in which they say things such as 'money is the great driving force of everything', and I've watched them scrambling to make money, so that I'm convinced that they were decent people but that they were businessmen, true capitalists in an age of booty capitalism, as some economic historians have called it. So they were willing to do all kinds of things: they would slip spies into the competitor's printing shop, they would steal things, they would speculate when they had their back to the wall in illegal literature and do very dangerous things.

So, yes, it was a business, and it was a business where economic interests were predominant; but what they were selling, in the case of the *Encyclopédie*, for example, was a book that had in it, in its text, the essence of the Enlightenment: it was radical in many ways, with wonderfully daring and shocking things scattered throughout the text, even in its cross-references. My favourite one is in the first volume, the one with the letter A, where there is an article about cannibalism (which is 'anthropophagie' in French), where you get a very straight description of cannibalism: how you make the fire, and put the water in the pot and eat people; then, at the end, it says only one thing in its cross-reference: 'see Eucharist'. And in the volume with the letter E, under 'Eucharist', you get a perfectly orthodox Catholic description of Holy Communion; and then at the end it just says 'see anthropophagie'. That's an extremely daring and irreligious thing to do. So the book they were selling was a very radical book, but they liked to hide it by inserting its radicalism between the lines or through techniques like these cross-references.

What I find fascinating is the combination of a modern, rational enlightened world view with this other kind of modernism which is raw capitalism with people out to make money. I think that in order to understand the eighteenth century and the Enlightenment you need both things: on the one side, you need to understand the texts and read them carefully, to see what is between the lines; and, on the other side, you also need to understand all of the economic and social interests surrounding them. If you could put them together you'd create what I call a social history of ideas, in which the ideas are not treated as if they were simply floating in some atmosphere, detached from social reality. The fascination, I think, of this kind of history is that it can change our notion of history in general, not just of the Enlightenment, by seeing how ideas become part of the everyday world, including the world of economic interests.

In one of your most lively and happy observations about the craft of the historian, you said that the best way for 'capturing the other', for understanding an alien culture, is to start with the most opaque documents. A joke, a proverb, a ritual, or anything in the past that does not make any sense to us is exactly what may enable us to grasp a foreign system of meaning. In your well-known book The Great Cat Massacre, *you have tried precisely to understand what was so funny about that massacre of cats, which made an event so repulsive to us seem the most hilarious experience to a group of eighteenth-century Parisian artisans. Since then you've shown that it was a rule in eighteenth-century France to place philosophical and pornographic books in the same category. Was this another of those unfunny jokes, whose unravelling might allow us to penetrate more deeply into the mentalité of those times?*

Yes, my point was exactly to show this, because I found the expression 'philosophical books' used everywhere in the literature about forbidden literature; and used not only by the publisher and the booksellers, but also by the police and the authors. So it was a kind of code name, but what did it refer to? It turns out that our categories don't coincide with the categories used by people in the eighteenth century at all, so that where we separate, for example, pornography from philosophy, they thought it natural that the two should be fused. There is, for example, something about sex which seems to trigger thinking. I wrote a little essay on pornography once which begins more or less in this way: 'Claude Lévi-Strauss says that most people don't think with abstract concepts, but they think with things; they manipulate objects and they put them together in relation to one another, rather as a handyman works when he repairs a table. This is thinking with the concrete, and so for most people thought is what he calls *la science du concret*, the science of the concrete.' Well, I think that people thought with sex in the same way, they took dirty stories and erotic episodes and then used them as a way to think about the nature of pleasure, the nature of love, the nature of power, and of all sorts of things. And specially, of course, the nature of men and women. So one of the best-sellers of the eighteenth century, the one that comes very close to the top of the list (when I did the research on the forbidden books I systematically measured demand from booksellers for books and came up with a best-seller list) was called *Thérèse philosophe* [Theresa, the philosopher, 1748; discussed in *Forbidden Best-Sellers*]. If you read that book you find real pornography, lots of salacious descriptions of making love, but as soon as the partners have had their orgasms, while they are restoring their energy for the next round of pleasure, they have metaphysical conversations. It's real metaphysics, and, in fact, I've identified some sections of the text just lifted from real philosophical treatises. So that what you see is a mixture of elements that to us are utterly incompatible. So, yes, your question is exactly on target. I found that it was curious that this phrase 'philosophical books' should be used for pornography, and then when I read the pornography I found it simply amazing that there was lots of metaphysics and indeed politics all mixed up with it. I think that's very instructive about the difference, the otherness of the eighteenth century. People simply didn't divide the world up the way we do. And the advantage of book history, of the kind when you do actual research and come up with real results – telling you what people were reading and, to a certain extent, how they were reading it – is that you can get at their way of organizing reality, their way of understanding the world. So, in fact, the interpenetration of politics, pornography and irreligion was to them as natural as killing cats was funny to the workers.

Your works, in general, do not discuss the meaning of the Enlightenment to women. Your study on Thérèse philosophe, *the best-seller in which the main character is a woman, could be considered your first incursion into the field of women's history. Is that correct?*

I think that it's right to say that I never did much work on the history of women and that is a missing dimension in my work. I try to repair that, to a certain extent, in this discussion of *Thérèse philosophe*, which was an anonymous tract that might have been written by the Marquis d'Argens. Not only does it have metaphysics, but I have also interpreted this book as a kind of manifesto for women's liberation. The idea is that women have a right to pleasure, and they have a right to pleasure on their own terms, and not as something dictated to them by men or by the social order. And furthermore, they should control their own bodies. It is a very radical text, not only for its anti-religious views (it's basically atheistic) but also for its views on women, since the heroine, Thérèse, who is a philosopher, doesn't want to have children and doesn't want to get married. Well, refusing the roles of both mother and wife, she was attacking the fundamental condition of women under the old regime. What she wants to live for is her own happiness on her own terms. This is, no doubt, a radical thought experiment and it was not possible for the vast majority of women to put it into practice in the eighteenth century; and yet, you've got a text that actually defines things in those terms. So for me this was a way to try to think a little bit about the condition of women in the past.

The book The Darnton Debate *has been causing quite a stir among the historians of the Enlightenment. Were you unhappy about the publication of this collection of essays organized around your books and articles and do you think that it has helped or hindered the understanding of the relation between the Enlightenment and the Revolution?*

I was certainly flattered that the Voltaire Foundation thought it worth publishing a volume about my work, but I must admit that I winced when I read some of the essays. I thought that some of the contributors had got me wrong – a sobering experience for someone who has attempted to develop the history of reading. Nonetheless, their attacks and my effort at a defence should help to clear up some misunderstandings. Contrary to what some of my critics maintain, I never set out to produce a history of the Enlightenment, much less to debunk the ideas of the *philosophes* or ideas in general. I wanted to create a social history of ideas – that is, to understand the way ideas travelled and 'took' in the society of the old regime. That general enterprise carried me down different paths in my research: the study of attitudes and value systems (at first in a version of the French 'histoire des mentalités', later as an effort to combine history and anthropology); the study of writers and the emergence of the intellectual as a historical phenomenon (life in 'Grub Street' and the policing of literature being central themes); the study of publishing and the book trade (I now am preparing the last volume of a trilogy based on the papers of the Société Typographique de Neuchâtel and related archives in Paris); and the study of public opinion (my latest work concerns news and the media in pre-Revolutionary Paris). In my own contribution to *The Darnton Debate* I tried to explain how these research projects are distinct and how they are related. I especially wanted to disavow the simplistic argument that treats books as self-evident containers of meaning and that finds lines of causality leading directly from the sale of the books to the reading of texts to the formation of public opinion and to revolutionary engagement in the form of action. But having acknowledged those complexities, I would not retreat from my conviction that we need to come up with some basic information by continuous labour in the archives. I still consider it important to learn what the French read and how the books reached them. I think it possible to put some historical questions in a way that can be answered – not definitively, perhaps, but in a manner that approaches 'truth' with a lower-case 't'. 'Truth' is a word that makes historians uncomfortable, as if it carried a commitment to positivism or some form of metaphysics. Nonetheless, I believe we can come to a meaningful understanding of the human condition in the past. Having done time with theorists – especially Clifford Geertz, Pierre Bourdieu, and Michel Foucault – I would not minimize the theoretical issues involved in this kind of work. But I would also emphasize its artisanal aspect – the attempt to follow trails through documents and to put words together in a way that will bring people back to life. A whole world remains to be explored in the archives, and I find it endlessly fascinating.

As you stated, one of your main ambitions in organizing, with Daniel Roche, a collective book about the press in France at the end of the eighteenth century was not so much to celebrate the principles of 1789, but to reappraise the power of the press and to contribute to the discussion of the role of media in public life today. What is, in your view, the role of the printing press in an age of multimedia communication?

One of the sad things is the decline not so much of the book as of the newspaper. I've been invited to I don't know how many conferences on the death of the book, the end of literature, etc. so that I'm beginning to believe that the book is very much alive. On the other hand, newspapers are dying, and television is elbowing aside newspapers as they used to exist. I once played with the idea of doing a study, as I said, of newspapers in the 1920s. It turned out that there were twenty-seven daily newspapers in New York

City in English, not to mention other languages. There were three in Yiddish alone. That was amazing. Today there are two or three daily newspapers in New York. From twenty-seven to two or three, it's a real change. And if it's true, as it's reported, that most citizens of the United States watch television for five or six hours a day, then we are indeed living in a world that has been transformed by this new medium. So, if I were to try to understand print as a force in the modern world I would have to look systematically at the competing media, and it seems to me that the impact of television on the way people think of the world is enormous. I mean, some semi-literate people in very remote parts of the United States follow events in Asia and Europe, and even know where the countries are now, in a way that was unthinkable twenty, thirty, forty years ago. So it seems to me that the newspaper is not what it was at all. That doesn't mean that it isn't important, but that it's important in a different way. I think there are, so to speak, circles within circles and that the influence of something like a newspaper is translated through different social layers, so that you get key people in the world of magazines who read the newspapers, key people who are television producers or whatever who also read them, and then apply what they read to their own television broadcasts, or magazines, or whatever. So a process of refracting takes place, and in that way journals or newspapers read by very few people can have a considerable influence. It seems to me, then, that to understand the way the media operate in today's culture, you need to look at the whole spectrum of the media, and of course you need to understand the way our culture, as a culture system, hangs together and often falls apart. That's beyond my understanding. I'm not someone who has worked on contemporary things, but certainly as a newspaper reporter I've felt all kinds of constraints that determined what finally appeared in print in the daily newspaper.

And going back to the eighteenth century, I think that I also need to broaden my scope and to look at all the other media. That's why I now plan to study songs, graffiti, images, and specially rumours and what were called 'public noises' in eighteenth-century Paris. All of this will point towards a book that is probably many years away, but a book that will be about the whole package, the whole ensemble of the media just in Paris, and the way they intercepted and transmitted messages. So I want to begin with a history of communication, with a systematic attempt to reconstruct the communicative systems of the old regime, and then to go on to a second stage, which will be a more intense study of the way these media construed a political crisis in France on the eve of the Revolution. That will, I hope, turn into a more narrative presentation of the events of the 1780s and the running commentary on the events that accompanied it. So I want to try to put this together in a general, large-scale book that will offer an in-depth understanding of the great founding event of modern history, the French Revolution. It's not going to explain, of course, the whole nature of the Revolution, but I think it will help us to understand the way the old regime fell apart and a lot of the revolutionary energy that was released in 1789. I'm shifting in my answer from your question and I'm already back in the eighteenth century and away from the present, but I do think that the idea is to be systematic, to look not simply at one aspect of a cultural system but to reconstruct the entirety, all the interconnections of what was in fact a series of systems of communication. In other words, I suppose I'd be moving from the history of the book in the strict sense of the phrase to a larger history of communication, which will in turn relate to the classic problem of the outbreak of the French Revolution. But I hope that other people who are interested in other things, in other revolutions, for instance, might also be interested in this attempt to conceptualize a history of communication and then use it for their own purposes.

Joseph Addison, the British essayist so admired in the French Enlightenment, says in the first issue of the Spectator *that readers are extremely curious about the lives of the authors of the books they read. Not only does this knowledge increase the pleasure of reading, but it is also extremely helpful for the understanding of the author's work. Following Addison's advice, would you like to satisfy the curiosity of your readers and tell them something about the man behind the historian Robert Darnton?*

I think that it would be fair to describe me as someone who is very much a family man. I have three children aged now twenty-two, twenty-six and twenty-nine, who have already finished their university studies. So I'm now intensely concerned and interested in how they are going to find a place in the adult world. I mean, it is a little bit frightening but it's also very exciting to watch them and to try to help them make their way in really rather difficult circumstances. Of course they have many advantages because they were brought up with bread always on the table and they were given a good education, I think. So I'm not really worried about their being able to find a job, but I am concerned that they get some satisfaction out of their lives, that they live life fully on their own terms, not on my terms. That may sound awfully abstract, but it is my main concern, really.

As for myself, I have a rather international life. I'm now living half-time in England and half-time in America, which is quite an unusual thing, and I have many connections with France in particular, and also to a certain extent with Germany. I try, however, to avoid travelling too much, jumping from one airport to another, because I find that unsatisfying. I want to talk with people and stay in a place long enough to make contacts, and I'm also extremely concerned with doing research and writing. But I find it is possible to combine that with travel. In other words, I think that scholarship in my case, and in the case of many others, has become an international enterprise and that we don't identify simply with a country, a home country. I mean, I hate nationalism and I believe in the idea of the Republic of Letters, a republic that has no police force and no boundaries, where everyone can say what they have to say, and you have a kind of open debate; so the fact that I can be accepted as a genuine fellow debater by French, Germans and English, and not simply catalogued as an American – because I know there is much anti-Americanism about – is for me a liberating feeling.

What else to say? American university life is very different from university life in Europe or, I think, in Latin America. We live on campuses and the campuses are, so to speak, oases in what is sometimes a cultural desert. The oasis is very rich: you have art museums, you have film theatres, you have your own professional theatre, in our case an amateur theatre as well, not to mention sports facilities, constant lectures and so on. And even housing is provided by the university. So that it is a very intense, rich existence in which to raise a family and to have an interesting life. But it has a disadvantage in that it cuts you off, to a certain extent, from the rest of the citizenry. And there is a danger in the United States, not perhaps in Brazil, of the college professor or the intellectual not sharing the same cultural universe as the rest of the population. When I wander off the campus I suddenly find myself not really speaking the same language as other people. That is why I often feel much more comfortable in France than I do in America. Princeton, my home town, is really a university town, very small and, as I say, an oasis. And just a few miles to the north of it or to the south of it are large cities with terrible slums and deep racial problems. I feel that I have done nothing to help that situation and sometimes, I must admit, when I get on a plane heading for Paris I feel guilty, because I'm enjoying this intellectually rich life but I'm not doing anything really for the quasi-literate or illiterate people trapped in the slums. So there is a little bit of bad conscience that accompanies me in these travels.

I guess a final point I could mention is that I find, now that I'm older and that there's been some recognition of my work, I do have a civic existence. I'm still not improving life in the slums, alas, but I'm very much involved in more public activities, like the work of the New York Public Library where I am a trustee. This library, unlike many others, is a democratic organization open to everyone; anyone can walk off the street and order a book, without any need to show a card or to pay any money. It's an enormous library, the second largest in the United States, a fabulous place that has traditionally been the place where immigrants and poor people came and educated themselves. Well, there is a great attempt by the trustees to keep up this tradition, which means raising money, developing lecture series, organizing exhibitions, and so on. And

I have devoted a great deal of my time to doing this. I find I also spend a lot of my time outside the campus as a member of boards of trustees of institutions and of groups that are doing things like, for instance, trying to publish the works of the founding fathers of America, the papers of Thomas Jefferson and Benjamin Franklin. Another thing I've done while I was president of the International Society for Eighteenth-century Studies was to create a summer seminar called the East–West Seminar to bring together young scholars less than forty years old from Eastern Europe and from the West, and this even before the Berlin wall fell. Its mission was to create a running dialogue between East and West, when the two were completely separated. It is also an attempt to give younger scholars a month in a great city like Paris, with no strings attached. They are given a generous book allowance, everything is paid for them, and they get to know scholars of their own age from other countries. This has actually occupied a great deal of my time over the last years. In other words, I find that along with this gypsy existence of travelling to different countries and doing research and teaching there, has come a kind of citizenship in the Republic of Letters that is international, that involves institutions like this where you try to bring people together and to reach out beyond the world of the campus to ordinary people and people in other countries. I think I can do a little bit in that respect; how much I don't know, but I do sense that the nation is no longer the only unit of scholarship and that people like me are international, not in some rather glitzy sense of the word, but in a deeper sense of trying to work out a genuine collaboration with people in other countries, so that we develop a common culture, even though we maintain our original cultural identity. In other words, when I talk about internationalism I'm not thinking of superficial, glamorous cosmopolitanism. I'm talking about genuine collaboration. Given the conditions of the twenty-first century – with cheap travel and computer contacts – we can really work across national borders much more than before; and of course I'd hope that it would be between North and South, as well as East and West. It remains to be seen.

Oxford, July 1996
(*Interview updated and enlarged, May and June 1999*)

SELECT BIBLIOGRAPHY

Mesmerism and the End of the Enlightenment in France (Cambridge, Mass., Harvard University Press, 1968); translated into German, French, Japanese, Dutch, Portuguese, Russian.

The Business of Enlightenment: A Publishing History of the Encyclopédie (Cambridge, Mass., Harvard University Press, 1979); translated into French, Italian, German, Portuguese.

The Literary Underground of the Old Regime (Cambridge, Mass., Harvard University Press, 1982); translated into Swedish, German, Dutch, Italian, Japanese, Portuguese.

The Great Cat Massacre and Other Episodes in French Cultural History (New York, Basic Books, 1984); translated into French, German, Dutch, Swedish, Danish, Italian, Spanish, Portuguese, Japanese, Hungarian, Korean.

The Kiss of Lamourette: Reflections on Cultural History (New York, Norton, 1989); translated into German, Dutch, Portuguese, Italian, Japanese.

Edition et sédition. L'Univers de la littérature clandestine au XVIIIe siècle (Paris, Gallimard, 1991); translated into German, Italian, Dutch, Japanese, Spanish and Portuguese.

Berlin Journal, 1989–1990 (New York, Norton, 1991); translated into German, Dutch, French, Italian.

Gens de lettres, gens du livre (Paris, Éditions Odile Jacob, 1992).

The Forbidden Best-Sellers of Pre-Revolutionary France (New York, Norton, 1995); translated into Italian, Portuguese, Swedish, German.

The Corpus of Clandestine Literature in France, 1769–1789 (New York, Norton, 1995).

The Darnton Debate: Books and Revolution in the Eighteenth Century, ed. Haydn T. Mason (Oxford, Voltaire Foundation, 1998).

8

Carlo Ginzburg

Few historians at work today are as original as Carlo Ginzburg, few write as well as he does, and even fewer share his remarkable breadth of interests. Ginzburg, who for the last few years has been teaching at the University of California and dividing his year between Los Angeles and Bologna, was born in 1939 into a family of Russian Jews who had settled in Turin. His father, Leone Ginzburg, who died in a fascist prison in 1944 when Carlo was just five years old, had been a professor of Russian literature, while his mother, Natalia Ginzburg[1], became one of the most famous and respected Italian authors of the twentieth century. Having given up the idea of devoting his life to literature, Ginzburg chose history instead, influenced especially by the Italian historian Delio Cantimori[2], known for his pioneering work on sixteenth-century Italian heretics. The academic community was soon astonished by the originality of Ginzburg's intellectual production. 'An intellectual to watch!' as one American reviewer remarked in the early 1970s.

His first book, *I benandanti* (*The Night Battles: Witchcraft and Agrarian Cults in the Sixteenth and Seventeenth Centuries*) published when he was only twenty-seven, was an extremely polemical and innovative work. The starting point for this study was the disconcerting reply given to the Inquisitorial court by a group of Friuli peasants accused of witchcraft:

1   Natalia Ginzburg (1916–91), author of *Lessico famigliare* (translated as *The Things We Used to Say*); *Le voci della sera* (translated as *Voices in the Evening*); *La famiglia Manzoni* (translated as *The Manzoni Family*); *Tutti i nostri ieri* (translated as *Dead Yesterdays*); etc.
2   Delio Cantimori (1904–66), author of *Eretici italiani del '500* (1939), *Prospettive di storia ereticale italiana* (1960).

calling themselves the *benandanti* ('wellfarers'), they said they were do-gooders who fought witches at night armed with stalks of fennel against the witches' sorghum reeds. This unexpected response, confounding the inquisitors' expectations, was the basis for this work which has made a notable contribution to witchcraft studies.

However, it was *Il formaggio e i vermi* (*The Cheese and the Worms*), a study of the cosmology of a sixteenth-century miller (also interrogated by the Inquisition on charges of heresy), which made Carlo Ginzburg internationally famous, almost overnight, in 1976. Again, while researching the Inquisition trials in Friuli, Ginzburg had come across the intriguing case of the miller Menocchio, who differed from most of the suspects, who spoke unwillingly, in that he adored talking. So the garrulous peasant used his trial as an excellent opportunity to explain to an audience from outside his village his view of the cosmos as an enormous cheese full of worms. According to Ginzburg, although Menocchio was literate and had read a few books, he could be seen as a spokesman for an essentially traditional, oral and popular culture. Citing Gramsci and using as an epigraph a passage from Brecht's 'Worker reading history' – 'Who built seven-gated Thebes?' – Ginzburg's book was acclaimed as a manifesto of 'history from below' and historical anthropology. From then onwards, too, despite his dislike of labels, he became known as a leading writer of so-called 'micro-history', a term which soon afterwards became fashionable when it was used as the title for a series of books published by Einaudi, edited by Ginzburg and his friend Giovanni Levi.

Other books by Ginzburg deal with the painter Piero della Francesca (1981), the history of the idea of the witches' sabbath over the last 2,000 years in Europe and Asia (*Ecstasies*), and a tragic episode in the recent history of Italian justice and the relation between the role of the judge and that of the historian (*The Judge and the Historian*). These reveal the diversity of topics and approaches used by Ginzburg in his work, making him a difficult historian to classify – something he finds very satisfying.

Ginzburg has published much of his ground-breaking work not as books but in the form of essays. The best-known of these, translated into thirteen languages, is intriguingly entitled 'Spie' (Clues), and itself provides clues to an understanding of Ginzburg's whole *oeuvre*. In this brilliant essay he stresses the importance of the apparently insignificant detail, the seemingly trivial phrase or gesture which leads the investigator – a detective like Sherlock Holmes, a psychoanalyst like Freud or a historian like Ginzburg himself – to make important discoveries. Using this special detective talent and almost always starting from apparently trivial details, he writes with elegance, verve and enthusiasm on topics and areas of knowledge about which he initially knew nothing. As he himself has remarked, when he is about to learn something that is totally new to him, he experiences an intense feeling of what he calls 'the euphoria of ignorance', which he compares to the pleasure a skier must feel when skiing on fresh snow.

Ginzburg gave this interview in his flat in Bologna. At first it seemed rather strange to be interviewing someone who has written at length about interrogations conducted by sixteenth-century inquisitors and twentieth-century police officers, but the interview soon became more like a conversation between friends. Always extremely pleasant, spontaneous and expressive, Ginzburg spoke for a long time with his characteristic enthusiasm about his intellectual trajectory and choices, his attitude to fame, his views on the role of the historian, his opinions of Foucault, Borges, postmodernism, and so on.

MARIA LÚCIA PALLARES-BURKE   *Which aspects of your origins and education do you consider crucial for the understanding of your ideas and interests?*

CARLO GINZBURG   There are many but, being a historian, I'm sceptical about the teleological approach that sees a sort of straight line going from the childhood of an individual to his or her maturity. I may not be able to recognize the crucial elements in my life, so I'm not the best judge. But having said that, I can try to tell you something about my background. Except for my maternal grandmother, I have a Jewish origin on both my father and my mother's side. My father was born in Odessa, came to Italy as a child, grew up in Turin and became an Italian citizen in his youth. He was extremely attached to his Italian identity as well as to his Russian identity. He studied Russian literature, translated Gogol's *Taras Bulba* and Tolstoy's *Anna Karenina* into Italian, and as a very young man became *libero docente* in Russian literature. I recall all this because immediately after that the Italian fascist regime demanded an oath of allegiance from all the university professors and my father refused to take such an oath; in fact, it was at this point that he abandoned his academic career and became involved in the anti-fascist movement. For him, to fight against fascism was part of being Italian (he had become an Italian citizen a few years before). Arrested in 1934 (at the age of twenty-five) as part of a small left-wing but non-communist group, he received a four-year prison sentence. Released under an amnesty after two years in jail, he was involved with Giulio Einaudi in the founding of the Einaudi publishing house, which was to become the leading anti-fascist publisher of the time. When Italy entered the war in 1940, as an anti-fascist he was sent into residence under surveillance with the whole family to a small village in the Abruzzi. So I, who was born in Turin, grew up in that village, where we lived for three years. The only dialect that I ever spoke was the dialect of that village, which I then forgot entirely. When Mussolini was arrested and the regime collapsed in 1943, my father went to Rome to return to his political activities as the director of an underground newspaper. Immediately after the Nazi troops occupied the city, though, he was arrested, recognized as a Jew and an anti-fascist and died in jail at the beginning of 1944, when I was five years old. Then we moved to Florence and ultimately to Turin where my mother – who had already published her first novel, *La strada che va in città,* under the pseudonym Alessandra Tornimparte – since after 1938 Jews were not allowed to publish – started working with Einaudi. It was also for this publishing house that she translated the first volume of Proust's *Recherche* into Italian and it was with Einaudi that she published all her works.

If I think about my life and about my choices as a historian, the question I put to myself (or, in fact, to anybody else) is: which choices were the crucial ones? In a way, it's like a chess game, in which the crucial moves take place early in the match. Obviously, there are crucial elements we don't decide, like our genetic inheritance, being born a male or female, and so forth. But when I select a moment in which I made a sort of crucial decision I can see that there was some freedom of choice, but also a lot of constraints. On the other hand, there was an enormous amount of unawareness. In fact, I'm always struck by the way in which all the crucial decisions in one's life – like falling in love or choosing a profession – are taken with blind eyes, with insufficient information. We think we are really choosing, but retrospectively one discovers that there was a powerful push, a drive that was not related to a real knowledge of the options. My choice to be a historian can illustrate this. When I was an adolescent I wanted to become a novelist like my mother, but soon discovered that I would be a bad one. Well, my involvement with writing as such is something that is still very much with me, as if my passion for writing fiction was diverted to my passion for historical writing. In a way it's like a dam or a ditch: when you block something there is a stronger push into a neighbouring direction, all the elements which were blocked becoming part of that new drive. The same happened with my wish to become a painter. Again, I soon discovered that I wouldn't be a good one and left all my paintings behind when we moved from one apartment to another; but this passion for painting became part of me, as if the negative moves were transformed into positive moves. I even thought of becoming an art historian, which I eventually tried in some way to do later.

You once confessed that the idea of becoming a historian never crossed your mind when you were an adolescent. All the same, you became a precocious historian who published a path-breaking article at the age of twenty-one. Were there any encounters which made you want to spend your life in the study of the past?

As I said, I used to read novels mostly, but when I was finishing the *liceo* I started reading Benedetto Croce's *History of Europe in the Nineteenth*

Century. The book disappointed me (other works by Croce, like his *Logic*, proved to be much more exciting). It had been given to my father by the author with a handwritten dedication, 'Con grato animo' (with gratitude). Some time later I discovered that my father, who had been a disciple and admirer of Croce, had also helped him for the section on nineteenth-century Russia. So my initial involvement with history was, in a way, mediated by the memory of my father and his intellectual activities and commitments. He had a lot of different intellectual interests: a philologist by training, he was also extremely interested in philosophy, criticism, literature and history. He wrote, for instance, about the relations between Garibaldi and Herzen, the Russian revolutionary. At the end of my school career I decided to take the entrance examination for the Scuola Normale in Pisa and spent the summer reading Croce, Gramsci, Auerbach's *Mimesis* and so forth. Through Leo Spitzer, Erich Auerbach and Gianfranco Contini[3], I became familiar with a textual approach based on a close reading of tiny fragments of a larger whole. So an approach implying close reading was already part of my intellectual experience before I even started my university studies.

When I was accepted in Pisa, I hesitated for some time between art history and literature – I was even tempted by philosophy. I started by studying literary criticism, but then, in my second year at the Scuola Normale, Delio Cantimori came for a week to give a seminar on Jacob Burckhardt's *Reflections on World History*. I vividly remember the first time I saw him. He was a large, white-bearded man, dressed in a sort of nineteenth-century way. I thought he was the oldest man I had ever seen. He was then only fifty-three years old. He dressed like his teacher, the philosopher Giovanni Gentile, a supporter of the fascist regime who was killed by the communist partisans in 1944.

Cantimori's seminar started like this. He asked around the table how many of us could read German, which only a few of us could. Then he began to compare the German text with several translations in different languages. After a week, we had read, I think, twelve lines. That was a most amazing experience, which still inspires me. Recently I started my seminar in UCLA saying to my students: 'In Italy there is a movement called "slow food", as opposed to fast food. My seminar will be an experiment in slow reading.' In the meantime I discovered a quotation, a sentence by Roman Jakobson saying 'philology is the art of slow reading', the source of which I later discovered to be Nietzsche. I liked very much this idea of slow reading. So Cantimori represented a definite turning-point for me, although I did not decide immediately to commit myself to history. Then Arsenio Frugoni, the medievalist, who taught at the Scuola Normale,

---

3   Gianfranco Contini (b. 1912), Italian literary critic, author of *Varianti e altre linguistica* (1970).

suggested that I could write a paper on the *Annales*, which was not so obvious a theme in 1958. When I started reading this journal I became fascinated by Marc Bloch and read *The Royal Touch* in the first 1924 edition – the reprint came a few years later. That was a real surprise, because until then I thought that historical books were basically boring, and this one was different. I was so impressed by it that I remember meeting Cantimori again in Pisa and saying that I wanted to work on Bloch.

Another prominent historian who fascinated me deeply, and whom I met through my family connections, was Franco Venturi, who had been a friend of my father's (Venturi had also been actively involved in the resistance). It was through him that I had my first paid job, translating Bloch's *French Rural History* for Einaudi. Once again, I was confronted with a choice: either to work with Venturi on some eighteenth-century topic, or with Cantimori, whose main interest was in the Italian heretics of the late Renaissance. The two men were very different from each other from all possible perspectives, starting from the political. Venturi had been actively involved in the Resistance; after the war he spent some time in Moscow working as a cultural attaché for the Italian government; he was a Russophile and a committed anti-communist. Cantimori had been a *fascista di sinistra*, a left-wing fascist; then sometime in the 1930s, he had become close to the communist party, which he joined after the war. I decided to work with Cantimori. That was a decision whose importance I didn't realize at the time. When I now look at it in retrospect I think that I was attracted by what in Cantimori was unfamiliar, distant, even sometimes painfully distant from me. Yes, I think distance was the crucial thing. Maybe I say this because I've just published a collection of essays about this topic of distance, *Occhiacci di legno*.

But now, thinking about Cantimori's approach and style, I would say that these elements were even more important for my decision than his political orientation. There was something about his intellectual style, full of allusions and innuendoes, that I didn't share at all and against which I was constantly reacting. I greatly admired him; he has been the historian of my time who has taught me most. In fact, I think that we learn more from someone who is different, who is distant from us. In retrospect, I would say that in my decision to work with Cantimori instead of with Venturi I was reacting against a too narrow allegiance to anti-fascism, to something that was at the very core of my background and upbringing. In an article on Dumézil I published in the 1980s,[4] I tried to articulate this idea, reflecting on the distinction between questions and answers and about the tendency of the left to ignore a question if the answer is unacceptable, not to say despicable. But even racism is an answer – scientifically untenable and

4   Georges Dumézil (1898–1988), French scholar, famous for his comparative studies of Latin, Celtic and ancient Indian cultures.

morally and politically despicable – to a perfectly legitimate question about the relationship between biology and culture.

You have referred to your taste for significant detail and have often been praised for your gift for story-telling. Would you say that your narrative style is related to the novelist you would like to have been, to your wish to follow in the footsteps of your mother? And what, in your view, is the relation between historians and novelists?

I think that my mother's example was important for me, but it also shows how constraints don't work in a definite direction. You can become an atheist because you are the son of a priest, but you can also become a saint. The outcome is predictable only retrospectively. The fact that I am the son of Natalia Ginzburg could have worked as a direct impulse or as an impulse to resist. You can see a connection, but what kind of connection is it?

As to the notion of narration in history, I think it has long been modelled on late nineteenth-century novels, but if one thinks about twentieth-century novels, like Proust's or Joyce's, you can see how the distinction between fiction and non-fiction can become blurred, even in the novel.

I'm very fond of thinking of the relation between fiction and history as implying mutual challenge and competition. History was a challenge for novelists like Balzac, for instance, who reacted to this challenge saying: 'I'll be the historian of the nineteenth century.' But then, after him, we have novelists like Stendhal and Flaubert who challenged historians in their turn. The relation between history and fiction is one of competition in which each challenges, responds to and learns from the other.

Who are your main interlocutors? Is there anyone you imagine as looking over your shoulder as you write, and criticizing or discussing it with you?

I'm involved in a constant intellectual exchange with a group of friends, and there are times when even after writing a single sentence I think about one of them reacting to it. Interaction with people is very important to me; but on a general level I think that too much communication is bad. Many years ago I suddenly had the feeling that I was somewhat in the mainstream and I felt rather uncomfortable about it. My first book, *I benandanti*, for some time had no audience, and there is certainly something very good in being isolated. This happened when I published a book called *The Cheese and the Worms*, which was an immediate success – although (and possibly because), it was less innovative than my first book, *I benandanti*. The same happened when I published my piece on 'Clues'. There was an immediate reaction, in part, I think, because the article was simultaneously published in a miscellaneous collection of essays (*Crisi della ragione*) as well as, without footnotes, in a small left-wing magazine, and this probably attracted a much wider audience. I remember that for two weeks I was inundated by calls from all over Italy, from Catania, Milan and elsewhere inviting me to speak about 'Clues' – which I did for a while. It was fun. But I also felt the danger of being swallowed up in a sort of flux of communication, losing all the advantages and the fun of being isolated.

Are you trying to say that there is something in success that can be disastrous for an intellectual?

Yes, there is something very dangerous about success – even in the case of a moderate success like mine. It's like a tiger that should be controlled. As in the case of gambling, there is a sort of temptation to repeat oneself in order to repeat the success. I myself am a failed gambler. I played roulette maybe five or six times and loved it. Once in Las Vegas I bet on a single number and won. I was terrified and fled, having realized how strong the drive was. I mention this because there is a gambling element in my research, a sort of temptation to go on to higher stakes, which can be dangerous.

Looking back, I would say that I was afraid of success and of being in a sort of mainstream, and this made me decide to resist. I agree that there is a kind of contradiction involved in all this, because I like talking, I like to communicate, I like writing a lot, I like very much to be translated, I love success. But on the other hand, I committed myself to research projects that would take me back to the periphery. I'm not saying that I thought of a conscious strategy to isolate myself again, but I soon realized that this was really the case. Maybe I'm wrong, but my perception is that this happened to me twice. First, the success of the essay on clues seemed to invite me to play the role of 'tuttologo', a derogatory Italian word meaning someone who writes about everything, who comments on all sorts of different issues. The essay was, in fact, so broad that it generated (it seemed to me) that kind of public expectation, which I felt I had to resist. All of a sudden I found myself immersed in a piece of research on Piero della Francesca – an unexpected revival of my interests in art history. And then I started a long-term project which I had postponed for some time: an offspring of *I benandanti*. The book I published after fifteen years – *Ecstasies* – disappointed many critics. And since then, I've become more and more erratic in my curiosities, more and more perplexed, as you can see from the essays that were collected in *Occhiacci di legno* (*Wooden Eyes*).

Your work sometimes reveals a vision of the world as an interweaving of texts and traditions that reminds one of Jorge Luis Borges [1899–1986]. Has he inspired you in any way?

My immediate answer would be: No. I read Borges in the early 1960s and enjoyed some of his pieces quite a lot. But I think he is a bit overrated. He was, I would say, an excellent second-class writer. There is a sort of self-indulgence in much of his writing; he decided not to take risks. But I might have been affected by Borges via Italo Calvino, who had a great impact on me, both as a person and as a writer. In his later writings Calvino was much influenced by Borges and maybe the Borges–Calvino influence has been deeper on me than I'm able to recognize for the moment.

A writer is somebody who is able to make us aware of certain dimensions of reality. This is the cognitive side of fiction, of which I became aware through Calvino (and through my mother since my childhood). What we call 'Kafkaesque' is a dimension of twentieth-century reality which was previously unknown – and unseen. I have been told that one of Kafka's nieces, who survived the war, once said: 'Uncle Franz was too optimistic.'

My latest book includes one essay entitled 'Ecce', in which I develop a topic which fascinated me from the start. I remember Luisa, my wife, asking me at the time what I was thinking of, and I used to reply: 'I am thinking of Jesus.' I became really obsessed with Jesus. I started from a fact which is well known to scholars, but not much spoken about outside scholarly circles: that is, that Jesus being born from a virgin was the result of a prophecy mediated by a mistake in translation. This led me to another well-known topic: the role of fulfilled prophecies in the gospels. The implications of this topic are far-reaching (to say the least). Well, the idea that a mistranslation can generate a reality is quite a paradox. But if you think about the sanctuaries to the Virgin spread all over the world, all the people who believe in the Virgin, the cults and everything else that was born from it, you see that a mistranslation can be a driving force and create realities. One might say: this is Borges. I would say on the contrary that this is reality and not Borges, but that he can certainly make us aware of it. It is in this sense that we can say that there is a Borgian side of reality.

I think it is important to emphasize that this is not a question of debunking. The debunking element is just one side of it. The other side is the compassion element, in the etymological sense of 'suffering with': a sort of empathy that tries to understand why people have the beliefs they have. This is a distinction I learned to make by reading Bloch's *Royal Touch*. On the one hand, Bloch was willing to unveil the conspiracy and to show that behind the English and French kings healing scrofula there was a conscious political strategy. But, on the other hand, Bloch was trying to understand why those poor people, beggars and women, made those long pilgrimages in order to be healed. The idea of working on both sides seems to me to be crucial in writing history. And if there is a contradiction in this, it is because reality is itself contradictory.

You have said that it is crucial for you to reach a wide audience. What would you say is the relevance of the history you write for a non-professional public?

I definitely recall that when I started to work as a historian, I consciously decided to write books simultaneously addressed to a professional and a non-professional audience. Simultaneously, that is without making any compromise in terms of rigour, footnotes and so forth. I don't know whether I achieved this. Recently the game became more complicated, since I began to collect in book form (as in the case of *Occhiacci di legno*) pieces which had been originally addressed to a more or less professional audience.

There is a paradox about writing. On the one hand, I try to control the reactions of my readers as much as possible. For instance, I am obsessed with punctuation: the different rhythms it creates are crucial for the way one perceives a text and gives it a meaning. On the other hand, there is no means of controlling the way in which people from different backgrounds will react to their readings, of knowing in which context my texts will be placed. This is why I have a somewhat ambiguous feeling when I see a book of mine being translated. On the one hand I am delighted, but on the other I feel that to a certain extent I will lose control of my writing, which besides being turned into another language will be read in a framework which I am often unaware of. Years ago I discovered an example of the strange way *The Cheese and the Worms* has been read, when I met John Murra, a specialist on the Andes, at a conference in Cornell. He told me that a group of his students in Lima who were trying to revive Quechua were using my book as a piece of evidence for an enterprise which involved, in their case, a clear political commitment. How could I ever foresee this sort of reading?

You have written about an amazing number of issues that range, for instance, from Mesopotamian diviners to Pope John Paul II, from sixteenth-century heretics to Leonardo da Vinci and Voltaire. How would you explain this encyclopaedic curiosity and this breathtaking productivity?

I am aware that this is not very usual. I'm definitely not an expert, and, in fact, I like to say that I'm an expert in anything. I know that some people would say that I am an expert on witchcraft, but this is not true either because after some time I didn't follow what was going on in that domain. So I'm not really an expert, because I'm involved with so many things, in so many different projects, which means that I'm ignorant about lots of things, about nearly everything, including the topic I'm writing on at the moment, or wrote about in the past. Actually, I've been thinking a lot about the relative advantage of being ignorant, of coming to a field from outside. I think more and more that the experts, including myself, of course, are ultimately blind to many things; the truth is that after some time we are all unable to see things in a fresh way. That is why I find that it is not absurd to shift to a domain which one knows nothing about, because then one might be able to ask significant questions which have been missed by experts. That is something I like doing a lot. Obviously, there is a price to be paid. On the one side, there is the question of competence. I know, for instance, that I'll make mistakes, that I'll say something that is naïve and so forth. On the other side, there is the problem of the reception, something that I noticed only recently when I realized that the specialists might not notice what I was saying. A reviewer of *Ecstasies* said more or less the following: 'I've read the book until page 213 [let's say] but the rest falls outside my competence.' Other people reviewed only the last section of the book. So I hope that *Occhiacci di legno*, a book that deals with so many themes, approaches and disciplines, will also get a professional audience, but I'm not sure.

The 'euphoria of ignorance', as you said, has prevented you from becoming a specialist. Would you, then, describe yourself as a historical essayist? And if so, what would you say to those who criticize the essay form for being superficial?

A historical essayist? No, definitely not. But certainly I've been more and more involved in writing essays, and much taken by the possibilities opened up by the essay as a form. I think that in this (as in much else) I have been influenced by Momigliano.[5] I have been lucky in getting involved in a kind of pupil–teacher relationship with him quite late in my life, and just at the end of his. It's partly from him that I got this passion for the essay form.

Thinking about the two kinds of intellectuals which Isaiah Berlin distinguished – the hedgehogs and the foxes[6] – which one is Carlo Ginzburg?

I think I'm becoming more and more a fox, but ultimately I regard myself as a hedgehog. Notwithstanding the variety of the topics I have been working on, I am still trying to cope with the implications of my initial work on witchcraft based on Inquisition trials. It was like fieldwork for an anthropologist. Even my lasting interest in methodological problems has been generated by that experience: by the challenge to read between the lines, to read those court records against the grain, against the way in

---

5   The Italian historian Arnaldo Momigliano (1908–87) was one of the most important classical scholars of the twentieth century.
6   Isaiah Berlin (1909–1997), *The Hedgehog and the Fox: An Essay on Tolstoy's View of History*, London, Weidenfeld and Nicolson, 1967 (1st edn, 1953).

which they had been constructed for the Inquisitors' aims. This is exactly what Marc Bloch suggested in *The Historian's Craft* when he refers to a sort of devious strategy for reading medieval hagiography as evidence for the history of medieval agriculture.

Although you were not trained as an art historian, you have more than once written about art: about Piero della Francesca, Titian, Jean Fouquet etc. What attracts you to this field? Do you think that the professional art historians fail to notice something that 'ordinary' historians can see?

Maybe. You know a quote by Clemenceau saying that war is too serious a subject to be left to the generals? I think that you can play with the same argument in different domains. So maybe art is too serious a subject to be left to the art historians (and history to historians, of course). You see, I'm not merely interested in paintings, I love them. I really love them. Actually, while I am in a library waiting for a book to be delivered, I'll probably be reading art historical journals, instead of historical ones. Although I approach a painting from a historical angle, my first reaction is a visual one. It is only then that there comes the attempt to translate visual curiosities or visual questions into historical questions. Learning to love a painter is for me a great experience, like meeting a new person. I still remember when, years and years ago, I was still blind to Rubens (which seems incredible to me now), the thrill in discovering him as a great painter. When I wander around Italy looking for new places, tiny villages, new churches, I have a very strange feeling that when I die most of Italy will still be unknown to me. One would need thirty lives in order to see all those places. And then, besides Italy, there is the rest of the whole world.

When I said before that I felt completely isolated for many years, I should have added that only in the Warburg Institute did I feel at home. My frequent visits, in the 1960s, to this centre for the study of the classical tradition – I worked there for a whole month on *I benandanti* – was very important for my intellectual development. But visual evidence is something so rich that it can be approached from different perspectives, and the gap (which is so wide in the USA nowadays), between the social-historical approach to visual evidence and that of a connoisseur is absurd and damaging. I'm fascinated by connoisseurship, that is, by the fact that there is something about visual evidence that can be translated into a sort of basic historical statement. When a connoisseur shows that a painting was made here, in such a place, at such a time, and maybe by such a person it is clear that the gap I mentioned is absurd because at the very core of connoisseurship is a basic historical statement. To show that a still life with a watermelon is by the painter who painted a portrait means that behind this sort of basic structural similarity there is something deeper that can be detected. In retrospect the relationship between morphology and history seems to me like a thread running throughout my entire work.

You have always described yourself as a great admirer of Marc Bloch. Considering that he strongly denounced what he called the 'idol of origins', how would you justify your work on the witches' sabbaths, in which you go back more than 2,000 years in the search for origins? Were you saying that, contrary to Bloch, the question of origins is not, in this case, the wrong question to ask?

In my view the target of Bloch's criticism was not the search for origins. What he criticized was an undue extension of this concern with origins; in other words, he rejected the idea of transforming an explanation of the early stages of an institution into one for the reasons for its persistence. What might have given the impression that I was contradicting Bloch is that I was very much interested in what Lévi-Strauss had to say about structure versus history and so was, in a way, opposing him to Bloch by giving so much weight to structural elements. But, in fact, my intention in *Ecstasies* was to combine the two elements, the structural with the historical, so as to show them in interaction: a goal which I attained only partially. I started with an event – the so-called conspiracy involving Christians, Muslims and Jews in 1331 – and then I tried to show what made this event possible by looking at something broader. So I was at the same time thinking of complementing micro-history with macro-history, and also events with structures: four elements involved in a very complex kind of interaction. I don't know whether I succeeded in showing this; I agree that this book is possibly the most ambitious I ever wrote, maybe too ambitious. However, there was a challenge there, which I decided to confront. Let me put the challenge in this way: if I had been lucky enough to discover the *benandanti*, I had also to make sense of them as much as possible.

Your work has attracted not only a great number of admirers and followers, but a great many critics as well. Have any criticisms of your work helped you with the development and rethinking of your ideas?

Yes, all of them – including criticism from inside. I have a sort of fascination with the devil's advocate strategy, something that was already with me but was reinforced by my conversations with Italo Calvino. The idea of learning from the enemy, of being myself my most formidable enemy appeals to me enormously – also because it's such a difficult task. (The risk of being self-indulgent is always there.) Even a silly criticism is ultimately instructive because it says something about one's audience, about the context in which one works. Constructive criticism is something different, of course. Some years ago John Elliott commented on a lecture I had given in Cambridge and mentioned Antonio de Guevara, whose work was at the time shamefully unfamiliar to me. Reading Guevara led me to complete a project on estrangement which had been dormant for thirty years, when I had come across a passage by La Bruyère.

Besides being your interlocutor, John Elliott is also one of the major critics of your book The Cheese *and the* Worms *for its role in encouraging the atomization of the past. How do you react to his criticism?*

Elliott's review of *The Cheese and the Worms* was very generous; it attracted attention to the book, and I am grateful to him for this. Later his attitude became more critical, aiming (if I am not mistaken) not so much at the book *per se* but, as you said, at the role which it might have played in bringing to the centre of history subjects which used to be peripheral. I didn't reply to Elliott's remark because the idea of opposing micro-history to macro-history doesn't really make sense. And even less the idea of opposing social history to political history. Some years ago somebody asked me which was, in my view, the most promising area in history; to which I answered: political history. Yes, because I believe that one should write this type of history, but in a new key, taking into account the fact that centres and peripheries necessarily imply each other.

Are you saying that the so-called 'history from below' has gone too far?

As I wrote in my book *The Cheese and the Worms*, it was important to show that the history of unknown people could (and should) be written. This statement had an obvious polemical edge. But as a research programme 'history from below' is clearly insufficient. Archives are full of stories of unknown people: the problem is why one has to choose that story instead of another story, why that document instead of another, and so on. A respectable intellectual programme may easily turn into a cliché, transmitting to its proponents a feeling of self-righteousness – something I really hate. The idea that 'history from below' might become a sort of slogan is for me unpleasant and also uninteresting, because this would mean replacing one orthodox approach to history with another. This is one of the reasons why I've been working on different themes and starting from different assumptions. So, in a way, I would say that my own aim is to disappoint all possible expectations derived from my books. Otherwise, I would be caught in a sort of cliché and would also be transformed into a preacher, which, once again, is a role I dislike enormously.

Having studied witches and witchcraft, you couldn't help dealing with women in history. Nevertheless, you do not seem to have any special interest in discussing your topics from the perspective of gender. Can you tell us why not?

Good and bad things have certainly been written from this perspective, and I have been rather slow in exposing myself to this trend. But, on the other hand, I must say that when I started my work on witchcraft I wanted to react against a sort of cliché (which was not based on serious research), according to which most people accused of witchcraft and condemned for it were women, since I found plenty of evidence to the contrary. Sometimes my intellectual reactions can be extremely quick, and occasionally wrong, maybe often wrong. On other occasions, though, they can be very slow, as if I had to digest a challenge gradually. My piece on estrangement, as I already said, is an example of this delayed reaction. My response to the history of women is another. Only gradually did I become aware that what I used to regard as a sort of neutral approach to history was, in fact, a man's approach to history. I might one day succeed in writing something about this, but I cannot wait another thirty years, as I did in the case of estrangement. Actually, a piece on Voltaire that I'm writing now might, I think, imply a sort of response to this, in a strange and devious way.

You once confessed to disliking your Nicodemismo, *and that your* Benandanti, *although not so successful as* Cheese and Worms, *was a more advanced book. Which of your works do you like best?*

I could say that my favourite book is the latest one, but this would simply be a sort of quick answer. I'm deeply committed to *I benandanti* because, being my first book, everything started from there. As Italo Calvino once wrote, the first book is a sort of initial gesture, and everything that one does afterwards will be out of that first impact. As in a chess game, the way you manage the opening creates an initial constraint, which prevents you from going back. As I said before, I think that that was perhaps the most challenging of my books and gave me the feeling of being very isolated. As to *Il Nicodemismo*, I don't like it because it is perhaps the most academic book I ever wrote. It was a way of continuing a dialogue with Cantimori, who had just died, and also to demonstrate to myself that I was a true historian, which is a need that I don't have any more; whether because in the meantime I've become a genuine historian, or because I don't care about this any longer. I wouldn't like, however, to repudiate this book completely (there being something in its research strategy that I still feel close to), although I have always refused permission for republication, since that would require a long introduction explaining what is wrong with some of its chapters. Another book that seems strange today is *Giochi de pazienza*, which I wrote with my friend Adriano Prosperi, telling the story of our joint research on sixteenth-century religious tracts. I never really understood why Einaudi decided to reprint it. It is in a deliberate way a rather unreadable book. But its research core was quite sound, as Adriano Prosperi will show in the book he has been working on for years on Giorgio Siculo, a sixteenth-century Benedictine monk put to death as a heretic.[7] But *Giochi di pazienza* was also a sort of methodological manifesto. I developed some of its themes in my essay on clues.

As you might imagine, *The Cheese and the Worms* has been by far the most successful and the most translated of my books. But it also had a peculiar reception in Montereale, the village in Friuli where the miller Menocchio was born. Aldo Colonnello, a schoolteacher from Montereale and a man of great intellectual energy (we became great friends) created a centre for elderly people and gave it the name Centro Menocchio. In recent years the Centro started many scholarly activities, including an international conference to celebrate the 500th anniversary of Menocchio's death. The conference took place in the village church. A heretic celebrated in a church – for the first time, I believe, since Joan of Arc. Now in Montereale you can buy a shirt and a poster in honour of Menocchio with a sentence from the trial: 'cercava uno mondo nuovo' (he was looking for a new world). I also became an honorary citizen of Montereale – something I am very proud of. Through a series of chain reactions my book had become part of the rediscovery of Friulian identity. This happened with *I benandanti* as well – I recently discovered that there is a rock band in Friuli called Benandanti Electronics. While I was working on *Ecstasies*, I asked myself: 'Should I aim at a big failure or a small success?' In Italian, *successo* means achievement as well. Obviously, a big success would have been the best: a big failure was the second best. That was the gambling element in me. I don't know whether *Ecstasies* is the best of my books; but it is certainly the one in which I invested the most, in which some very personal elements are involved.

According to Jack Goody, comparison is one of the few equivalents in the historical and social sciences for the kind of experiments the scientists carry out. Would you agree with him about the importance of the comparative approach for the understanding of the past?

I think that it was Marc Bloch who said that the only alternative to experiments is the comparative approach, since it would be either impossible or immoral to start a religious movement, for instance, as an experiment. And it's striking to think that the programme Bloch sketched so

7 *L'eresia del Libro Grande*, Milan, Feltrinelli, 2000.

long ago in that famous article 'A Contribution towards a Comparative History of European Societies' is still very much alive, and that so few people have actually engaged in that sort of approach. So I totally agree with the importance of making explicit comparisons. On the other hand, it is impossible not to compare, because the way in which the mind works always involves implicit comparisons. The continuous interference of recollections of the past in everyday experience always implies comparison.

Nevertheless, when it is a case of making systematic comparisons in order to understand, for instance, what was so unique about European civilization which allowed it to conquer the world (I'm not saying that this is good, but the facts are undeniable), many difficulties arise. The one that relates to the unspoken assumptions is the most serious, I think, because they have to be made explicit when comparing different cultures. And this is difficult. In a way, every historian is a foreigner in the past, but when confronted with a very different culture from ours, like the Chinese or African, for example, we are even more foreign. Written as if it were with invisible ink, all unspoken assumptions become even more difficult to grasp.

You have already declared that you would like to be on the fringe, not only of the historical profession, but on the fringe of everything. Many times, as you admit, you go to your office to meet your students as if you were going to a movie. Would you say, then, that you try to relate to the world as a spectator?

Going to a movie – well, I said this ages ago, when movies were still fun (getting older, I find most of them boring). But I am still curious about students. Concerning your question: yes, the devil's advocate who exists in me already asked me this. I understand the intellectual virtues and potentialities of this position, and since I've been staying half of the year in Los Angeles and half in Italy, I've doubled the possibilities of being an outsider. But I also see that there are disadvantages in this position and that being a simple spectator is morally unacceptable. Strangely enough, I was compelled to counteract this tendency of mine soon after I started leaving Italy every year, by becoming involved in the trial of my friend Adriano Sofri, who was being condemned for a crime he did not commit. This has been the only time in which I've been personally committed as a historian to a present event, realizing that what I write might make a difference – which, unfortunately, was not the case. But if, on the one hand, I recognize the danger of being a mere spectator, I've always been sceptical about the idea of being a historian *engagé*. To choose a topic of study just because it is related to contemporary preoccupations is to have a myopic and provincial approach to history. What you regard as totally distant from present concerns might become the focus of engagement just two days later. I remember that when I was in Rome in 1969 my students were frantically interested in only one event: the occupation of the factories by the workers in Turin in 1920. They couldn't think about anything else. And I, who was working on witchcraft and the *benandanti*, was some thousand light-years distant from them. And then, some time later – and I always like to remember this – there were rallies in the streets in Italy, with the feminists shouting: 'tremate, tremate, le streghe son tornate' (look out, look out, the witches are back).

In an age in which history is often described as becoming increasingly fragmented, is there anything, in your view, that unites all historians?

I am aware that many historians complain about the fragmentation of history; I don't. The emergence of a fragmentation of points of view seems to me productive. After all, history is a pre-paradigmatic discipline – in the Kuhnian sense, or at least in one of the Kuhnian senses. In other words, history is like chemistry before Boyle or mathematics before Euclid; that is, there has never been a Galileo or a Newton in history who would have created a strong unifying paradigm. And maybe there will never be any, which means that history may always remain in a pre-Galilean or pre-Newtonian stage. As a result of this, if we look at historians working all over the world, it is impossible to say that this one or that one is within the paradigm or outside the profession. I would describe the situation only in terms of negative paradigms. If somebody were to say something like, 'God is directly intervening in human affairs' (as medieval chronicles used to say about the crusades), this person would be placing himself or herself outside the profession. But apart from extreme cases like this, one can say a lot of different things, even conflicting things, in history and still be in the profession, which is not something you can say about a science like physics, for instance.

As a consequence, the relevance of a historical topic is not immediately evident. This last point is, in my view, extremely important. I think we've been used to pre-existent hierarchies of relevance that were related to national as well as to world history. Within British history, for instance, the role played by Britain in world history implied the relevance of certain events, which meant that Brazil and Italy, for example, were intrinsically peripheral in the nineteenth century. Well, this is fortunately something that has probably gone, because a distinction has emerged between, on the one side, topics whose relevance is given *a priori* (like the French Revolution), and, on the other side, those topics whose relevance is given *a posteriori*, depending on the results of the research (like, let's say, the study of a single community in northern Italy or southern Brazil). This is, after all, one of the implications of micro-history. When I was still a student there was a definite hierarchy of relevance and the *benandanti* were regarded as people of no importance, merely colourful and picturesque. I had, therefore, to stress the fact that there was much more in them than that.

I see the change as being related to the impact of anthropology on history, because in anthropology the relevance of a given piece of research is not linked to the relevance of such and such a tribe, as Malinowski would have said. Instead, it is linked to the general quality of the questions and answers it will raise. I was confronted with this issue when I worked on my miller Menocchio, and felt compelled to justify in the introduction why I was studying a miller, and why that specific miller. So the idea was to show the relevance of studying a Friulian miller to a non-Friulian audience and potentially to everybody, because there are larger questions which could be addressed through this example. I wouldn't justify my work in the same terms today because I think that that battle has been won (at least to some extent). But I would like to add that research which deals with topics the relevance of which is given *a priori* is not better or more important than research the relevance of which is given *a posteriori*. I would simply say that better research is better.

You are often described as a historian of mentalities, although you have often criticized this approach. Are you in favour of a reformed history of mentalities, or do you reject this approach altogether? Does the new history of the 'imaginaire social' answer your criticisms?

I am not interested in labels, including micro-history, because they can easily become slogans, and I don't really care if people call me a micro-historian or a historian of mentalities. On the other hand, I think that a book like Bloch's *Royal Touch* certainly opened up that domain of research, although he didn't use that label. Anyway, he was not opposing that approach to others and, in fact, succeeded in connecting political history with what one could call history of mentalities, and that seems to me very important. 'Imaginaire social' is one more label, and as such it is not particularly interesting. What really matters are the results generated by a certain approach, as well as the specific difficulties raised by them.

When you talk about your career, you refer to your visits to the archives without knowing what to look for, to the casual nature of your discoveries and to the great importance of chance, risk and intuition in your way of writing history. Wouldn't you say that such assertions are disconcerting, contradict what is conventionally told to students and show that there is not, in fact, much to teach future historians?

I'm very much intrigued by those chance events which trigger or stimulate something in us. I'm not saying, though, that there is something irrational, mystical in this. We are surrounded, exposed to all sorts of random events, and the problem is, to which event will we react, since we are not passive recipients. All our life, to this second, predisposes us to a certain range of reactions, which is very wide; now, only a fraction of that range will become reality; in other words, we could react to so many different things, but we react only to some of them and in certain ways. When I discovered the document on the *benandanti*, for instance, I was more or less working at random, but when I saw it as potentially relevant, it's because I was already involved and interacting with it, so to speak. Usually my works start from a flash, from a sort of Aha! reaction, and then I have to unfold this Aha! in order to discover the question. This may be related to the idea that I stressed in the piece on estrangement, in which starting from a quotation from Proust (which I slightly misquote), I suggest that history should be written backwards, starting from the conclusion. So the most important and difficult thing is to be potentially open to the unknown and to the unexpected.

Being older than my students and having read more books that have become part of my pre-existent background, my possible reactions to the chance events will be necessarily different; my Ahas – so to speak – will be closely related to my previous readings which are not part of my students' backgrounds. So there is something in me, in the historian I became, which I cannot teach. In fact, I think that teaching is a sort of impossible task; yet it happens. I know I have learned from so many people, and sometimes from people whom I met for only a few hours, or maybe a few seconds. So I suppose I have also taught something to somebody else but, in a way, I have my doubts about that; many more doubts about my teaching than about my writings. After all, I can be wrong, but if I can avoid self-indulgence – and I hope I can – I am the best judge of my writing. Teaching, on the other hand, since it involves other people, is difficult to test. Being a process that sometimes cannot be fully articulated in words, perhaps the only way of teaching something is, like cooking, by showing. Who can learn cooking from a cookery book? I think that like most of human activities, it is taught in this way: look, practise; look at the way I'm doing it, and so on.

Many years ago I had an interview with my friend Adriano Sofri, who asked me what my advice for young historians would be. My answer at that time was: 'read many novels', since my point was that young historians should develop what I call moral imagination, that is, that which allows us to make guesses about human beings, about ourselves and about other people as well. Well, those guesses are based on what we have learned from our interactions with other human beings; and a lot of this is based, I think, on what we read, from fairy tales to contemporary novels. Reading opens up to us a range of human possibilities and if we had the luck to have read Dostoevsky's *Crime and Punishment*, the encounter with Raskolnikov will always affect our way of thinking about human beings. Nevertheless, I would hesitate to give the same answer today, because I wouldn't like to associate myself with the current trend that blurs the distinction between fiction and history. I am still very much in favour of reading a lot of novels, but I would add the following warning: 'read novels, but be aware that history and fiction are distinct genres which relate to each other by a sort of competition and mutual challenge.'

With other disciplines such as medicine and divining, history, as you once said, shares a conjectural character that makes the knowledge they produce inevitably speculative. All the same, you suggest that they are also scientific. Could you develop this apparently contradictory idea?

The problem is that the process of knowledge is very complex, does not follow a straight line, but progresses by making moves in opposite directions. That's the reason why debates and even fights are so important. So it's true that I made a move in the direction of insights; but then, because this might have become a sort of slogan, I decided to try to complicate it again and focused on the question of proof, of evidence (I must add that I felt compelled to do this as soon as I became aware of the moral and political implications of the sceptical attitude towards history). This was a way of correcting a false image, and also of stressing the role of the constraints of the outside world. I'm still very much interested in the reason why some insights can be either proved or disproved, while others are more or less resistant to verification. That's certainly the reason why Adriano Prosperi and I tried to describe the false trails in a research experience in *Giochi di pazienza*, discussing why certain strategies, approaches or guesses don't work and are abandoned.

The idea of proof, which was very fashionable in the late nineteenth and early twentieth centuries, has become extremely unfashionable in the last twenty years, when historians have become more and more seduced by the idea of blurring the distinction between fiction and history and stopped concerning themselves with proving anything. And that was a very bad thing. I think that the idea of proof is becoming relevant again, and I certainly try to contribute to the growth of this interest as much as I can. But if this sceptical attitude has been harmful, the challenge it represents has been important because it shows that there was a real question behind a somewhat superficial answer. In other words, it shows that there is a sceptical question that historians should take very seriously. I would like to describe my attitude in the following way: on the one hand, I would like to keep the distinction between fiction and history as clear-cut as possible, and to show that, in spite of the fact that historians are situated people and knowledge is also situated, there is an objective side of things which can be proved and accepted by people working on different assumptions. After all, I'm committed to science and there is a sort of impersonal quality in my writings; they are not fiction, they have a lot of footnotes. This commitment to science as an ideal has some personal implications – or associations. My maternal grandfather, Giuseppe Levi – readers of my mother's book *The Things We Used to Say* will recall him – had a great impact on me during my childhood. He was a great biologist, who was considered for the Nobel Prize and never got it, but three of his pupils got the Nobel Prize – something which is very unusual. He was a man of strong personality and very powerful intellectually, and I think that I have a sort of nineteenth-century model of science which is related to him; and so when I wrote about Morelli I was thinking a bit about my grandfather.

That knowledge is provable, and that everybody who is ready to accept the rules of the game must accept even the truths that are unpleasant is a lesson that I learned from Freud. One has to face what is unpleasant, even what is painful.

Your study of Menocchio, together with Le Roy Ladurie's Montaillou *and Natalie Davis's* The Return of Martin Guerre, *has been praised for belonging to the postmodernist tradition in historiography. Do you agree with this view?*

Not at all. I think Ankersmit and others have completely misread all these works. I've realized, especially in the United States, that people who read my *Cheese and Worms* and my essay on 'clues' regard me as a postmodernist historian, which sounds bizarre to me. My ambition would be to be attacked by both positivists and postmodernists, to be regarded as a postmodernist by the positivists, and also the other way around, as a positivist by the postmodernists. Not because I am in the middle. In fact, I think it is impossible to be in the middle: the truth is not in the middle and the solution to the problem does not consist in putting in a bottle 50 per cent of positivism and 50 per cent of scepticism. At least at an earlier stage, a compromise should not be sought; on the contrary, the contradiction should be pushed as much as possible so that its full potential can emerge and the arguments on both sides be evaluated. Such a debate entails many problems, such as, for instance, that of knowing to what extent a piece of evidence is related to social reality and how can this be assessed. This relation is not so obvious and clear as many positivists would argue. As I wrote somewhere, I think that evidence should neither be regarded as a sort of window open onto social reality, nor an enclosed wall that prevents us from seeing anything beyond the evidence itself, as the postmodernists would say. It's more like a distorting glass, and the problem is to see which way the glass is distorting, since this is the only way to have access to reality. Another bigger problem implicit in the debate is related to the issue of 'situated knowledge' (to use an expression of Donna Haraway's), because it involves a serious political danger: a society in which each group – Jews, blacks, gays, and so forth – speaks for itself and to itself, writing its own history from its particular set of assumptions, and not bothering to prove anything. 'Situated knowledge' is undeniable, but one should take it as a starting point, not as the last word, in order to make communication and understanding possible.

You have suggested that to demand from the study of the past the solution of our problems is a superficial approach to history. In what way, then, is the study of the past meaningful?

By contributing to the perception of different cultures, to the perception that people can be different, have been different and will be different, history can enlarge the boundaries of imagination and promote a less provincial attitude towards the past and present. This has often been said. But the impact of scholarly work is unpredictable.

Let me add another example to what I said before. At the beginning of this year [1998], I received a letter inviting me to a conference on the opening of the Inquisition archive in Rome. I replied that I couldn't go but received a phone call from an archivist in the Vatican saying that it would be a great pity for me not to go because, as he explained, I had contributed to that event with a letter. In fact, at the conference which I was unable to attend, Cardinal Ratzinger made a speech quoting a passage from a letter I had written to Pope John Paul II in 1979, sometime after his election. I had written more or less the following: 'I am a Jewish-born historian, I am an atheist, I have been working on the Inquisition for many years and I think that you should open this archive, because in this way you would demonstrate that the Church is not afraid to submit itself to the judgement of scholars, even in a case like the Inquisition.' A Jew asking for the opening of the Inquisition archives certainly contributed to the Pope's historic gesture.

Do you have any theory or philosophy of history yourself?

I'm sceptical about a philosophy of history as a way of recapitulating the history of humankind, but I've been thinking of writing a piece on this theme having as a motto this very short children's poem which says: 'Questa è la storia della vacca Vittoria; morta la vacca finita la storia' [This is the story of the cow Vittoria. The cow is dead and the story is finished]. In Italian *storia* means both 'story' and 'history'. This, I'd say, is my philosophy of history – humankind will perish, hopefully as late as possible, but it is definitely mortal. The fact that a collective suicide has become possible, that the end of history is at hand, represents a real turning-point in human history. The retrospective impact that such a possibility has on our perception of history has yet to be dealt with by historians. So I'm thinking of using that 'storia della vacca Vittoria' as a sort of gloss to a poem by Raymond Queneau, 'Petite cosmogonie porta-tive', in which he recapitulates human history in two lines, from the ape to the splitting of the atom.

You often refer to the work of Freud. Are these references an important clue to your approach to history?

Yes, he has been very influential on me, but less through his theories and much more through the case studies reported in his *Psychopathology of Everyday Life*. The analytical Freud fascinates me enormously. Two of his ideas, in particular, have been especially important to me. First, that truth, no matter how painful, must be looked at. And second, that it is possible to combine positivism with openness to what is irrational. My approach to intellectual matters can be described, in fact, by an effort to confront the tension between what is rational and what is irrational and to analyse irrational behaviour or beliefs from a rational perspective. There is a tendency to take for granted that the right approach involves some mimicry, that is, that the approach has to fit the content and that therefore the irrational cannot be approached from a rational perspective. Well, I don't share this idea at all and I'd say that my aim, from my adolescence (even if this sounds a bit too emphatic), has been to disclose the rationality of the irrational. So not mimicry but distance is the key. Or, if you like, emotional involvement combined with distance.

Could you situate yourself in relation to Marxism?

I first read Marx in my student years and was immensely taken by his writings, which were so pervasive then. I never declared myself a Marxist for modesty, let's say, because I think it would have been pretentious to call myself a Marxist, as I was too ignorant of his work. In any case, I always resisted the idea of involving myself too deeply in Marxist debates. I don't regret this, since it seemed to me that it would be too easy to get bogged down in some not very interesting scholastic distinctions. Never-theless, I wouldn't deny that I started my researches with some sort of crude Marxist hypotheses, which were part of the general atmosphere of the 1960s. What I retained from this afterwards was the importance of the conflict between the Inquisitors and the *benandanti*, contrary to the continuity of beliefs that many scholars who were studying the issue were stressing. I don't deny that those trials could be studied from different points of view, including the one that stresses the circulation of beliefs. Nevertheless, it seemed to me that the approach that insisted on the divergence (and sometimes clash) of their respective beliefs was more productive. I can imagine that, if I had started with a sort of unifying hypothesis, I could have dismissed the *benandanti* trials as uninteresting. It is like a fish which cannot be taken in a net because it is too small. So to have started with a hypothesis based on conflict was certainly a choice related to the leftist atmosphere I was breathing and to the leftist attitude to which I was committed. I've been thinking of going back to Marx, and the fact that Marxism as such seems to be dead is an additional reason for reading him again.

Is your attitude to politics that of an observer or a participant? By writing a defence of Adriano Sofri, did you mean to take a political stand?

I always voted for the communist party (as long as it existed), but was never a member of it. My mother, on the other hand, joined the party after the war, but then left and was elected to Parliament as a sort of independent MP. I have been fascinated by the communist party but from a distance, although Gramsci's *Letter from Prison* had a great intellectual and emotional impact on me. As to my defence of Adriano Sofri, I must say that *The Judge and the Historian* was related to my friendship with him. I wouldn't like to pretend that it is something else. If politics played some role in it, it was a very small one. I sympathized with Lotta Continua, but I would never have written such a book if Adriano Sofri had not been my friend and if I had not been convinced that he was not guilty of the death of the police officer Luigi Calabresi, for which he was condemned to twenty-two years in prison. So for me it was a question of using my expertise to help my friend. It was painful work. I read an enormous amount of court records, which are in principle available to everybody, but nobody reads; made the public aware of how a trial works; reflected on the question of proof (which is an area of convergence between judges and historians); and argued that the sentence against Sofri was a judicial error which had to be corrected. Unfortunately, this did not happen.

You seem not to appreciate Foucault's work and have even criticized him for being populist. Could you explain your reserves about him?

First of all, I think that Foucault is much more interesting than his followers. What is so uninteresting about them is that they take his metaphors as explanations, and that is absurd. And I would even say that Foucault *before* his metaphors is much more interesting than *with* his metaphors. In fact, I was struck by a thin volume published a couple of years ago that gives some résumés of the courses he gave at the Collège de

France. Well, this volume reveals a much better Foucault, a Foucault without all the usual Foucaultian panache. There are several Foucaults, and one of them was extremely brilliant. But as an original thinker he has been in my view highly overrated. He was a footnote to Nietzsche – but there are so few original thinkers, after all. He certainly discovered new areas of knowledge, and launched some challenging metaphors. Microphysics of power is one of them. There is certainly a lot to be done in that direction, which, in my view, Foucault didn't do, and his followers even less.

Personally, he was probably the most aggressive person I ever met. And also egocentric in a maniacal way, which allowed him to sell his image very effectively. I remember being in Paris in a café with E. P. Thompson and I don't know why we started to talk about Foucault. And then he said something that I thought I had misunderstood and asked him to repeat, which he did: 'Foucault is a charlatan!' I was really surprised but I agree that there was much of a charlatan in him, though not only that. I suspect that in the long run much of his work will vanish, especially the empty rhetoric. But there is also something interesting to preserve. That is why a sober approach to Foucault by someone who is not a follower would be very refreshing. A lot of rubbish has been written on him, and actually all those eulogies ultimately belittle him. It would be very good if somebody could rescue Foucault from this silly idolatry.

You have been teaching in the States for the last ten years, and have considered this situation to be one of great intellectual fertility. Has this experience of comparing Italy with the States made you see both cultures in a new light?

I had strong anti-American feelings and when I first went to the States I was very ignorant about the country and had many crude stereotypes and assumptions about it. I remember that the first time I saw an American flag not being burned was when I went to the American consulate in Florence in the early 1970s to get a visa. Living in the States changed my attitude. I got a feeling of the great, tragic and bold social experiment which is going on there. There is a lot in this experiment which I dislike, but its scale is so huge and our time perspective is so short that I wouldn't like to be hasty in my judgement.

As to the comparison between Italy and the States, I would say that to compare cultures which are so different is, in a way, impossible. Everything is different between them, beginning with the fact that Bologna is made for pedestrians, while in LA one can hardly walk, everything being built for cars. Starting from this, everything else is different: the huge empty spaces, the educational institutions, the absence of an *Ancien Régime* in their past, etc. But in spite of so many differences between

Italy and this unique, gigantic experiment which is the United States, there is something in it that raises questions that Europeans are having to confront more and more. I'm referring to the coexistence and conflict between different cultures, which has become our problem now. The scale is, of course, different and will demand a different answer. But the question being comparable, we have something to learn from the Americans. I remember that as soon as I arrived in the States I had a conversation with a distinguished scholar and when I mentioned the problem of the blacks he said that their situation was comparable with that of other immigrants. They were just in line like the Irish, Italians and other ethnic groups, and they would also eventually get a slice of the American pie. He was wrong. It's only when you look at the history of the blacks in the long perspective, starting from slavery, that what is happening makes sense and explains why their situation is very different from that of other ethnic groups.

Some of your latest essays in the book Occhiacci di legno [Wooden Eyes] – *like the one on the political use of myth as a lie or the one on the grip of the intolerant tradition exemplified by the Pope's slip of the tongue – seem to reveal a more pessimistic Ginzburg than in the past. Do you agree with this impression?*

I have been told that already, but if I'm becoming more pessimistic it's beyond my control. I don't really know if things are getting worse, or if I'm seeing them in a clearer light, something which may be related to age. In the past I never had so many opportunities to speak about the present, so probably my view about it was already gloomy and is still gloomy. There is a motto by Romain Rolland,[8] which became famous in Italy through Gramsci, which talks about the pessimism of intelligence and the optimism of the will. I like this motto because it emphasizes the distinction between reality and our wishes, between what reality is and what we would like it to be. This, in fact, goes back to the idea that one should learn from Freud: that reality is unpleasant but we have to look at it. Nevertheless our fears, wishes and desires tend to protect us from reality. Seeing reality is a difficult achievement.

Bologna, October 1998

---

8   Romain Rolland (1866–1944), French novelist, author of a ten-volume novel, *Jean-Christophe* (1904–12).

SELECT BIBLIOGRAPHY

The Night Battles (1966; English translation, London and Baltimore, Johns Hopkins University Press, 1983); also translated into French, German, Japanese, Dutch, Portuguese, Swedish.

The Cheese and the Worms (1976; English translation, London and Baltimore, Johns Hopkins University Press, 1980); also translated into French, German, Japanese, Dutch, Portuguese, Spanish, Swedish, Polish, Serbo-Croat, Hungarian, Greek, Turkish, Romanian, Albanian, Estonian, Czech.

The Enigma of Piero (1981; English translation, London, Verso, 1985); also translated into French, German, Spanish, Portuguese, Japanese.

Myths, Emblems, Clues (1986; London, Hutchinson Radius, 1989); also translated into French, German, Spanish, Portuguese, Dutch, Japanese, Swedish, Finnish, Danish.

Ecstasies: Deciphering the Witches' Sabbath (1989; English translation, Harmondsworth, Penguin, 1991); also translated into French, German, Spanish, Portuguese, Japanese, Swedish, Dutch, Romanian, Norwegian.

The Judge and the Historian: Marginal Notes on a Late Twentieth-Century Miscarriage of Justice (1991; English translation, London, Verso, 1999); translated into German, Japanese, Dutch, Spanish, French.

'Just One Witness', in S. Friedlander (ed.), *Probing the Limits of Representation: Nazism and the 'Final Solution'* (Cambridge, Mass., Harvard University Press, 1992), 82–96, 350–5.

'Montaigne, Cannibals and Grottoes', *History and Anthropology*, 6 (1993), 125–55.

Wooden Eyes: Nine Reflections on Distance, English translation, London, Verso, 2002, also translated into German, Spanish, French, Portuguese, Japanese.

History, Rhetoric and Proof (Hanover and London, University Press of New England, 1999); also translated into Japanese and German.

No Island is an Island: Four Glances at English Literature in a World Perspective, Columbia University Press, New York, 2000.

9

Quentin Skinner

Since October 1997 the University of Cambridge has had a new Regius Professor of History: Quentin Skinner. His appointment has crowned the swift and brilliant career that Skinner began there in 1962 at the age of twenty-one. In 1978 he was chosen for the Political Science chair at Cambridge in recognition of his contribution to the methodology and practice of the history of ideas in general and political history in particular. His early articles in the late sixties showed he was a polemical and innovative thinker and drew reactions ranging from the highly positive to the profoundly critical. Some would say that Skinner's 'reign' began in the seventies, when his historical studies on the political ideas of the Renaissance and his philosophical and methodological reflections fuelled an extremely enriching and fruitful debate, extending beyond the Anglo-American world. *The Foundations of Modern Political Thought*, published in 1978 and winner of the Wolfson Literary Award, established Skinner as a compulsory reference in the historiography of political ideas. This position has since been confirmed by the impact of a series of innovative and provocative articles, the success of his short book on Machiavelli, and his more recent substantial book on Hobbes, *Reason and Rhetoric in the Philosophy of Hobbes.* He is now working on an even more ambitious project, a large-scale book entitled *Visions of Politics.*

In contrast to studies which deal with the classical texts on political theory as if they were vehicles of eternal wisdom, Skinner's intention is to approach them in terms of their context: not so much their social context (which is not, however, excluded from his analyses) but rather their

---

The cover photograph of Quentin Skinner reproduced by kind permission of Susan James.

intellectual and political context. The objective of his work may be summed up as an attempt to discover the intentions of the authors of classical works such as *The Prince* and *Leviathan*. In other words, considering these texts as acts – or 'speech acts', as Skinner calls them in the tradition of the philosopher J. L. Austin – he tries to understand these works as interventions by Machiavelli and Hobbes in the political debate of their times. This view contrasts with the history of ideas as propounded by Arthur Lovejoy, founder of the influential *Journal of the History of Ideas*, and his followers. By isolating 'unit-ideas' and following them down the centuries, that kind of history attempted, for instance, to recover the transformations in the Platonic idea of the Great Chain of Being until the nineteenth century, so as to continue to give a rational explanation of the world. Skinner and others such as John Dunn, Richard Tuck and John Pocock criticize that form of history as anachronistic, and try to show that thinkers such as Hobbes or Locke spoke a language and dealt with questions that were very specific to their own time, the seventeenth century.

Apart from his intellectual qualities, a contributing factor in Skinner's appointment to his high post in the British academic hierarchy must have been the fact that he can be called a genuine 'Cambridge Man'. His more recent appointment as Pro-Vice-Chancellor of Cambridge may be explained in the same way. Having begun his connection with Cambridge in 1959 as a student at Caius and embarked on his academic career as a fellow of Christ's three years later, Skinner is thus regarded as a man who upholds the spirit and the rules of this ancient university. He is so closely identified with Cambridge that certain colleagues of his thought he was the inspiration for the main character in a detective story (unfortunately not a very good one) portraying certain aspects of life in this university city!

Although swamped by the administrative duties that come with his new chair and the attention he is known to give to the many students who surround him, Skinner was willing to set aside several hours for this interview. In the fine suite of rooms he occupies in Christ's College he spoke at length about his work, his critics, his methods, interests, views on Marxism, idea of freedom, today's historiographic trends, etc.

Extremely pleasant and polite and yet also formal and serious, Skinner impresses the listener with the brilliant, fluent and enthusiastic manner in which he talks about his subjects of study. The order and clarity of his ideas seems to reflect the meticulous neatness of the papers, books and objects in his room. His extremely articulate speech, without digressions, hesitations or grammatical slips differs little from the elegant, limpid prose that characterizes his historical and philosophical works. A colleague of his jokingly compared Skinner's remarkable fluency with one of the concepts central to his theory of interpretation: 'When he speaks,

Skinner gives the impression of being a computer programmed to produce forceful and highly effective "speech acts"!'

MARIA LÚCIA PALLARES-BURKE   *What led you to become a historian
of political thought?*

QUENTIN SKINNER   I had a remarkable schoolmaster who set me going
by getting me to read several of the classical texts in English political
theory. He had an enormous influence on my adolescence and first fired
me with enthusiasm for my subject. I'm certainly struck when I think
about the texts I worked on at that early age. One of them was Thomas
More's *Utopia*, which we read as a text for examination at school; and the
other, which he insisted we should all read, was Hobbes's *Leviathan*. I still
have the copies of these texts I acquired in my schooldays, and I've
written and lectured about these texts ever since.

After that fortunate start, my interest was quickened by some very
good teaching I had as an undergraduate at Cambridge. I was specially
influenced by two people. One of them was John Burrow, who was then a
young research fellow of Christ's College (and is now Professor of Intellectual History at Oxford) and who gave me some of the most exciting
teaching I received as an undergraduate. But the other person who was
even more important to me from the point of view of how I've tried to
study my subject was Peter Laslett. I was deeply impressed by his lectures,
wide-ranging and full of insights, and also by his edition of Locke's *Two
Treatises of Government*, which was published while I was an undergraduate and remains one of the great works of modern textual scholarship
in my subject. I remember John Burrow telling me I must be sure to write
an essay on Locke because Laslett's new edition was going to introduce not
only a new standard for the subject but also inaugurate a new approach.

I recall being overwhelmed by Laslett's Introduction to his edition
when I duly read it. I found it wonderful in many ways. First, it was a
beautiful piece of English prose, with a grace and clarity which I found
quite exceptional, especially when compared with anything by the supposedly major historians I was being asked to read at the time. Secondly,
the new edition showed that Laslett had made a number of discoveries
about Locke which seemed to me methodologically interesting. Locke's
Treatise had always been seen as a justification of the English Revolution
of 1688 and a celebration of the establishment of a balanced Parliamentary constitution. Laslett proved that it had, in fact, been written ten
years before it was printed, that it was not a justification for any kind of
revolution and that it was produced under the rising tide of absolutism
in the reign of Charles II. What was especially important to me was
Laslett's insistence that we should not be thinking of the text in isolation from the circumstances in which it was written. He showed the

importance of understanding the context in which Locke's text was written in order to understand its meaning. The *Treatise* had become a celebration of the Revolution, the great text of liberalism, the founding text of British constitutionalism. Nevertheless, none of these things were part of its historical identity; they had nothing to do with what Locke thought he was doing in writing it.

Do you think that your family and childhood experiences played any special role in the choice of your career as a historian?

Not really. I have thought about it and I don't think that they had a direct influence on my academic development at all. It's true that my mother had specialized in English literature at university, and had been a school-teacher before she was married, and that much of my early reading was due to her influence. But there is one thing about my young life which is relevant here, and which is not an uncommon English story. The fact is that I didn't live with my parents until I was much older, because they actually lived in Africa, where my father was a member of the colonial administration in Nigeria. Not only was I not born there, but I never set foot in Africa, not even during my school holidays. The British Colonial Service didn't encourage young children to go to Africa because it was still a dangerous area, medically speaking, and because there were no schools – well, at least no schools of the kind that the English would have recognized. My parents used to come back to England when my father had leave, but that was only every two years. So I lived with my guardian, who was my mother's sister, until I went to boarding-school – in fact, to Bedford School – at the age of seven; and after that I would also spend my holidays with her. Possibly my aunt, who was a doctor near Manchester, did have some influence on my later career. She was a remarkable person and an enthusiastic reader of history, and her house was full of history books. She also had a passion for visiting the great English country houses, and often took me along with her. Maybe I should have become a social historian, considering all those early guided tours. I can still remember a visit we made soon after the war, when there was still petrol rationing (being a doctor she had special allowances), to Chatsworth in Derbyshire, the mansion of the dukes of Devonshire, about fifty miles south-east of Manchester. Little did I know that forty years later I would spend a lot of time working in Chatsworth, where Hobbes's archives were lodged after his death.

When I think, though, about my early life, the great direct influence was exerted by the person I've already mentioned, my schoolmaster, John Eyre, with whom I'm still in touch. It was he who was very keen on my sitting the entrance scholarship examination to Cambridge, since he believed that I could win a scholarship. These awards have long since been abolished, but at that time it was felt quite an honour to win one. When any boy at my school managed this feat, we all got an extra half-day's holiday. By this time I was living with my parents, because after my father's retirement they bought a house in Bedford, and I stopped being a boarder and became a day boy at Bedford School. I remember that, when it came to applying for Cambridge, I got my poor father to write a rather impertinent letter to Gonville and Caius College, where my brother had read medicine. In the letter my father said that his elder son had been at Caius because it was the great college for medicine, but that his younger son wanted to read history. Was Caius a good college for history? I was most impressed by the answer he got back from the college, a two-line letter from the admissions tutor saying: 'Caius is the best college in all subjects'. So that sounded good enough, and I was entered for a scholarship at Caius, which I won.

You once professed to being perplexed when hearing your critics describe you as an idealist, a materialist, a positivist, a relativist, an antiquarian, a historicist and even a mere methodologist. How would you describe yourself?

It isn't easy. Among these titles, the one I would least disavow is probably that of being a relativist, if that does not mean a conceptual relativist, which I'm definitely not. I don't believe, that is, that the concept of truth can simply be equated with whatever it may be rational to hold true at some particular time. But I think that all historians are inclined towards a kind of mild relativism. By that I mean that all historians who are interested in trying to understand cultures in which the beliefs and practices are very different from their own are already embracing a mild relativism. They see their project as being one of translation in a very broad sense, that is, of trying to get inside a different culture and then trying to render the terms of that culture in a way that is at the same time faithful to its differences.

As to the other titles, I've always been very interested in the Idealist tradition in philosophy, with many of my heroes coming from the anti-positivist, Idealist tradition of British philosophy. In fact, one of the writers who I suppose has had the most direct theoretical influence on my practice as a historian has been R. G. Collingwood; and so, if he is an Idealist, then that is not a label I would want to disavow. However, the label I want to put on myself is the one I used when I had to think of a title for the series I edit for the Cambridge University Press, a title which expresses the kind of intellectual history I'm interested in and which I try to practise: 'Ideas in Context'. In other words, I suppose that if I had to describe myself it would be as a historian whose work is intertextual, contextualist in approach.

Robert Darnton has confessed that he owed much of his historical work to his immense luck in having walked into 'a historian's dream', that is, a treasury with documents waiting to be discovered. In his case this was the finding of untouched papers in the archives of the Société Typographique de Neuchâtel, the largest publishing house in Switzerland in the eighteenth century. Has anything similar happened to you?

I had no such luck, but I think I can remember exactly what it was that did in fact set me off. And here I need to come back to Peter Laslett (who was my first adviser when I graduated) and also say something about the astonishingly different way in which academic careers could start in the early sixties, since that is (to use the title of Laslett's famous book) 'a world we have lost'. I belong to that generation which could still hope for appointment to a tenured university position before and even without having a Ph.D. I graduated in 1962 and my college, Caius, still had the option in those days of electing someone to a research fellowship on the strength of their undergraduate examination results. The college decided to make such an election in my own case, and so, without having done any academic research to justify my election, I moved immediately from being an undergraduate to being a fellow of my college. But in fact I never took up the fellowship, for later in the same summer a yet more extraor-dinary thing happened to me. One of the main teachers of history at Christ's College, John Kenyon, a very distinguished seventeenth-century historian, suddenly accepted a professorship at Hull and left the college at very short notice. That was when Neil McKendrick, who was my director of studies at Caius (and is now Master of the college) recommended me to Sir Jack Plumb, then one of the most successful teachers of history in the university. I was thereupon elected to a teaching fellowship at Christ's and made assistant Director of Studies in History, although I was still only twenty-one. In a way it was a very exciting start and for a while I was submerged in a big and challenging job: I helped with undergraduate admissions in history, did a lot of college examining and taught about fifteen hours a week. On the other hand, that made it difficult for me to start doing research. That was when Peter Laslett made another import-ant contribution to my career. He saw that what had happened to me might look wonderful, but could actually be terrible for my intellectual life. Since I did not have a formal supervisor, because I was not doing a Ph.D., the attention he gave me and the endless conversations we had in his college rooms and at his home were of extreme value to me at the time.

I remember talking to him about his new edition of Locke and feeling that he had a strange idea of what he had achieved in that work. He told me that, whereas commentators used to link Hobbes and Locke together as systematic theorists of politics, he had sought to dethrone Locke as an architectonic thinker and to show that, by contrast with Hobbes's

Leviathan, Locke's *Two Treatises* was a mere *pièce d'occasion*. But he still seemed to think of Hobbes as the author of a system of politics capable of being appraised independently of its historical context.

Well, the problem was that Laslett's own work had persuaded me that, contrary to what he seemed to believe, there must be similar work to be done on *any* philosophical text. That was when I decided to try to do for Hobbes what Laslett had done for Locke. I never properly succeeded, of course, for the task is a vast one, but Laslett was very helpful in getting me going. In particular, he advised me to go to Chatsworth to find out if there was any manuscript material there which might help to relate Hobbes to his political context. My earliest publications were, in fact, based on my taking Peter's advice seriously. To my surprise, hardly anyone had gone to Chatsworth to look at that material and to ask that question before. I think I was one of the first scholars to make use of Hobbes's unpublished correspondence, and one of my earliest articles was about the significance of that source. It didn't help me to work out the ideological context of Hobbes's thought, but it did begin to give me a sense of the intellectual traditions within which he was working. It was on the same occasion that I came across a brief manuscript by Hobbes commenting on a particular political crisis – the so-called Exclusion Crisis – which cropped up in the year of his death. To me that was extremely exciting because it showed a great political theorist commenting on something going on in Parliament at the time.

So I would say that I began my career with three big pieces of luck. One was to have had the benefit of Laslett's excellent advice. Another was to have started my career in a faculty of history, not philosophy, where there would have been no interest in the kind of contextual questions which, I quickly found, attracted me above all. But my greatest luck, and this is a point I'd like to return to, was in my contemporaries, for I began research at the same time as a remarkable group of young scholars who likewise benefited from the huge expansion in British higher education in the 1960s.

Considering the importance you give to authorial intentions in order to recover the 'historical identity' of a text, what could you say about your own intentions when writing what seems to be your manifesto of 1969 – 'Meaning and Understanding in the History of Ideas'? Have all your other works been a response to the same problem?

Very much so. I suppose that my practice as an historian has always been to try to go in the direction I pointed to in that early article. It was a manifesto, as you rightly call it. It was written in order to shock and irritate and it succeeded. My aim was to challenge two prevailing approaches to intellectual history, and it is perhaps not surprising that I had the utmost difficulty in getting the article published. It was turned down by several journals before it was finally accepted by *History and Theory*. It's very much a work of its time, very polemical, and I would never write like that now, not least because the two approaches I was engaging with are not nearly so much practised any more. One of these approaches treated the philosophical works of, for example, Plato, Hobbes, Hume or Hegel as if they were floating around in a kind of eternal present. My aim was not just to say that I wanted the subject approached differently, but also to show that no one could ever hope properly to understand such texts by purely textual analysis. Using *The Prince* of Machiavelli as an illustration, I tried to show that there are masses of very important things about many philosophical texts that you will never understand if you just read them. You will never, in particular, understand what they are *doing*, whether they are satirizing, repudiating, ridiculing, ignoring, accepting other points of view, and so on. In my recent book on Hobbes I still move in the same direction, trying to give answers to questions of that form.

The second target of my manifesto was the Marxist tradition of intellectual history which was very important at that time, specially after the publication of C. B. Macpherson's Marxist interpretation of the political theory of the seventeenth century, *The Political Theory of Possessive Individualism*, which came out in 1962. That book disturbed me enormously. I thought it was a tremendous piece of writing, a tremendously insightful way of thinking about Hobbes's and Locke's texts but, at the same time, I thought there was something profoundly wrong with seeing their doctrines as a kind of reflex of the deep social and economic structures of their society. I didn't like that at all, although I now feel I wasn't at all successful in explaining in my manifesto what I didn't like about it. What I wanted, though, was to argue that the way to get at such texts is to try to find out not the social but the intellectual context in which their doctrines were worked out.

Do you reject Marxism en bloc, or do you see some value in the work of Marx or some of his followers?

The short answer is that I do not in the least reject Marxism *en bloc* and that I think, furthermore, that it is an unfortunate feature of contemporary social theory that Marxism has become so discredited as a social philosophy. Considering the importance of this subject, I'd like to talk about this at somewhat greater length.

I'd like to start by referring to three ways in which Marxism has been valuable and important to me. The first is at the methodological level. It seems to me that all of us have now internalized one of the fundamental assumptions of Marxism, namely that social being determines consciousness. Nobody would now try to write history without assuming that that is so at some level and to some degree. The problem, of course, arises when we ask about the exact degree and level of that determination. No one, I take it, thinks that the determination is complete. I'll try to say something more about that in a minute. The second point is related to the kind of social diagnosis – and diagnostic vocabulary – Marxism has bequeathed to us. We surely cannot deny that Marxism has given us a valuable vocabulary for talking about social relations in any society. No one nowadays would think that they could investigate the social world without taking up a number of explanatory concepts – for example, alienation, or exploitation – that are specifically Marxist in provenance. This brings me to my third point, which is that, ironically, some of Marx's predictions have never seemed more perceptive than now, at the exact moment when Marxism has become widely discredited as a social philosophy. Certainly Marx was not thinking on the global scale, but the relationship of the capitalist world to the third world – the first getting richer while the second gets poorer as a result of its debt to the first – seems to me a very serious problem for the coming century.

Having said that, I must also make the point that my own thinking has been, I wouldn't say anti-Marxist, but certainly non-Marxist, and this for two main reasons. As I mentioned before, I was very critical of Marxism in my polemical writings of the 1960s, when the Marxist approach was very influential due to works such as those of C. B. Macpherson and Christopher Hill. One of the tenets I most of all opposed was Marx's theory of ideology, that is, the suggestion that people's beliefs can be explained not just as causal products but as mere epiphenomena of their social circumstances. One of my main aspirations at the time was to show that this notion is a mistake, which I think I did, and in the following way. One of the fundamental purposes of ideological structures is to legitimize or de-legitimize social arrangements. But if this is true, then the capacity of any group to make changes in their social arrangements, and to carry people with them in any debate about the moral value of those changes, will depend on their having access to a moral vocabulary which is itself capable of being used to criticize those arrangements. Well, such moral vocabularies are not given *by* us, they are given *to* us; in other words, if they have any normative force, this will be because they are historically embedded and available in consequence as recognizable weapons of debate. But to the extent that that is so, then what we can do by way of reforming and changing our society will depend on how far we can make our proposed programme of change fit onto one of these pre-existent moral vocabularies; because unless people can recognize reform projects as being moral projects, they won't embrace them. The point I wanted to stress is that what you can do in social practices depends on the moral descriptions you can give of what you are doing. And if that is so, the Marxist theory of ideology is identifiably mistaken, because these descriptions are not epiphenomena, are not causal products of some other processes, but, on the contrary, will have to be ranked among the causal conditions of social change.

My other main reason for being a non-Marxist is related to the positivism of Marxism, a weakness I became increasingly aware of in the seventies. During those years I was working at the Institute for Advanced Study in Princeton, and so had the amazing good fortune to be a colleague of Clifford Geertz and Thomas Kuhn. (I had the office next to Kuhn's.) They helped me to see the importance of the fact that Marx still inhabited an unduly simple world in which he felt able to speak of true consciousness and false consciousness. But in a more postmodern culture – of the kind I found myself exposed to at Princeton – in which consciousness is seen more in the nature of a construction, Marxism begins to look like a very crude way of looking at the social world. The more interesting questions seem to be about how to negotiate different constructions, since all of them might have something to be said for them. The historical or anthropological task is then to vindicate the rationality of different constructions by trying to make sense of them from the inside. Now, Marxism with its very strong true–false dichotomy doesn't really allow for that kind of approach. But I'm tempted to say that the aspiration to vindicate so far as possible the rationality of our ancestors is the approach any historian *must* adopt.

Finally, I would like to insist that I remain of the view, like many other people in the Western world, that there remains something noble about Marx's diagnosis of what is wrong with capitalism. It is true that we've discovered that capitalism is the most effective – perhaps the only effective – means of delivering prosperity to very large numbers of people. But the fact that no other economic system has ever achieved that prodigious feat should not blind us to the fact that it has large human costs embedded in it. I don't see why we should pretend it doesn't have those costs simply because it's more efficient than any other system. The fact that communism has been discredited doesn't mean that there isn't anything discreditable about capitalism. It remains a very unfair system just as Marxism remains a very interesting way of thinking about those unfairnesses.

The type of intellectual history you practise has been described as 'a revolution in the historiography of political thought'. How revolutionary do you think it really is?

Wittgenstein says in the epigraph to his *Philosophical Investigations* that all advances are less important than they look. I think that some scholars of my generation did change the way that intellectual history was written, but you can easily see where we were getting our ideas from. I certainly don't think I produced a revolution. I did begin to write intellectual history a bit differently from the way in which it was generally being written. But it is easy for me to recall the people by whom I was deeply influenced, either because they had already theorized the position I took up, or else because their practice seemed to me exemplary. It's fair to say that there were very few of these people when I started off; very little to admire had been produced in the 1950s. But in my memory four names unquestionably stand out, two of which I have already mentioned, but the other two of which were at least as important for my development, if not more so.

Chronologically, R. G. Collingwood comes first. My teacher John Eyre put me onto Collingwood's *Autobiography* while I was still at school, and I came back to it when I first started to do research, encouraged that time round, I think, by some fine work published about Collingwood's philosophy of history by John Passmore in the early 1960s. I was enormously taken with Collingwood's core idea – which originally came out of his aesthetics – that all works of art (including works of philosophy and literature) are intentional objects, and thus that to understand them we must aim to recover and understand the purposes underlying them. These purposes are never written on their surface, but it's part of the hermeneutic task to find them out. By directing us away from surfaces towards purposes, this approach in turn suggests that we shall need to look at immediate contexts in quest of the understanding we seek. This was the idea that struck me so forcibly when I first started out. This already shows that the alleged revolution was not so revolutionary, since that theoretical work had already been done.

Next in order, as I've already said, came Peter Laslett. With his name, however, I need to couple a third, that of my friend John Dunn, who was also a student of Laslett's and was an exact contemporary of mine at Cambridge. When we started off I took Hobbes and John took Locke. He was much quicker than me and by 1969 he had published his absolutely classic monograph on the political theory of Locke. At the level of method this book was and remains exemplary. In 1968 he also published his classic article 'The Identity of the History of Ideas' in which he theorized the approach embodied in his book. I felt that that essay and that book really showed how to do the subject. In those days John and I used to meet and talk constantly about our work, how to do our subject, what would be the interesting questions to ask, which books were wonderful and which were junk. John was always enormously confident and always emphasized how much junk there was to be cleared away. From him I think I learned most of all.

The fourth name is that of John Pocock. I did not meet him until the late 1960s, after we had corresponded for quite some time, but when I first read his work as an undergraduate he seemed to me to be Collingwood put into practice. I was overwhelmed by his book *The Ancient Constitution and the Feudal Law* (1957), especially by the intertextual quality of the text and by the way he wrote the history not of an idea, but of people using ideas and working through arguments. To me that was the most exciting book I read as an undergraduate. It seems now a rather dry book to be so excited by, but it shows that I was already interested in a kind of intellectual history which was not usually being done.

Your work has given rise to a whole school of followers here and abroad and also, as you say, 'a distressingly numerous group' of critics. How important have these criticisms been for the development of your ideas?

There is one criticism of my philosophical work that has made me reconsider my position about the theory of interpretation quite extensively. In the book about my work edited by James Tully, *Meaning and Context*, so many critics converged on this specific point that it enabled me to see that I hadn't formulated my views about interpretation as carefully as I should have done.

The point is a purely philosophical one, but it's of enormous importance to me in my historical practice. Perhaps I can best put it as follows. There's a distinction one would want to draw that would be extremely important if one were asking questions, as I've done, about the relations between authorial intentionality and the interpretation of texts. The distinction is between questions, on the one hand, about what an author may have intended to say; and, on the other hand, about what an author may have intended or meant by the act of saying what he or she said. Although these are two completely different issues, postmodernist critics often confuse them and suppose that, when someone like me talks about intentionality, that must mean that they're talking about it in the first of the two senses I've just isolated. That's why there has been so much postmodernist criticism of my kind of work, in which my critics have emphasized that authors are not necessarily the best authorities on their own texts, that the meaning of their works is a public matter and separable from what they may have intended, that one has to take on board Derrida's points about the polysemic character of virtually all our utterances, etc. etc. Well, I have never doubted any of that and I'm pretty much a postmodernist in relation to these issues. So all these critics of my work have been attacking a position I've never defended. What I have defended is a completely different position. I am interested in intentionality not with respect to meanings but with respect to speech acts. I am interested, that is, in trying to recover what may have been the meaning of the act of writing particular texts.

As a result, in my recent book, *Reason and Rhetoric in the Philosophy of Hobbes*, I've tried to reformulate and advance my argument about interpretation in a way that protects it against the criticism I've mentioned. The question that underpins the book is not so much what Hobbes means in his various texts, but what he is *up to*, what he may have *meant* by writing as he did. Answering my own question, I argue that he was questioning, criticizing, seeking to discredit, seeking to supersede a particular understanding of the relations between eloquence and argument, an understanding that had been central to Renaissance ideas about civil science. Now, the kind of approach I try to put to work in this book is founded on my having been made to see more clearly than I saw before the nature of the distinction between the two concepts of intentionality. My critics in this case really helped me to reformulate that distinction, thereby enabling me to clarify where I take issue with postmodernists and where I don't.

Your book about reason and rhetoric in Hobbes seems to have a certain analogy with Starobinski's interpretation of Rousseau as a thinker who found 'le remède dans le mal'. Do you think that this was also the case with Hobbes and the art of rhetoric?

I've never thought of this parallel, but I think the analogy *is* an appropriate one. Hobbes was educated in the rhetorical tradition, as was everybody who went to school in Elizabethan England. In the 1630s, though, a dramatic rupture occurred when he became deeply interested for the first time in the new sciences and encountered scientists like Galileo and Mersenne: he became seduced by the idea that the methods of the physical sciences could be applied to all forms of human enquiry. His first work of civil science, which he called *De cive*, reflects this commitment. Wishing his own civil science to be a closed deductive system, he proceeded entirely by giving definitions, and then pursuing their logical and material implications. As to the literary problem of how to write that kind of science, Hobbes made it clear in the Preface to *De cive* that he would write in as anti-rhetorical a style as possible. But then, in later works, one sees that Hobbes fell into despair about the reception of his own philosophy, especially his *De cive*. Although he believed that he had arrived at the truth about the best kind of political system, he realized that he had not succeeded in persuading anyone. So he was left confronting the question of whether he couldn't use persuasive techniques in the service of science.

Now, reflecting on your quotation from Starobinski, I see that it really does apply, for I see Hobbes's *Leviathan* as an attempt to answer his own question by way of making the disease part of the cure. Basically, Hobbes detests rhetoric for the same reasons as Plato detested it: for its appeal to emotion instead of reason, for its aspiration to persuade instead of teach. Nevertheless, in order to get his own message across, he was led to use the methods of persuasion, and especially of ridicule, to underpin and so advance what he took to be the cause of reason. This is why I feel that, although Hobbes's *Leviathan* is rightly aligned with the works of Gassendi, Mersenne and above all Descartes, there is also a case for associating it with the works of Montaigne, Rabelais and other great satirists of the Renaissance.

Most of your work has been centred on two political writers who were famous for being cynical realists: Machiavelli and Hobbes. What attracts you to them and not, say, to more idealistic ones like Locke and Rousseau?

That is something I have thought about a lot and I would say that there is a methodological as well as a substantive reason for my choice. The substantive point is that I turn out to be interested as a historian in writing about figures whom I don't find personally attractive, towards whom I do not have a great feeling of emotional affinity. I seem to enjoy tackling bodies of philosophy where I have to work against my own grain. This is more or less the same attitude as I try to adopt in my more workaday intellectual life. For example, I subscribe to *The Economist* in spite of its politics causing me to spit blood every time I read it. The reason I continue to subscribe is not only because this is the best-informed magazine about current affairs. It's also because I feel that it is going to educate me far more than if I only read the *Guardian*, with which I probably agree too readily.

As to the methodological reason for my choice, I think it carries me quite deeply into my motivations as a scholar and it takes me back to the time when I was talking a great deal to Peter Laslett about his work on Locke. As I've mentioned, Laslett's own view of what he had achieved greatly surprised me. He thought he had removed Locke's *Two Treatises* from the canon of classic treatises of political thought. But he still seemed to think that there was a canon of such treatises, that these at least could be understood independently of their time, and that the paradigm case of such a treatise was Hobbes's *Leviathan*. But having been so influenced by Laslett's work on Locke, I thought that it was bound to be true that any work of political theory was going to be motivated by an immediate political context which needed to be uncovered. So, in an act no doubt of aggression towards my revered teacher, I set forth to try to uncover the ideological context in which, and for which, Hobbes's *Leviathan* was composed. And I believe I eventually succeeded in showing that Hobbes's *Leviathan* was written in order to provide an answer to an urgent question of political obligation that had arisen in the immediate aftermath of the execution of King Charles I and the success of the Cromwellian revolution: should a government be obeyed even if it does not have a right to rule? Hobbes addresses that question and offers a deliberately eirenic answer by way of disjoining questions of obligation from questions of right and linking them instead to questions about whether we are being effectively protected.

In your Liberty before Liberalism *there is an intriguing assertion, which seems to have a specific target: historians, you say, should try 'to write about the past with as much seriousness as their talents allow'. Could you, in a Skinnerian way, explain what you intended to do in writing as you did?*

Yes, there was a target there that I decided not to identify because I thought it might seem aggressive towards some of my colleagues. But now I would love to say a word about what lies behind that remark. I wrote it partly, of course, in a spirit of realism about the fact that it's difficult for me and most other historians to write anything serious at all, simply because the talents required are greater than we possess. But at the same time I wanted to criticize a quite widespread belief in the historical profession, both in this country and in the United States, which seems to me to have the effect of undervaluing the seriousness of the vocation of being a historian. The belief in question may be summarized as follows. It is not enough, we are told, and it may be even a mistake, for professional historians to address themselves exclusively to their own professional colleagues; they ought instead to see their real task as that of reaching out to a wider audience. As a result of this belief, some historians spend much of their time turning out reviews and articles for general cultural magazines, as well as books intended not for a professional audience, but rather for people who enjoy reading a bit of history on the side.

When I say that this view undervalues the seriousness of our vocation, I am thinking of the work of great historians like F. W. Maitland, for instance, who addressed serious theoretical questions in a historical spirit. The brilliant essays he wrote a century ago on the concept of the state and the theory of corporation are still eminently worth reading, and show the profound cultural significance of writing genuinely philosophical history. To this it is often objected that this is an unduly elitist view of the historian's task. But this objection strikes me as completely mistaken, as we can easily see if we reflect for a moment on the work of a great historian like Max Weber. His work – which has been translated into every major language and is still read a century after he wrote – asks fundamental questions about our understanding of social structure and social change. So, if you happen to be as gifted as Weber, the audience is enormous. The irony is that if Weber had written a textbook about the history of Germany aimed at 'a wider audience', he would not only have misused his talents but would not have reached nearly as wide an audience as he eventually did. I am aware that my vision of what the historians should do may seem rather austere, in the sense that I do think we should be addressing ourselves to our professional colleagues. But that itself, I must insist, is at least potentially a huge audience. When you think about the excellent series edited by Keith Thomas, Past Masters, in which some of the titles have been translated into over twenty languages, you get a good idea of its very large size.

Do you think that your new approach in studying Machiavelli in his intellectual and political context has done anything to counteract his sinister reputation for duplicity and immorality?

I hope my approach has done this in various ways. When I first started to write about Machiavelli in the early seventies there was a pronounced view, especially in Italian scholarship, that saw in his political theory a complete divorce of politics from morality. According to this view, Machiavelli was seen either as a realist critic of Christian morality or as an anti-Christian, an immoralist. This latter view became extremely important in American historiography, especially in the hands of Leo Strauss and his disciples, who saw Machiavelli, to use Strauss's phrase, as 'a preacher of evil'. What I tried to do was to show that both those views of Machiavelli were seriously mistaken. First, to say he was not a Christian moralist is not to say he was an immoralist. Christian moralism was not the only form of moralism available to a well-educated figure in sixteenth-century Italy. There was also the whole Roman tradition of moral philosophy in which Machiavelli was saturated. He knew by heart his Sallust, Livy and Cicero, and in their works he could find a particular view about *virtù* – which should not be translated as 'virtue' but as the means by which princes are able to attain their ends, that is, bring security to the people and honour and glory to themselves.

To me a second very interesting point about Machiavelli was that, while he was a classical moralist, he was also the most profound critic of classical and Renaissance moral philosophy. According to his humanist contemporaries, the actual qualities that enabled rulers to attain their ends were the princely virtues of clemency, liberality, justice and so forth. Repudiating these values, Machiavelli insists that a willingness to act according to the dictates of necessity, without considering whether one's actions are essentially good or bad, is what enables political leaders to attain their ends of civic glory and greatness. Rather than being an immoralist, Machiavelli's political theory announces a new moral claim: that humanistic virtue is not, as they had claimed, the road to glory and greatness, but the road to ruin. According to Machiavelli, if you want to succeed in this dark world, you must do good so far as possible but evil whenever necessary. Therein lies the true *virtù* of the prince.

You have argued that the 'business of the historian is surely to serve as a recording angel, not a hanging judge'. But is it always good – and is it even possible – to be neutral on historical matters?

I make a kind of optimistic distinction here. On the one hand, the task of the historian is that of a recording angel in the sense that his or her aspiration must be to try to recapture the past in its own terms. In the case of Machiavelli, for instance, what I tried to do was to see him within his own intellectual setting and thereby find out what kind of debate he was taking part in, what kind of intervention his work constituted, what kind of historical understanding we can acquire of the position he came to adopt.

But, on the other hand, I would be critical of scholars who, in selecting the questions they are going to study, do not allow themselves to be guided by some sense of what might be important for us to know here and now. In other words, I think that our values should be expressed at the level of our motivations as scholars. But then, once we have chosen a subject, we must, as far as possible, act simply as scholars. I began by saying that I had made an optimistic distinction. I must confess that I am not sure that we can hold motivation completely separate from practice, because, no doubt, one's practice is contaminated by the desire to get certain things to come out in certain ways. Nevertheless, the historian's duty is to minimize that so far as possible; otherwise the study of history stops being proper scholarship and just becomes ideology.

There is a case that provoked a huge debate in the United States in the 1980s, which illustrates what I'm trying to say as well as its difficulties. A young scholar called Abraham, whose approach seemed to some critics to imply hostility to capitalism, put forward the argument that big business played a major role in the downfall of the Weimar Republic. Well, his critics claimed that in order to uphold that thesis he had to falsify a lot of the documentation. I am not, of course, taking sides here, and in fact Abraham had many defenders, but I offer the example as an instance of the distinction I'm trying to draw. Of course it is of the first importance to understand how democracies come to be undermined and how tyrannies come to supersede democracies. So if that was Abraham's motivation for investigating such a disastrous event, it was certainly an honourable and morally important motivation. But once you enter the archives, you must do so armed only with hypotheses, not with ready-made judgements. If it was true, as some critics seemed to imply, that this historian wanted to accuse big business because he was a Marxist, then that would have been a kind of *trahison des clercs*. Our motivations must be held apart from what the documents say. Of course we can't talk as positivist historians used to do about letting the documents tell us the facts. We can't ever report all the facts, so we always have to select and all selections are inevitably partial. Nevertheless the documents constrain us; there are things they will and things they won't let us say.

In your Liberty before Liberalism *you claimed that the task of intellectual historians is to refrain from any enthusiasm or indignation, leaving readers to make their own judgement. Nevertheless, you seem to have infringed your own rule when you judge the republican ideal of liberty (with its emphasis on people's duties) preferable to the 'libertarian form of contemporary liberalism', with its obsession with self-interest and individual rights. Would you agree that, in this case, Skinner the reader has become confused with Skinner the historian?*

I have to admit that the division between motivation and practice that I advocated earlier in our conversation may have been breached here. What I should like to say in my own defence, though, is that there's another distinction that interests me in the way historians set about their task. On the one hand, they can be motivated to try to find a particular set of values in the past that they want to excavate and bring back to view. On the other hand, they may simply be engaged, in so far as this is possible, in a kind of neutral or scholarly investigation, in the course of which they may happen to come upon structures of thought which seem to them to have got lost or muddled in later times. And if these look to them morally valuable, they may find it worth excavating them and trying to make people ruminate about those structures of thought once more.

Now, I truly believe that my own case falls into the second category. I was undertaking a quite neutral scholarly enquiry into the development of early Renaissance republicanism as a background to the understanding of Machiavelli's works. In the course of this investigation, I came upon the accounts of the paradoxes of freedom that were worked out so brilliantly in Renaissance moral theory, and above all in Machiavelli's *Discorsi*. I mean the paradoxes that speak of freedom as the product of service. At first I was only interested in understanding these paradoxes, but soon I fell in love with them and came to feel that they represented a kind of model which could still be deeply relevant today. So I started to write on freedom and citizenship because I was inspired by the wish to re-present to an audience which had become obsessed with notions of rights and interests a completely different model, in which the notion of duty was prioritized and citizens were not encouraged to see themselves simply as consumers of government. Mine was a kind of essay in retrieval, so to speak, in which I wanted to reintroduce a way of thinking about individual liberty that comes from within our own tradition, but of which we had lost sight. I ended up by writing about a missing theory of citizenship in our current debates. This is the reason why Foucault's image of the historian as an archaeologist who brings to the surface layers of meanings and of lost traditions is so important for me.

You have taken on the task of bringing to light the neo-Roman tradition of liberty that was silenced by the liberal tradition. What contribution can this revival make to the current debate about theories of liberty?

I believe that this tradition can help us to contest classical liberalism because it gives a completely different account of the circumstances in which individuals might claim to have been deprived of their freedom within a civil association. Think how discussions about the relations between the freedom of citizens and the powers of the state have developed in the Anglo-American tradition of classical liberalism. In this tradition you find an analysis of the freedom of the individual in terms of the coercive powers of the state, and the view taken is that the less coercion there is, the more freedom. Now, that suggests that forms of government are not particularly important, because what matters for freedom is not who coerces you but how much you are coerced. You tend to end up with the view that who governs best governs least.

It is clear that underlying this picture of the relation of freedom to the state is a recognizable political agenda, which is powerful but contestable. By bringing back to the surface the neo-Roman view of freedom, I wanted to show that classical liberalism has bequeathed us a very narrow sense of the conditions under which we can properly claim that we are unfree. Governments may not have to coerce their citizens in order to cause them to do what they want. When people are rendered dependent on the goodwill of the powerful, they will internalize a sense of the dangers of behaving in certain ways, and therefore will not behave in those ways, not because they know that something bad will happen to them if they do, but because they know that something bad might or could happen to them it they do, simply because of the discretionary powers held by those on whom they depend. I felt that bringing these neo-Roman insights into the debate might help us make a larger but justifiable claim upon the liberal state in the name of liberty.

It is rather significant that early liberal theorists noticed this challenging power of the rival neo-Roman view and, as a result, sought to marginalize it as incoherent and dangerous. In fact, the story of the hegemonic success of classical liberalism in Anglophone political theory is, in part, the story of the discrediting of the neo-Roman theory of liberty. The book I am now trying to write is about exactly this historical development.

In an article which well illustrates your way of writing history, you showed that the Royal Society was not originally a centre of learning and research, but, on the contrary, a gentleman's club which excluded Hobbes because he was socially inadequate, or, as you put it, 'a club bore'. What led you to such an original interpretation?

This article is a Cinderella amongst the essays I have written about Hobbes, so I'm very glad that you mention it. It was, in fact, strongly criticized because people thought I had overemphasized the extent to which the Royal Society did not have a project of an identifiable intellectual kind. I think I was led to my interpretation first of all by the influence upon me of Thomas Kuhn's writings, especially his insistence that we should never read back into earlier societies the paradigms we have for understanding our own society and its institutions and practices. I remember being overwhelmed by Kuhn's *The Structure of Scientific Revolutions* when I first read it in the mid-1960s, and especially by his point about the debate between Galileo and the Pisan professors. The dispute about the use of the telescope had very little to do with factual information, argued Kuhn, but was a theoretical debate between two different paradigms for viewing celestial objects. When studying the early years of the Royal Society I realized that most people who had written about it had had the modern Royal Society in mind, and thought about it as a competitive learned society in which scientific expertise was the only criterion for admission. According to this view, Hobbes could never have been a fellow because he was not a proper scientist. But I was struck by the fact that, although the institution had kept the same name throughout its existence, it seemed a very different kind of institution in the time of Hobbes. But what finally led me to my conclusion about the personal reasons for Hobbes's exclusion was my examination of his correspondence. This source showed that there was nothing in principle that stopped him from being a fellow of the Society. At one point he was excluded because of personal hostility from other members, and at a later point he refused an invitation to join the Society as a response to that previous hostility. I thought my interpretation was the one best supported by the relevant evidence.

How different is your notion of linguistic context from the notion of mentalité, *as the French* Annales *historians use it?*

It is very different because mine is a much more modest enterprise. Bloch and Febvre, for example, were interested in whole mental worlds, the whole *Weltanschauung* of people at different periods. I have never had the confidence to work on that kind of broad canvas, have never asked myself about the mental world of the Renaissance, and, in fact, if I found a book with that title I am not sure I would want to read it. Although Bloch and Febvre were great historians who wrote wonderful texts, I would not recommend a student to study a *mentalité*. To ask about an entire ensemble of beliefs is, for me, the wrong type of unit to take. When I talk about linguistic conventions, beliefs and practices, I do so because I am interested in understanding individual texts. Say that you are interested, as in my case, in understanding the theory of republican liberty as it was developed in Machiavelli's *Discorsi*. You need to identify the context that both takes meaning from and gives meaning to that particular text. The questions to ask are: what are the sources of his view, what sort of theory is being advanced, what does it seek to discredit, whom is it siding with, etc.? All those are questions which would certainly lead one into a mental world, but it's the very specific mental world of Renaissance political theory and of its sources in Roman antiquity.

I am fundamentally interested in linguistic contexts, that is, in the study of whatever texts make sense of the vocabulary, the preoccupations, the organization and the themes of whatever particular text I happen to be basically interested in. All my work is about how, and the extent to which, the understanding of any one text presupposes an understanding of its relationship to other texts. But while I concentrate on such intellectual contexts, I assume at the same time that nobody ever writes political theory in a political vacuum. There wouldn't be any political discourse at all if no one had any political motivation to engage in that kind of discourse. There is always going to be some story to be told about the politics of the society in which a text like *Leviathan*, for instance, was written; always some story about what immediate political problems set the questions that it sought to answer. So my books tend to have rather elementary bits of political history in them at the beginning, and then a great deal of intertextual material. In short, the hermeneutical task I am interested in is much more modest than the ambitious one aimed at by the historians of *mentalité*.

The so-called 'minor works' seem to gain importance in your intellectual approach. Would you advise historians to enter, as Meinecke put it, 'the catacombs of forgotten literature by mediocrities'?

Well, I am really a quite traditional intellectual historian in this respect. When I talk about the kind of explanatory context I am interested in – explanatory not in the sense of giving causal explanations but of shedding light on the meanings of texts – I do presuppose that there will be a whole variety of texts worth exploring. And when I say 'texts', I have in mind the widest possible sense of that term, so that buildings, pieces of music and paintings, as much as works of literature and philosophy, are all texts to be read. But, having said that, at no point do I endorse the idea that we should always enter the catacombs of forgotten texts, because they may have been forgotten for very good reasons. My only reason for being interested in catacombs – and I do spend a lot of my time reading small-scale and uninteresting texts – is the hope that they will illuminate other texts of unquestionable importance.

Do you agree with Passmore's distinction between the aims, emphases and methods of the history of philosophy and cultural history, and his placing of intellectual history in between these two?

I do not agree at all with this view, developed by Passmore in an influential article in *History and Theory*, although as I've mentioned I was greatly impressed by the article when it first appeared. The reason is that, by contrast with my approach, Passmore is centrally interested in the truth-content of the beliefs he studies. I, on the other hand, am not primarily interested in the truth of the doctrines I examine. I'm interested in the circumstances that generated them and made them the doctrines they were, in getting a sense of their internal coherence, of their relationship to other texts, and so forth. I don't at this stage ask myself whether I'm disposed to *agree* with the doctrines concerned.

According to this latter view, there is no point in distinguishing the history of philosophy from intellectual or cultural history, since they deal equally with texts to which we want to put the same sorts of questions: what they are doing within their culture, what their motivation is, what their character is, what their role is, and so on. In this sense, I suppose I'm a bit more postmodernist than Passmore, since I do not make any strong distinctions between types of historical document. I do not go as far as Derrida in extending the notion of a text to encompass everything, because I want to preserve the notion for something less metaphorical than that. But I am very sympathetic to Derrida's point that all philosophical texts are literary constructs, and that it is therefore worth putting to them the same range of questions we have always asked about literary texts.

If, as Collingwood insists, 'all history is the history of thought' because to penetrate the inside of events and to detect the thoughts which they express is what historians aim to do, what is distinct about intellectual history?

The reason why Collingwood says that we must seek to re-enact past thoughts is that he thinks, rightly of course, that human action is the product of human thought in the shape of beliefs and desires. Nevertheless, human action is not in fact the subject matter of a great deal of history – most obviously, it is rarely the subject matter of social or economic history. Such historians tend to be interested not in actions but in processes, not in events but in statistical findings, and in this and other kinds of history the notion of human action has much less importance.

Collingwood's proposition is, therefore, an extreme overstatement. But as far as intellectual history is concerned, the suggestion seems to me very fruitful, but in a way that might have surprised him. I will try to explain. When Collingwood said that all history is the history of thought, I think he was connecting up in his mind the idea of rethinking people's thoughts with the idea of getting at the intended meanings of texts. Now, as I've already indicated, I would not myself want to say that this is the task of the interpreter of any complex philosophical text. I am sufficient of a postmodernist to want to question the relationship between author and authority, and to want to say that a text may bear all kinds of meanings which will not have been intended by its author. But another and quite different project is to try to discover what the author may have intended by saying what he or she said. In this case, what is of interest is what I've already called speech acts. By this I mean that any speech has a meaning but is also an act. If you take a simple utterance, like 'the ice over there is very thin', the phrase has a meaning but it also has a force – the force in that case being that of warning the skater. So what seems very fruitful about Collingwood's remark is that, if all speeches are at the same time actions, then we want to bring to bear on the interpretation of speech and writing some of the same criteria we bring to bear on the explanation of any other kind of voluntary act. That means asking about motivation, about intentionality, and so forth. But not as questions about the intended meaning of the author's words. Rather as questions about what may have been intended by the act of writing those words.

You confess to preferring the study of discontinuities in our intellectual heritage to the continuities. But how is it possible to study discontinuities without studying continuities, since each seems to be defined against the other?

That remark, which comes from the little book I recently published called *Liberty before Liberalism*, was indeed an incautious one. I agree that it ought not to be the motivation of a scholar investigating some episode in the past to make an effort to find discontinuities. What I really wanted to say could best be put as follows. When a historian studies different theories within different communities of discourse in very remote periods of time, he or she will, I think, generally come upon two contrasting states of affairs. On the one hand, we certainly find continuities in concepts between even our remote forebears and ourselves. That seems to be the case for very deep concepts like freedom, rights, authority, obligation, and so forth. But on the other hand, the way in which these concepts are put together to make theories can differ enormously. Consider again the example I took of the familiar idea of freedom as absence of constraint. The modern liberal tradition supposes that all that can count as constraint is actual coercion of the individual by some other individual or group. An earlier tradition construed the concept of constraint differently and argued that individuals are also constrained if they live in conditions of dependence on the goodwill of others. What we find here is that, although both schools of thought are recognizably talking about our concept of freedom, they will nevertheless disagree in a large number of cases over the question of whether or not some particular agent is or is not free. Now, that is really a discontinuity within a continuity, which I think very commonly happens in the history of philosophy. Discontinuity in the application of the concepts, continuity in the underlying meanings of the terms used to express them.

You have insisted that intellectual history does not have any lesson for us, and that to demand from the study of the past the solution to our problems is not only 'a methodological fallacy but also a moral error'. In which way, then, is the study of the past meaningful?

This is a quotation from an early essay of mine and it is likely to look not merely an overstatement but a contradiction of some more recent points I have tried to make. Nevertheless, I still hold to this idea and would like to say something more about it. Throughout my career as an intellectual historian it has seemed to me that the best way to write about it is in the traditional manner of the historian of any other sort of human activity, that is, by trying to recapture the meaning or purpose of the activity in question from the point of view of the people engaged in it. Well, that is very different from the belief that the purpose of intellectual history is to assemble a small list of texts from all over our culture and label them the great texts that have something of timeless value to offer us. That was, in fact, a very prevalent view about the subject when I first started writing in the sixties. So by not approaching the past from our point of view, I was accused of trying to turn the study of political theory into a merely anti-quarian undertaking.

Having said that, I must stress that at no point did I suppose that there was not some kind of moral point or purpose in the history I was writing. On the contrary, I always hoped that, if we could reconstitute past theories in their own terms, thereby illuminating both their strangeness and their continuities with us, this might enable us to gain a richer sense of our own intellectual heritage and of our relationship to it. The moral interest of studying the past stems from the fact that it can reveal discontinuities perhaps even more readily than continuities. The discontinuities are just as capable of being illuminating to us. To uncover the reasons, quite often ideological, why some of our traditions became hegemonic while others were sidelined, so moving beyond what Gramsci describes as the hege-monic ideologies of our own period, is an important way in which history can educate us.

The title of your book The Foundations of Modern Political Thought *seems to announce a teleological approach. How do you reconcile the contextual message of the text with the forward-looking message of the title?*

This metaphor of foundations is inherently teleological, so there is a teleology built into the book which troubles me now. I would not write like that today. I was trying to tell the story of how, out of the destruction of feudal and Catholic Europe, a secularizing and purportedly neutralist and universalistic idea of the state emerged. That was recognizably an agenda set by Max Weber's idea of state formation. Designed and written in the late sixties and early seventies, that book was definitely based on an agenda of its day. I tried to write it in the light of that 'manifesto' of '69 that we talked about, presenting the book as the practice of that theory, but people have pointed out that it is much more forward-looking than my theory allowed.

In my defence I would say that, considering the complicated transformation I was interested in, I did not write teleologically in a gravely mistaken way. I did, however, write about the whole tradition of neo-scholasticism in an unduly selective way, and that is, as I see it now, the big weakness of the book. Because I was interested in that enormously important tradition of natural law, I pulled the texts out of shape in order to make them tell my story, forgetting that they were also telling very different stories crucial for them, especially stories about the ethics of empire and of war. I recruited them into a story of my making and not theirs, and to that degree my text violated my own principles.

I think, however, that the book followed up my principles at the basic level of trying to place the major texts of early modern political theory within the intellectual contexts that best made sense of them. And since that was the basis of the anti-textualist and pro-intertextualist methodology I had been advocating, I think that the book illustrated my principles far more than it violated them.

You specialize in European political thought. Does this choice imply a belief that political thought is essentially a European achievement?

I have thought a lot about this and I suppose that upon the answer I am going to give reposes part of the explanation why I chose in my late thirties to return to Europe rather than stay in America, where I had by then been living and working for several years. I am far from believing that the European tradition represents an exemplary achievement, nor am I even learned enough to be in a position to assert that it remains the most interesting tradition for us to be looking at today. For all I know, we should be studying the fate of Confucianism, or the mystical religions of India, or the history of American political thought. But what I have come to realize, especially through working in the United States, is that I am far more of a local historian than I used to suppose. The questions that preoccupy me are, I must admit, essentially about the European Renaissance and Reformation, about the rise of absolutism and the challenge to it and, more generally, about the relationship of the culture of early modernity to the classical world of antiquity. My questions are questions about fifteenth-, sixteenth- and seventeenth-century Europe, questions that in turn require me to have at least some understanding of the languages of Western Europe and of classical antiquity. Now, those are, I believe, enormously important questions because it so happened that the art, literature and philosophy of that period remain of huge human significance. But they are obviously local questions at the same time.

I must admit that, in a way, there is problem of cultural relativism here. When I lecture in France or in Italy or in other parts of Western Europe, I do not feel that I am a local historian in a parochial sense, since all these countries, like Great Britain, remain deeply marked and formed by the historical movements in which I'm interested. It is true that I lecture, if you like, largely about white European males, but not dead white European males, for these figures are still alive, in the important sense, for my audiences, which are of course European audiences too. When I lecture in the United States, however, or in China or Australia, I feel a much greater nervousness. The cultural traditions I know about are not in the same way part of the ordinary furniture of people's lives, and I am fully prepared to agree that there may be much less reason, perhaps no reason, why such people should be interested in the evolution of European culture.

Worried about the historical trend of thinking that everything is discourse and construction, Robert Darnton suggested that historians should start by being trained as reporters covering robbery, murder and rape. This would be a way to learn respect for the facts, since if they'd get the name of the murderer wrong, for instance, they could be sued. Would you give similar advice to would-be historians?

Well, I think that Bob Darnton speaks hyperbolically here, because in order to learn respect for factual information you would not necessarily have to become a reporter. You could learn the necessary respect in many other ways. I can see that, if you write the kind of history that Bob himself has increasingly written, then a preoccupation with reporting rape and murder might, no doubt, be a valuable training. But I have never been interested in that kind of history and I fail to see how being a reporter of the sensational tragedies of everyday life would help you become a better intellectual historian.

My advice to anyone who is interested in starting intellectual history would be to read exemplary studies by great practitioners of our own generation, since the linguistic turn of the 1960s and 1970s gave rise to some major works of cultural history and cultural anthropology. I would not tell my aspiring student to go away and become a reporter, but instead to read writers like Michel Foucault or Clifford Geertz or John Pocock, first of all because they are extraordinarily original practitioners and secondly because they explicitly theorize their practice.

The demands upon historians are great because, as Bob Darnton rightly suggests, they have to follow the facts patiently. But, of course, unlike the reporter, the historian has to be a person of imagination and theoretical skills as well, skills that were developed to an extraordinary degree by, for example, Foucault. I do not want to be seen to choose between accuracy and imagination, but I do want to stress that merely getting the facts right is not what matters in history. It also matters that we should ask new, important and truly imaginative questions, questions that enable existing facts to be seen in new ways.

You have been in Cambridge since you were an undergraduate, and will probably stay here until your retirement from the prestigious chair of Regius Professor. Do you see any danger of intellectual provincialism in this?

Well, of course there is a serious danger. I cannot but feel that I would have benefited immeasurably if I had had the good fortune to work in some other really major intellectual centres besides Cambridge and Princeton. The four years I spent in Princeton were extraordinarily formative, especially because I had the privilege of having Clifford Geertz and Albert Hirschman and Thomas Kuhn as my closest colleagues. Although they never set out to teach me in an explicitly pedagogical way, I must admit that I came back from Princeton thinking very differently. I can even identify one specific and very large change. When I arrived there I had a strong belief in a kind of trans-cultural notion of rationality as an element in social explanation. I thought that the interesting question to ask of a belief in an alien culture was whether it was rational to hold it. If it struck me as less than rational, then I took it that I needed to ask a strongly causal question, namely, what was stopping those people from seeing that they ought not to hold that particular belief? After talking with Kuhn and Geertz about these issues, and especially with Richard Rorty, who was then at Princeton University and whose thinking likewise influenced me very much, I came to feel that the question of what it is rational for someone to believe primarily depends on what else they believe, and not at all straightforwardly on something called the evidence or the facts. Now, the implication that what it is rational for you to believe may not be something it is rational for me to believe was very liberating for me. It turned me into the kind of mild cultural relativist that I now think all intellectual historians need to be.

Apart from this long stay in Princeton, I have made other more short-term visits, especially to Australia and France (where I spent part of last year as *Professeur invité* at the Collège de France). And I must say that these visits too, although in less clearly identifiable ways, have also been hugely fruitful and liberating. So I have no doubt that, had I travelled yet more widely and had the chance to learn from scholars from yet other traditions, I would have benefited correspondingly.

On the other hand, I have always had very strong intellectual reasons for wanting to make my base here in Cambridge, and family reasons too. My partner also teaches in Cambridge, and the town has been a wonderful place for our children to grow up in. As for the intellectual reasons, the Faculty of History is large, self-confident, has brilliant scholars in it and remains a spectacular intellectual community in which to work. The students at Cambridge, who increasingly come from all over the world, are also wonderful, and I have learned more and more from them in recent years, especially from the remarkable Ph.D. students I have taught, several of whom have already become really major figures, like James Tully and Richard Tuck.

But now I'm beginning to sound complacent. I do, of course, agree that by living most of one's life in one intellectual community one loses as well as gains a lot. I'm conscious of the losses as well as the gains of remaining in Cambridge. But maybe I shall suddenly freak out and go somewhere else.

Of the books in your area of interest, which would you like to have written?

Peter Laslett's edition of Locke seems to be a model of how to do a critical edition of a major work of political theory. Keith Thomas's *Religion and the Decline of Magic*, astoundingly published as early as 1971, is a masterwork of intellectual as well as social history. John Pocock's *The Machiavellian Moment* is likewise a masterly study, and one that directly influenced my own practice. These are people who do much the same thing as I try to do, but they do it better. They are more learned than I am, and above all they are more imaginative; I would certainly love to be able to do as well.

Cambridge, March and April 1998

SELECT BIBLIOGRAPHY

'Thomas Hobbes and the Nature of the Early Royal Society', *Historical Journal*, 12 (1969), 217–39.

'Meaning and Understanding in the History of Ideas', *History and Theory*, 8 (1969), 3–53.

The Foundations of Modern Political Thought (2 vols, Cambridge, Cambridge University Press, 1978); translated into Spanish, Italian, Portuguese.

Machiavelli (Oxford, Oxford University Press, 1981); translated into Czech, French, German, Hebrew, Hungarian, Indonesian, Italian, Japanese, Portuguese, Spanish, Swedish.

ed., *The Return of Grand Theory in the Human Sciences* (Cambridge, Cambridge University Press, 1985); translated into Japanese, Portuguese, Spanish, Turkish.

Meaning and Context: Quentin Skinner and his Critics, ed. J. Tully (Cambridge, Polity, 1988); translated into Japanese.

'Modernity and Disenchantment: Some Historical Reflections', in James Tully (ed.), *Philosophy in an Age of Pluralism*, (Cambridge, Cambridge University Press, 1994), 37–48.

'From Hume's Intentions to Deconstruction and Back', *Journal of Political Philosophy*, 4 (1996), 142–54.

Reason and Rhetoric in the Philosophy of Hobbes (Cambridge, Cambridge University Press, 1996); translated into Portuguese.

Liberty before Liberalism (Cambridge, Cambridge University Press, 1997).

Machiavelli: A Very Short Introduction (Oxford, Oxford University Press, 2000).

Index

Acton, Lord, 98
Africa, 8–12, 15, 21–2, 26, 28–9, 46, 72, 74, 80, 215
Agulhon, Maurice, 77–8
Ainsworth, Harrison, 82
Allen, Woody, 77
American Historical Review, 76
amnesia, structural, 134, 156
Anderson, Perry, 18, 148
Anderson, Benedict, 148
Ankersmit, Frank, 138, 205
Annales, 85, 103, 106, 109, 124, 153–4, 167–8, 189, 231–2
anthropology, 7–30, 51, 60, 62, 67, 80, 85, 90–1, 97, 125, 133–5, 147, 168, 202
appropriation, 22, 115, 120
archaeology, 10, 13, 19
archives, 59, 95, 107, 110, 113, 115, 122, 125–6, 139–40, 152, 162–3, 167, 202–3, 206, 228
Ariès, Philippe, 24, 124
Ashmole, Elias, 97
astrology, 97
Auerbach, Erich, 3, 188
Austin, J. L., 213
Ayer, Alfred, 144
Aylmer, Gerald, 87

Bakhtin, Mikhail, 81
Barker, Ernest, 36
Barraclough, Geoffrey, 93
Barry, Jonathan, 99
Bartlett, Robert, 104
Baudrillard, Jean, 108
Beatty, Warren, 5
Beauvoir, Simone de, 88
Begriffsgeschichte, 146
Bèze, Théodore de, 62
Blair, Tony, 40, 47, 102
Bloch, Marc, 3, 76, 85–6, 104, 121, 134, 148, 150, 155, 164, 168, 189, 192, 195–6, 199, 202, 231
Bloom, Harold, 77
Borges, Jorge Luis, 191–2
borrowing, cultural, 22
Bourdieu, Pierre, 2, 4, 134
Braudel, Fernand, 4, 8, 85, 110–11, 120, 124, 137, 146, 150, 153, 155
Brazil, 22–3, 32, 43, 45–6, 155
Brewer, John, 116, 120
Briggs, Asa, 3–4, 31–49
Brissot, Jacques Pierre, 166
Buddhism, 27
Burckhardt, Jacob, 3, 104, 141, 150, 163, 168, 188
Burke, Peter, 3, 32, 129–57

Burrow, John, 214

Callaghan, Jim, 33, 46
Calvino, Italo, 192, 196, 198
Cambridge, 7–9, 31, 33–4, 142–3,
    212–13, 216, 238–9
Canada, 50, 52
Cannadine, David, 42
Cantimori, Delio, 184, 189, 198
capitalism, 16, 35, 46, 174, 220–1
Caribbean, 42, 44, 46, 72, 74, 91–2
Carr, E. H., 131
Carroll, Lewis, 5
catholicism, 14, 20, 60, 206
Cecil, Robert, 87
Certeau, Michel de, 111
Chagall, Marc, 28
Chartier, Roger, 107, 115, 118, 123,
    125, 158, 169
Chekhov, Anton, 150
Chesneaux, Jean, 115
Childe, Gordon, 8, 13, 19
childhood, 17, 24, 90
China, 12–13, 15–16, 18–19, 46, 141,
    143, 150
Christine de Pisan, 57
classes, social, 35, 51
clothes, 116–18
Clough, Arthur Hugh, 38
Cobb, Richard, 158
Colie, Rosalie, 57
Collingwood, R. G., 216, 222, 233–4
comparison, 17–19, 31, 42, 72–3,
    120–1, 147–8, 164–5, 199–200, 209
Conan Doyle, Arthur, 5
conflict, 45–6, 58
consumption, 115–16
context, 212–16, 219, 225
Contini, Gianfranco, 188
contradiction, cognitive, 26–7
Conway, Jill Ker, 50, 78
Cooper, John, 87, 97, 38
corruption, 38
counter-factuals, 93
Croce, Benedetto, 187–8
cultural borrowing (*see* appropriation)
cultural mixing, 42, 66, 74–5

cultural translation, 136, 141,
    193, 216

Daniel, Glyn, 83
Darnton, Robert, 2–3, 47–8, 118, 125,
    148, 158, 237
Daunton, Martin, 83
Davis, Natalie Z., 4, 50–79, 138, 144
Delumeau, Jean, 60
Dépardieu, Gérard, 51
Derrida, Jacques, 23, 138, 223, 233
Descimon, Robert, 125
Diana, Princess, 13–14, 47
Dickens, Charles, 38
Diderot, Denis, 119, 159, 174
distance, distanciation, 21, 60, 71, 80,
    91, 151, 189, 200, 207
Douglas, Mary, 62, 134
Duby, Georges, 7, 127
Dumézil, Georges, 189
Dunn, John, 213, 222
Dupront, Alphonse, 113
Durkheim, Emile, 63

east and west, 14–18, 40, 63, 154
eclecticism, 43, 62–3, 92, 122,
    144–5
Eco, Umberto, 141
ecology, 16
economics, economies, 8–10, 15, 36
education (*see also* schools), 11–12,
    88–9
Edwards, Thomas, 87
Elias, Norbert, 81, 94, 122, 144–5
Eliot, George, 38–9
Eliot, T. S., 18
Elliott, John, 20, 68–9, 96, 197
Elton, Geoffrey, 95, 104, 137
empiricism, positivism, 95, 110, 137,
    143–4, 167, 205, 207, 228
Encyclopédie, the, 107, 159, 162, 167,
    170–2, 175
Enlightenment, 48, 106, 113–14, 118,
    158–9, 172–3, 177–8
essay, 59, 185, 193
ethnocentrism, 17, 63, 73, 98–9, 132,
    142–3, 147, 156

Evans-Pritchard, Edward, 80, 90–2,
    97, 134
everyday, 108, 119–20
evidence (*see also* archives), 70–1, 161,
    204–5, 229
evolution, 58–9, 186, 204, 236

Fabian, Johannes, 74
facts, *see* empiricism
family, 9, 17, 21
Farge, Arlette, 118, 123
Fayel, Gilles, 119
Febvre, Lucien, 85–6, 120, 168, 231
feminism (*see also* women), 67, 88, 117
Fernandes, Florestan, 155
Feyjóo, Benito Jerónimo, 65–6
fiction (*see also* literature), 69–70, 100,
    149, 187, 190, 203–4
fieldwork, 18, 20, 133–4, 194
Figes, Orlando, 104
films, historical, 51, 68–70, 149
Finlay, Robert, 76
Finley, Moses, 93
Firth, Charles, 86, 141
flowers, 12–13, 15–16, 20
Fortes, Meyer, 9
Foucault, Michel, 4, 122–23, 125,
    127, 138, 145, 152, 208–9, 229–30,
    238
Frazer, James, 7–8, 18
Freud, Sigmund, 61–2, 89, 94, 122, 145,
    185, 205, 207
Freyre, Gilberto, 32, 41–5, 155
Frugoni, Arsenio, 188
Furet, François, 110, 116

gardens, 16
Gardiner, Samuel, 86
Gay, Peter, 158
Geertz, Clifford, 92, 125–6, 134, 159,
    168, 221, 238
gender (*see also* women), 88, 198
Gentile, Giovanni, 188
geography, 108
Germany, 7, 18, 36
Giddens, Anthony, 131
Gide, André, 1

Gierke, Otto von, 36
Gilroy, Beryl, 71
Ginzburg, Carlo, 3–4, 67–8, 77, 80, 96,
    107, 126, 137–8, 144, 148, 151,
    184–211
Ginzburg, Natalia, 186–7, 190
Girard, René, 123
Gladstone, William E., 40
Goody, Jack, 2–3, 7–30, 72, 89, 121,
    134, 147, 154, 199
Gossman, Lionel, 70
Goubert, Pierre, 109–10
Grafton, Tony, 70
Gramsci, Antonio, 185, 188, 210,
    235
Granet, Marcel, 146
Greece, 14, 24
Guerre, Martin, 20, 51, 67–70, 96

Habakkuk, H. J., 83
Hahn, Barbara, 64
Halévy, Elie, 34
Hallpike, C. R., 94
Hanawalt, Barbara, 90
Haraway, Donna, 206
Hardman, Charlotte, 90
Hauser, Henri, 59, 61
Hayek, Friedrich von, 36
Hazard, Paul, 114
Heal, Felicity, 128
Henriques, Fernando, 42, 44
hermeneutics, 222–3, 232
Hill, Christopher, 80, 83–4, 86–7, 130,
    134, 150, 220
Hirschman, Albert, 238
history
    of art, 135, 187, 191, 195;
    history from below, 136, 197;
    history of the book, 106–7, 115–16,
        118–19, 169–73, 176;
    history of communications, 32,
        179–80;
    comparative history, *see* comparison
    cultural history, 123, 129, 142, 147,
        159;
    diplomatic history, 39;
    economic history, 93, 174;

history (*Cont.*)
 intellectual history, 113, 120, 147,
  218–19, 221–3, 233–4, 238;
 history of mentalities, *see* mentalities
 microhistory, 20, 51, 67–9, 96, 126,
  185, 188, 196–7, 201;
 political history, 39, 86, 124–5, 133,
  197, 202;
 prehistory, 25;
 professional history, 75, 193, 226;
 psycho-history, 94;
 quantitative history, 93, 106–7, 138;
 radical history, 75;
 serial history, 114, 153;
 social history, 32, 36–7, 42, 123, 147,
  152, 174, 177;
 total history, 69, 146;
 urban history, 8, 13, 31, 45, 51, 106,
  127–8, 153;
 history of women, 50, 57, 63–6, 76,
  81, 86–8, 90, 151–2, 177, 198;
History and Theory, 219, 233
Hitchcock, Alfred, 129
Hobbes, Thomas, 217–19, 223–5, 231
Hobsbawm, Eric, 7, 35, 130, 150–1
Holocaust, 61, 65
Homer, 29
Hufton, Olwen, 88
Huizinga, Johan, 104, 150, 168
Hurstfield, Joel, 87

imagined, imaginary, 138, 202
images, 20, 26–8
imperialism, 40–1
India, 10, 12, 15, 19, 46
Industrial Revolution, 15, 31
innovation, 36–7
insularity, *see* provincialism
intentionality, 213, 218, 222–4, 234
interpretation, *see* hermeneutics
interview situation, 1–6, 186
Islam, 22–3, 136, 156

Jakobson, Roman, 3, 188
Japan, 16, 18, 73, 121, 148–9
Jaurès, Jean, 107
Joslin, David, 83

Journal of the History of Ideas, 58, 213
journalism, journals, *see* press, the
Jouhaud, Christian, 125
Judaism, Jewish culture, 14, 27–8,
  51–4, 60–1, 64, 72–4, 133

Kapur, Shekhar, 68
Kenyon, John, 217
Kilito, Abdelfattah, 63
Kipling, Rudyard, 5
Koselleck, Reinhart, 146
Kuhn, Thomas, 3, 201, 221, 231, 238
Kula, Witold, 155
Kurosawa, Akira, 149

Labrousse, Ernest, 106, 110, 112–14
La Capra, Dominick, 100
language, 74, 99, 213, 223, 232, 234
Laski, Harold, 36
Laslett, Peter, 214, 217, 222, 225, 239
Leavis, Frank, 10
Le Goff, Jacques, 45, 109
Le Roy Ladurie, Emmanuel, 67–8, 77,
  80, 95–6, 106, 110, 114–15, 127
Levi, Giovanni, 185
Levi, Giuseppe, 205
Lévi-Strauss, Claude, 4, 18, 25–6, 92,
  134, 176, 196
libraries, national, 102, 124, 181
literacy, 11–12, 21–2, 24–6, 89
literature, 7–8, 10, 18, 34, 38–9, 100,
  149, 187, 203–4
Lloyd, Geoffrey, 24, 154
Locke, John, 214, 217–19, 222, 225
London School of Economics, 36
Lovejoy, Arthur O., 213
Luria, Alexander, 94
Lyons, 51, 59

McFarlane, Bruce, 93
Machiavelli, Niccolò, 227, 229
McKendrick, Neil, 116, 120, 217
Macpherson, C. B., 219
Maitland, F. W., 226
Major, John, 39–40
Malinowski, Bronislaw, 81, 92, 134
Mandrou, Robert, 115, 120

Mannheim, Karl, 152
Marguerite de Navarre, 63
Martin, Henri-Jean, 107
Marx, Karl, Marxism, 9, 14, 19, 35, 43, 54–5, 57–8, 83–6, 106, 108, 110, 114, 138–9, 144, 151, 168, 207–8, 219–21
material culture, 32, 36, 41, 106–8, 117, 120, 149
Mauss, Marcel, 63, 17
media, *see* history of communications, press
Mehta, Ved, 5
Melbourne, 31
memory, 29, 134, 156–7
mentalities, 15, 24, 94, 100, 117, 124, 141, 154, 158, 176, 200, 202, 232
mentors, 76–7, 83–4, 109, 150, 188, 214, 217, 222
Merton, Robert, 168
methods, 17–18, 43–4, 146, 194, 212, 214, 219, 222, 236
Michelet, Jules, 101, 107
microhistory, *see* history
Mill, John Stuart, 89
The Modern Quarterly, 83
Mitterand, François, 95
modernity, modernization, 16, 58–9, 175
Momigliano, Arnaldo, 194
Montaigne, Michel de, 63, 150, 225
Moore, Barrington, 148
morality, 37
Mornet, Daniel, 114
morphology, 196
Mousnier, Roland, 110
myths, 28–9, 101, 140–1

Namier, Lewis, 146, 150
narrative, 68–70, 86, 162, 190, 236
Needham, Joseph, 15
Nietzsche, Friedrich, 138, 145, 188, 209

Oakeshott, Michael, 36
objectivity, 138, 140, 205
Oman, Charles, 98
Opie, Iona, 90

orality, 4, 11, 28–9, 134
orientalism, *see* east and west
Ortiz, Fernando, 155
Overton, Richard, 97
Oxford, 45, 80–1, 129–30, 135, 142–3, 167
Oxford Magazine, 90–1

Panofsky, Erwin, 153
Paris, 59
   Collège de France, 4, 106, 127, 239;
   École des Hautes Études, 109–10, 114, 116;
   École Normale, 108–9, 111;
   Linguistic Society, 74;
   Maison des Sciences de l'Homme, 115;
   Sorbonne, 108, 111, 115
Passmore, John, 222, 233
Past and Present, 21, 87, 91–2, 96, 101
Pepys, Samuel, 96
periphery, 143, 155, 197
Perrot, Jean-Claude, 115
Perrot, Michelle, 115, 123
philosophy of history (*see also* Marxism), 58–9, 206–7
Pico della Mirandola, Giovanni, 54
Piero della Francesca, 185
Plumb, Jack, 116, 120, 217
Pocock, John, 158, 213, 222–3, 239
Polanski, Roman, 5
politics, 10, 46–7, 54–6, 61, 85–6, 111–12, 131–2, 165, 186, 189, 193, 199–201, 208, 225
Popper, Karl, 144
popular culture, 106–7, 114–15
population, 15
pornography, 47–8, 118, 172, 176
positivism, *see* empiricism
postmodernity, postmodernism, 18, 23, 67, 137–9, 205, 221, 223, 234
Poullain de la Barre, François, 65–6
Power, Eileen, 36, 76
press, the, 3, 38, 42–3, 47–8, 118–19, 125, 160–2, 166, 178–9
Prestwich, John, 86
proof, *see* evidence

prosopography, 146
Prosperi, Adriano, 199, 204
Protestantism (*see also* Reformation), 14, 20, 27, 38–9, 57, 60, 66–7, 82–3, 87
provincialism, 132, 142–3, 156, 200, 237
psychology (*see also* Freud), 44, 55, 89
public opinion, 38, 172, 178

Queneau, Raymond, 207

Rabelais, François, 63, 74, 225
Ranke, Leopold von, 139, 142
Reformation, 13–14, 57
Reinhard, Marcel, 113
relativism, 23, 139, 216, 237
religion (*see also* Buddhism, Catholicism, Islam, Judaism, Protestantism), 16, 18
Renaissance, 136, 148, 227, 229
Renouvin, Pierre, 110
revolutions
    American, 166;
    French, 47–8, 114, 117–19, 159, 165–6, 172, 179–80;
    1688, 214;
    Industrial, 15, 31, 35;
    urban, 8, 13
Richet, Denis, 115
Rimbaud, Caroline, 119
Roche, Daniel, 3–4, 106–28, 158
Rodrigues, Nina, 23
Rolland, Romain, 210
Romano, Ruggiero, 112–13
Roncayolo, Marcel, 115
Roper, Lyndal, 69
Rorty, Richard, 238
Rousseau, Jean-Jacques, 174, 224
Russell, Bertrand, 142
Ryle, Gilbert, 144

Sahlins, Marshall, 134
Said, Edward, 22, 40–1
Samuel, Raphael, 84, 150
São Paulo, 45, 81
scepticism, 138–9, 204

schools, 10, 34, 41, 82–3, 109, 129, 214–15, 222
Scott, Joan, 78
Scott, Walter, 82
Scribner, Bob, 69
Sen, Amartya, 7
serendipity, 202–3
Serres, Michel, 123
Simmel, Georg, 122
Skinner, Quentin, 3, 130, 146, 148, 158, 212–40
slaves, slavery, 22–3, 45–6, 66, 74, 210
Smiles, Samuel, 33
sociology, 42, 44, 85, 113, 122, 147
Sofri, Adriano, 200, 203, 208
sources (*see also* archives), 42, 70, 90, 96, 100, 107, 119
Southern, Richard, 84–5
speech acts, 213, 223, 234
Spence, Jonathan, 150
Spitzer, Leo, 188
Starobinski, Jean, 224
statistics, *see* history, quantitative
Stone, Lawrence, 17, 24, 86, 91, 104, 146, 150
stories, *see* narrative
Strachey, Lytton, 35
Strauss, Leo, 227
Stretton, Hugh, 84
The Sun, 48
Sussex, University of, 33, 41–2, 44, 130, 143, 147

Tawney, R. H., 82–3, 86, 104
Taylor, A. J. P., 5
Taylor, Charles, 84
teleology, *see* evolution
Thatcher, Margaret, 5, 39, 102
theory, 62–3, 81, 95, 143–4, 178, 238
Thirsk, Joan, 21
Thomas, Keith, 3, 6, 15, 57, 80–105, 130, 133–4, 140–1, 144, 148, 150, 154, 227, 239
Thompson, Edward, 7–8, 21, 35, 65, 78, 104, 145, 151, 209
Tilly, Louise, 78
The Times, 48

The Times Literary Supplement, 93
Topolski, Jerzy, 58
tradition, 36–7, 218, 227, 229–30, 234–6
translation (*see also* cultural
    translation), 192–3
Trevelyan, George M., 32, 36, 42
Trevor-Roper, Hugh, 86, 130
Trollope, Anthony, 38–9
Tuck, Richard, 213, 239
Tully, Richard, 239
Twain, Mark, 5

Venturi, Franco, 189
Victoria, Queen, 34, 40, 47
Victorian values, 37, 39
Vigne, Daniel, 51
violence, 61–2
Voltaire, 173
Vovelle, Michel, 124

Warburg, Aby, 153
Warburg Institute, 195
Watt, Ian, 8, 24, 26
War, Second World, 7, 9, 26, 36, 131
Weber, Max, 8–9, 14, 18–19, 57, 94,
    144–5, 150, 226, 236
Wells, H. G., 5
west, *see* east and west
Wheeler, Mortimer, 10
White, Hayden, 69–70, 100, 140
Williams, David, 83
Williams, Eric, 46
Williams, Raymond, 7
witchcraft, 80, 97, 185, 196, 201
Wittgenstein, Ludwig, 144, 221
women, 21, 41, 50, 52, 57, 63–4,
    117–18, 136, 151–2, 176, 198
Wood, Anthony, 84, 87
writing, *see* literacy